Europe after 1918

COURAGE
REMEMBERED

To the
one and three-quarter million fallen
who never came home

QUO FAS
ET GLORIA
DUCUNT*

Whither duty and glory lead.
Motto of the Royal Regiment of Artillery

Major-General Sir Fabian Ware KCVO KBE CB CMG LLD 1869–1949
Creator of the Imperial War Graves Commission 1917.

COURAGE
REMEMBERED

The story behind the construction
and maintenance of the Commonwealth's
Military Cemeteries and Memorials
of the Wars of
1914–1918 and 1939–1945

MAJOR EDWIN GIBSON MBE and
G. KINGSLEY WARD

INTRODUCTION BY MAJOR F.A. TILSTON VC

LONDON
HER MAJESTY'S STATIONERY OFFICE

© Crown copyright 1989
First published 1989

ISBN 0 11 772608 7

HMSO publications are available from:

HMSO Publications Centre
(Mail and telephone orders only)
PO Box 276, London, SW8 5DT
Telephone orders 01-873 9090
General enquiries 01-873 0011
(queuing system in operation for both numbers)

HMSO Bookshops
49 High Holborn, London, WC1V 6HB   01-873 0011 (Counter service only)
258 Broad Street, Birmingham, B1 2HE   021-643 3740
Southey House, 33 Wine Street, Bristol, BS1 2BQ   (0272) 264306
9–21 Princess Street, Manchester, M60 8AS   061-834 7201
80 Chichester Street, Belfast, BT1 4JY   (0232) 238451
71 Lothian Road, Edinburgh, EH3 9AZ   031-228 4181

HMSO's Accredited Agents
(see Yellow Pages)

and through good booksellers

Printed in the United Kingdom for Her Majesty's Stationery Office
Dd 291406   C25   2/89

Contents

Acknowledgements

We thank Sir Arthur Hockaday KCB, CMG, Director-General of the Commonwealth War Graves Commission, for his advice, and his permission for us to have the support of his staff. Our thanks also to Mr Roger Dalley, Director of Secretariat of the Commission, for his help.

We were well guided around, and informed about, the War Cemeteries and Memorials in the area of Ieper (perhaps better known as Ypres) by Mr Ken Lane BEM, an infantryman of the 1939–1945 War, now retired after 30 years with the Commission.

We are grateful for the assistance of the staff of the Maidenhead, England, and Ottawa, Canada offices of the Commission. Every request for information to these dedicated people (particularly those in Records) was promptly and efficiently handled.

For editorial and research services by Mr Sidney Allinson, Toronto, Canada and Mr David Knott, in attendance at Oxford, we are thankful, as we are for the secretarial support in Canada of Mrs Tania Ellis, Mrs Carmen Goodsell, Mrs Leila Deegan and in England, of Mrs Pat Smith and last, but by no means least, Mrs Sally Gibson. We also appreciate the interest of Mr Peter Bennett of London.

And finally, we acknowledge the work of Mr Laurence Cotterell, whose professional and literary talents were essential for the work to proceed from manuscript to publication.

Preface

OVER THE PAST FEW YEARS THERE HAS BEEN RENEWED interest shown – by many, including veterans and their relatives, historians, students and others – in visiting military cemeteries and memorials to the fallen of the 1914–1918 and 1939–1945 Wars. Why has there been this increased interest? Probably for a variety of reasons. First there seems to be a revival of memories among those who are old enough actually to have lived through either world conflict. Then there is a growing desire among descendants of the fallen to locate the burial place or memorial of a family member. Still further, there is evident a growing curiosity among younger people which draws them to the various sites to see the tragic results of war. Or perhaps there is a generally heightened historical interest owing to the passage of time since the two world wars ended. Whatever the reason, more and more people now wish to pay their respects to our fallen.

The authors have three main purposes in writing this book. First, to help perpetuate the memory of the war dead. Second, to provide some background knowledge to assist people who visit the cemeteries and memorials. The third reason is to recognize the often little-known work of the Commonwealth War Graves Commission in building and maintaining the sites throughout the world over the past 70 years.

Few people today realize the enormous initial effort that was made by the Commonwealth countries, led by Great Britain, in preparing these sites. This task involved many questions of international relations, and called for much planning and innovative policy, vast expense; and long years of work – some 1914–1918 Great War memorials were only completed a scant couple of years before the outbreak of the 1939–1945 Second World War. The heart and soul and personal dedication which the people of the Commission put into the creation and maintenance of the sites go to make an intensely moving story.

Today each location under the Commission's care is a place of exquisite craftsmanship, where a moment's view allows the visitor to observe the classical beauty which has been created and maintained. Sites such as Etaples with 11,000 graves or Tyne Cot with 12,000 graves and 30,000 names of the missing carved on the long rear wall can often take away the breath of a first viewer. Other small cemeteries containing 50 or so graves pull at the heartstrings. At any location most visitors are amazed by its moving beauty, created to perpetuate the memory of those who made the supreme sacrifice.

Many people probably think that visiting these areas must surely be a very sad experience, one not to be particularly desired. Yet more often than not, the thoughts of a pilgrim after a visit are of wonderment at what has been seen. Perhaps this book will help to encourage you also one day to stand before these sites of silent tribute. If so, you may then ponder on Laurence Binyon's immortal words:

At the going down of the sun
and in the morning,
We will remember them.

For the Fallen

Foreword

I CONSIDER IT A GREAT PRIVILEGE TO BE ASKED TO write a Foreword to this story about the British Commonwealth's Military Cemeteries and Memorials, which mark and recall the one and three quarter million who fell in the service of their countries in two World Wars.

For no one who visits these cemeteries today, whether they be in Flanders, North Africa, Italy, Normandy or in South-East Asia, or, indeed, in many other places too, can be left untouched or can fail to be moved by the extent of the sacrifice recalled. Partly it is the shock of the sheer scale and numbers of the fallen, reflected by the immaculate and symmetrical rows of white headstones which confirm only too vividly the statistics of War.

Then there is the added poignancy of the youthfulness of so many of those recorded – the flower of the Nation, the great majority of whom were killed in action between the ages of 18 and 25. If mankind needed a salutary reminder of the horrors of modern warfare, and why Deterrence and Peace with Honour is the only sensible course to follow, the War graves provide all the evidence that is needed.

Thanks, however, to the Commonwealth War Graves Commission there is a grain of comfort in all this, because we have at least been able to put into effect the universal and heartfelt aspiration of all those who were spared, that we would remember individually those who never came home and that we would do it with pride and dignity.

The scale of the problem was immense because the nature of battlefields and the circumstances of death in action could so easily have lead to so many inadequate interments, so many of the fallen unrecorded and missing without a trace, and so few visible and tangible memorials to those who lived and hoped and died as individuals, carrying out individual acts of will, and often showing great personal heroism.

As it is, thanks to the whole grand concept of Fabian Ware and the tireless and dedicated work over the years of the Commission which he founded, triumphant steps have been taken to overcome these problems, and the fallen have been found, traced and recorded, wherever they lay, and they have been reinterred, not in mass graves surmounted by heroic sculpture, as favoured by some nations, but, wherever possible, in single graves in beautiful settings. These maintain for those who mourn and for posterity the sanctity and dignity of the individual.

Courage Remembered is, therefore, the story of a most important contribution to our Twentieth Century Civilisation. It also provides a fascinating account of the construction and maintenance of these lovely cemeteries and memorials so in keeping with their surroundings and so appropriate to the everlasting peace that we wish for those who lie there.

I commend this book not only to all those who have personally experienced the loss of loved ones, but to all those who, at the going down of the sun and in the morning – and indeed at other times – want to remember all who, in the lovely words of the memorial at Kohima, 'gave their tomorrow for our today'.

Field Marshal THE LORD BRAMALL, GCB, OBE, MC, JP.

Introduction

Man lives each moment of his life in a
world of certain beliefs, the greater
part of which are shared by his fellows
then living, these beliefs constitute
the spirit of the time.

Quotation of José Ortega Y. Gasset,
cited by Joe Chamblin,
in the Therapy of Landscape.

ROM TIME IMMEMORIAL, MANKIND HAS RESPECTED his dead. Whether Christian or Non-Christian, aboriginal or other civilization, there is a common denominator at time of death, respectful disposal and remembrance for all.

The account you are to read of the Commonwealth War Graves Commission is a proper memorial to its founder Sir Fabian Ware. He realized that the 'exigencies of war' resulted in hasty burials under difficult conditions, lost graves due to destruction by later battles, and lack of proper reporting and recording.

I am like most readers of this book. What little I know of the 1914–1918 War (The Great War) has come from my grandparents with whom I lived (they had a son, recently graduated from university, serving with the Canadian Corps), or from my teachers at school, or newspaper articles and books read during and after 1914–1918.

My knowledge of the 1939–1945 War is that of experience as an officer of a Highland Infantry Regiment of the Canadian Army from May 1940 to December 1945. In 1983, at the invitation of one of the authors of this book, I accompanied him on another of his trips to the battlefields, memorials, and cemeteries of WW I. Of course, areas of the 1914–1918 War and the 1939–1945 War overlap in places like France, Belgium and Flanders. In addition, we visited parts of Holland and Germany where fighting had taken place in the 1939–1945 War, and where our dead are buried.

In 1970 and again in 1985 (the anniversaries of the 25th and 40th year of the liberation of Holland) as a member of the official Canadian Delegation, I was able to visit cemeteries of 'My War'. It was in 1980, at Groesbeek Military Cemetery in Holland, when after the service someone commented on how well the cemeteries were maintained. I said to that person 'they are more than well maintained, they are manicured'. I have heard that expression used many times since.

Although the object of the authors in this book is to chronicle the history of the Commonwealth War Graves Commission – its planning, construction, principles, responsibilities and ongoing business – it is also a capsule account of why the wars of 1914–1918 and 1939–1945 were fought, and some indication of how they were fought.

Let us remember that both wars were ones of defence, fought by the Commonwealth Armies and their allies to avoid conquest by a dictator.

As adjutant of my regiment when we went to Normandy in 1944, one of my responsibilities (along with the unit Padre) was to ensure burial of our dead, the proper marking of the grave, and the reporting to higher authority of other details, including location of the grave or graves.

A burial site was chosen, and dug by comrades of the dead. The bodies were wrapped in their own (or a friend's) gray blanket and laid to rest. The Padre read the brief prayers of committal, and the graves were filled in and marked. 'The Union Jack' was the flag our regiment used at these burials, and it hangs today, framed, in the Chapel of our Regiment's Headquarters – The Armouries in Windsor, Ontario.

Larger and more elaborate services have been, are, and will be, held in funeral homes, palaces, and cathedrals throughout the world, but few if any will have the sincerity and poignancy of a burial in the field where the congregation is but a handful of their comrades.

To tell you of the dedication of the Commonwealth War Graves Commission, I will give one personal experience with the Commission's agents. In the early stages of the Normandy campaign, we were located in the fields south of Caen. Our position was overlooked by a hill – not too big a hill, but it did provide an excellent observation point for the enemy. Our Commanding Officer ordered an attack of about 100 men to capture this feature. The battle was successful. Our casualties included eight men killed.

The top of the hill was occupied by a farm and large orchard. Six of our dead were adjacent to the farm building, the remaining two at the far end of the orchard. All were buried close to their place of death.

Five months later, during the Ardennes Battles – when acting as a reserve unit for Monty's offensive counter attack – we were visited by two representatives of the Commission. They could not locate the two graves at the far end of the orchard.

A short description of the ground and reference to our maps resolved their problem. Two reported graves, but which they were unable to locate, were important to them, for in death the great and not so great are equal.

'Conquest of my country and rule by a foreign dictator?' was the question of these men, and 'Never!' was their reply.

They realized, as we should too, that free government is not lightly come by, nor is it lightly held. Freedom is not to be bought, received as a gift, or hit upon as an accident. Nor can it be maintained by compromise with its enemies, by hired groups or professional soldiers, or by the determined efforts of a few of its citizens.

It must be earned by a whole people, lived by a whole people, and fought for to the death by everyone who shares in its glorious benefits.

Sir Arthur Currie, GOC Canadian Corps, acknowledging Canada's Prime Minister's message of congratulations after the 1914–1918 War, said 'Our hearts go out to those to whom there remains only the cherished memory of those loved and lost, sacrificed in the noblest cause for which men have died.'

We share Sir Arthur's sentiments.

The Commonwealth War Graves Commission, founded and directed by Sir Fabian Ware, and his staff of gardeners, caretakers, and administrators, has ensured that the memories and glory of the Commonwealth Armed Forces, whom the Supreme Commander-in-Chief bade to stack their arms and appear before him in a last grand review, shall remain in perpetuity.

MAJOR F.A. TILSTON, VC, CD, LLD

PART I

Historical

{ 1 }

Sarajevo and the road to war

*Just a word – 'neutrality', a word which in wartime
has so often been disregarded, just for a scrap
of paper – Great Britain is going to make war*

Theobald von Bethmann-Hollweg (1856–1921),
German Chancellor, 1914.

WHEN FIRST SEEN, THE THOUSANDS OF GRAVES IN A
twentieth century military cemetery can cause a profound shock.
The evidence of so many young lives snuffed out in battle always
raises the anguished question, 'What causes war?' All kinds of complex
reasons are then often put forward, but at the bottom lies this simpler
answer: war is caused mostly by politicians through a mixture of too much
greed and too little honour. Twice in recent times, it stemmed from the
shortcomings of a few leaders, who had reached the peak of power and
become drunk with it; arrogant men who were willing to spill the blood of
nations over an isolated incident; conscienceless men too dull to foresee the
deadly consequences of their actions.

The death of an entire generation was directly caused by an isolated
incident of political murder that occurred in the summer of 1914. The greed
in this case was that of Austria-Hungary, then in the last days of its
once-impressive power, the remnants of the Habsburg Empire fading away
under the rule of Emperor Franz Joseph I. The heir to the throne was
Archduke Franz Ferdinand, who was to be, involuntarily, the cause of world
tragedy.

An arrogant man with no sympathy for the democratic ideals growing
in Europe after the turn of the century, the Archduke was consumed with
pride over his country's recent military occupation of two small Balkan
states: Bosnia and Hercegovina. Previously under Turkish rule, they had
been the scene of several rebellions since being annexed by Austria-Hungary
in 1908. The Slav, Serb and Croat inhabitants resented their new Habsburg
rulers, and passionately wished instead to be united with the small kingdom
of Serbia. Despite this violent hostility, Archduke Franz Ferdinand gloried
in his new domains, and welcomed the opportunity to inspect his army of
occupation on summer manoeuvres at Sarajevo, Bosnia's capital.

Splendid in his field marshal's uniform, he arrived there with his wife,
the Duchess of Hohenberg, on Sunday 28th June 1914 – one of the most

3

momentous dates in history. That afternoon the royal couple drove in an open motor car through the streets of Sarajevo, and experienced the fright of having a bomb thrown at them, which narrowly missed. Though understandably upset, Archduke Franz Ferdinand went on to attend a civic meeting and later ordered his chauffeur to drive him out of the city. The driver lost his way and stopped the car to reverse. At that moment a 17-year-old schoolboy, a fanatic named Gavrilo Princip, stepped forward and killed the Archduke with a single shot from his automatic pistol – 'the shot that echoed round the world'. The Duchess died a moment later from a second bullet, moments before police arrested the youth. Princip was convicted of the assassinations and imprisoned; he died in gaol of tuberculosis a few years later.

Initially there was small concern elsewhere over what was then regarded as 'just another of those Balkan political murders'. But a flicker of wider interest arose over speculation that the killing had been plotted by Serbia, when it was found that Princip's pistol had been supplied by the Serbian chief of intelligence. Though there was no further proof of Serbia's complicity, this discovery was enough to provoke a reaction on the part of Austria – a dangerous reaction as each country in Europe had a good deal of blind nationalism in its make-up (this was especially true of its leaders). To this factor was added the pressures of alliances which had been forged in the previous decade, with on the one hand Austria-Hungary and her main ally Germany, and on the other a political alignment between Russia, France and Great Britain.

These nations were among the most powerful in the world. Any hint of interference with their carefully structured empires was met with exaggerated pride, and the certainty of quick revenge. In such a competitive atmosphere, it was small wonder that Austria-Hungary's immediate reaction to Archduke Franz Ferdinand's assassination was to consider sending a punitive force into Serbia.

However, as such a move involved calling up reservists and widespread issuing of equipment, it would require the total mobilization of the army, which would surely provoke Russia, protector of all Slav states. So, Austria first asked Germany's Kaiser for advice. He and the Chancellor, Bethmann-Hollweg, encouraged Vienna to take a tough line, with promises of full German backing against any Russian threats. Thus reassured, Austria sent an ultimatum to Serbia, followed by a declaration of war on 26th July – an action that set the powers on the road to war.

Russia immediately took exception. This was not only in the cause of Slavic pride, but for more practical fears of the Germanic partners being able to dominate the Balkan approaches to the strategic Bosporus. In mixed outrage and self-protection, Russia ordered complete mobilization 'just in case'. This was a necessary precaution, because it would have taken that chaotically disorganized country many weeks to start the railroad transport of conscript armies and war material across its vast distances. Meanwhile no doubt the diplomats could sort things out, with no need for actual shooting . . .

But Germany felt its own apprehensions, too. As a nation which had long been rehearsing for the opportunity of a war of domination in Europe, she knew she had little hope of winning a fight on two fronts, against both France and Russia. Since 1892 Berlin's military strategy had been based entirely on the 'Schlieffen Plan', a lightning attack through Belgium aimed at capturing Paris before the ponderous Russian war machine could get moving. Clearly, Germany would either have to bluff Russia into cancelling its preparations, or start the war without delay. Accordingly, Berlin sent an ultimatum, demanding Russian demobilization within 12 hours. Moscow refused and Germany declared war on Russia next day – 1st August 1914.

Meanwhile France also hurried towards mobilization. With a huge standing army, and thirsting for revenge for its defeat by Prussia in 1870, France was itself in belligerent mood. When Germany declared war on France on 3rd August, celebrating crowds surged through the streets of Paris, singing 'La Marseillaise'.

All this Continental sabre-rattling deeply concerned Britain, though her own immediate territorial interests were not being threatened. Without any formal military alliance with France, Britain nevertheless felt bound by the 'Entente Cordiale'; and also had a form of understanding with Russia, as part of the balance of power. In addition there was the matter of honouring a scrap of paper, an international treaty signed by Britain and Germany (among other nations) to guarantee Belgium's neutrality.

Until the Germans launched the 'Schlieffen Plan' against France and demanded free passage through Belgium, Britain had been reluctant to get involved in 'a Balkan squabble'. But when that small nation refused, Britain went to its support, sending an ultimatum that the Kaiser stop his invasion. It was a popular stance in Britain, with much talk of 'defending little Belgium against the Hun'. While his nation waited, Britain's Foreign Secretary, Sir Edward Grey, remarked perceptively: 'The lamps are going out all over Europe. We shall not see them lit again in our lifetime'.

On the night of 4th August crowds of Londoners gathered in front of the Prime Minister's residence at 10 Downing Street as the last minutes ticked by to the expiry of the ultimatum. When Big Ben chimed eleven, confirming that war was declared, a great cheer went up. So it went up around the world, in all Dominions of the British Empire, in Toronto, Auckland, Sydney and Cape Town with equally supportive outbursts of patriotism. The same sentiments were strong in Berlin, where exultant crowds threw flowers to troops on the march with happy cries of 'Nach Paris!' One of the cheering crowd in the Odeonsplatz in Munich was a certain Adolf Hitler, aged 25. 'The war to end all wars' had begun.

{ 2 }

How the 1914–1918 War
was fought

*War is much too serious a thing
to be left to the military*

Georges Clemenceau (1841–1929),
Premier of France, 1917.

THE UNEQUIVOCAL ANTI-WAR SENTIMENTS WHICH ARE
accepted so widely in Western countries today sometimes make it
difficult for the modern person to comprehend the ardour with which
men of both sides marched off to battle in 1914. The wisdom of hindsight
makes their intensity of feeling seem almost strange or pointless. Yet the fact
is that patriotic spirit on both sides then was so high that millions of men
eagerly volunteered for the chance to fight for their country. This was
particularly so in the British and Commonwealth forces, whose countries did
not have conscription as did those on the Continent.

Within hours of the declaration of war, hordes of eager men and boys
swarmed around recruiting stations in Britain to enrol for military service.
Posters blossomed everywhere with Field Marshal Kitchener's pointing finger
urging 'Your Country Needs You!' These were part of an intensive
programme to recruit a massive new army of volunteers to reinforce the
regulars who were already fighting in France. Within the first month over
half a million enlisted in Britain and a proportionate number of men stepped
forward in every country of the British Commonwealth of Nations. The
widespread eagerness of volunteers in far-off Dominions to cross the seas to
fight for the 'Mother Country' perhaps indicates better than anything else
the degree of loyalty and enthusiasm which prevailed. An officer of the
Green Howards wrote of the simple morality of the time:

'People in England then were far more influenced by the traditional attitudes of
right, wrong and duty. While few of the officers had a clear idea of the history and
politics of the Balkans which had brought on the war, every private knew that
Belgium had been brutally attacked and that unless Belgium was rescued, it might
be Britain's turn. It was that point that brought the crowds to the recruiting offices
and it was that point which maintained morale until 1918 in spite of colossal
casualties.'

6

Enlistment in Britain averaged over 100,000 a month for the next 18 months and eventually totalled three million volunteers (later augmented by a similar number mobilized after conscription was introduced in Britain in 1916). In all, the British Commonwealth and Empire mobilized nearly nine million men. They and the Commonwealth troops were to be sorely needed because by as early as October 1914 the small British Expeditionary Force (BEF) had been badly depleted by an early war of movement following the Retreat from Mons.

But the nature of the fighting was to change. When the BEF returned north to counter the German thrust for the Channel ports, both sides collided in a fierce battle at Ypres (the 'First' Ypres). Although the Germans sustained enormous casualties, the dwindling British force was in worse condition with few reserves. Having learned from the German example of entrenchments along the River Aisne, the British dug in. By the year's end the armies faced each other from a continuous line of opposing ditches which ran all the way from the North Sea coast of Belgium to the neutral Swiss border. It was the way they were fated to fight from now on: trench warfare.

Trenches had been used in the Crimea, the US Civil War and at the siege of Port Arthur just a decade earlier. But never before had they been dug on such a scale, or used for over four years, as they were on the Western Front. Certainly trenches were never dug in a less suitable place. On much of the war zone the ground was a thin layer of soil over non-porous clay, poor material indeed for digging ditches when combined with the area's heavy rainfall and frequent watercourses.

Water seemed to be everywhere, coming from rain and streams and marshes; it filled each trench like a dyke and was slow to drain away through the clay bottom. Permanently damp at the best of times, trenches could turn into streams from persistent rain, so that men sometimes had to stand up to their knees in water. Soldiers lived here a week or more at a time with little shelter from the weather. Throughout four years of war men were often wet, cold, muddy, sleepless; without proper sanitation or hot food; sometimes suffering from frostbite and trench foot; and distressed by lice, fleas and rats. Added to this was the ever-present danger of death: from shellfire, drowning or gas, to name but a few.

Germany conquered so much strategic and industrial territory in 1914, including most of France's coal and steel-making regions, that General Erich von Falkenhayn could afford to withdraw his army from less defensible ground and fortify generally higher and advantageous positions. This placed British and French troops at a disadvantage throughout the war; they continually had to occupy militarily less suitable areas and impermanent earthworks. In addition to this, as Germany was the occupier and defending her gains, most of the attacking between First Ypres and spring 1918 was done by the Allies in attempts to oust that occupier – and the attacker almost always suffers more heavily than the defender.

In the 1914–1918 War about 12 per cent of all active-service soldiers died. Total battle casualties on the Western Front, killed and wounded, have been estimated at over 50 per cent. Because of the determination to 'lead from the front', officers in combat suffered more severely than other soldiers, with about 17 per cent being killed. To realize fully the appallingly high level of death and mutilation, one should also remember that the ratio of *fighting* soldiers to support troops was about one to five, so that statistically very few actual frontline men could escape at least some form of wound.

Individual soldiers relied on their bolt-action rifles, the British .303 inch Short Magazine Lee Enfield (SMLE – 'Smellie' to the soldiers) and the German 7.92mm Mauser. But this was a dramatically 'modern' war with an ever increasing range of new weapons. The Germans brought out the flamethrower; the British the tank – a revolutionary tracked armoured fighting vehicle, armed with guns. A dreadful new weapon appeared early in April 1915 – poison gas – introduced by the Germans at the Second Battle of Ypres, where Canadian and French troops were first to experience it. Soon the British were retaliating with their own gas, discharging it regularly with the prevailing westerly wind for the rest of the war. In all, Commonwealth forces had an estimated 250,000 gas casualties, of whom 10,000 died immediately, while the rest suffered to varying degrees.

However, artillery claimed by far the largest number of casualties. Both sides used guns in unprecedented numbers (sometimes thousands were concentrated almost wheel to wheel), bombarding each other's troops with high explosive, steel fragments and shrapnel. About half of all wounds sustained by troops who were medically treated were found to be caused by shellfire, either from fragments or shrapnel-balls. Rough, tumbling, shell fragments caused far more shock and damage to the human system than did a smoothly flying bullet. Consequently, more of those struck by fragments died at once, or before medical aid could be given; this was the main reason why the proportion of killed to wounded was much higher for artillery casualties than from other causes.

Apart from its death-dealing capability, sustained artillery fire could break the will of men and bring on 'shell shock', a widespread and serious nervous disorder. However, lengthy artillery bombardments could be self-defeating, the ground becoming so cratered and boggy as to be impassable to the troops the artillery was supporting. At other times (on the Somme in 1916, for example) several days' preliminary bombardment induced over-confidence in the attackers. Most shells were incapable of reaching down the 20 feet or more into the dugouts, from which the German machine-gunners emerged when the barrage lifted and caught the attackers struggling through the barbed-wire entanglements.

The second most effective weapon was the machine gun. Early in the conflict General (later Field Marshal) Douglas Haig had classified this weapon as being 'of limited use', yet by the end of the war Britain had an entire Machine Gun Corps, with an allocation of up to 50 machine guns for each of its battalions. The Germans recognized early the 'efficiency' of the machine gun and equipped their army lavishly with them.

Average British losses between battles exceeded 300 men a day. 'Quiet' sectors of the front could kill troops at a rate of up to 500 a week. Even out of the line, most battalions lost an average of eight men a week, from training accidents and so forth. For all the valiant contribution of British, Commonwealth and Belgian troops, it should be remembered that it was the soldiers of France and its colonies who bore the heaviest burden of fighting on the Allies' side on the Western Front. By the war's end French dead totalled one and a half million; Germany lost at least two million.

However, the near stagnation of movement on the Western Front between the end of 1914 and the German breakthrough in March 1918 was not reflected elsewhere. The 1914–1918 War eventually involved over a score nations as belligerents and fighting took place in many distant corners of the earth – in Macedonia, Mesopotamia and East Africa, for example. By far the most ambitious of these so-called 'sideshows' was in the Dardanelles, Turkey.

The amphibious landing by British (with a battalion from Newfoundland), French, Anzac and Indian troops took place on the Gallipoli Peninsula in April 1915. Although ostensibly aimed at capturing Constantinople (now Istanbul) it was partly a response to Russia's appeal for some action to distract a new enemy – Turkey – and gain an ice-free access to Russia. The Allied landings were made with great gallantry, the Lancashire Fusiliers earning 'six VC's before breakfast'; the Australian and New Zealand troops in particular made their mark at Gallipoli, where so many of them were to fight and die half a world away from their homelands.

Trapped on narrow beaches below cliffs that commanded the entire landing area and unable to move inland, the Allied force held on desparately throughout the entire summer. The fierce Turks were able to bring batteries of guns and machine guns to bear on the invaders below, who fought with their backs to the sea, burrowing as best they could into the rocks and sand. The Gallipoli Peninsula Campaign ended, its objects unattained, with the evacuation of the Anzacs in December 1915 and the British in January 1916.

The French and British also landed at Salonika, Greece, to support Serbia and counter Bulgaria. Despite much bitter fighting, very little strategic gain was made by opening this new front and it tied up over half a million troops (they were nicknamed the 'Gardeners of Salonika' by Clemenceau) who might have been better employed elsewhere.

There was perhaps more understandable logic in military operations aimed at defeating Turkey in Mesopotamia (now Iraq) and in Palestine (now Israel). While Colonel T.E. Lawrence ('Lawrence of Arabia') united and led the desert Arabs in a guerrilla war against the Turks, a conventional British and Australian army pushed north from the Suez Canal eventually to free Palestine.

Things did not go so well at first in Mesopotamia where a British and Indian force surrendered after months of siege at Kut-al-Amara; its men died in great numbers as prisoners of war. However, by late 1917 Britain had taken Baghdad and driven the Ottoman forces out of Mesopotamia, which led to the eventual total defeat of Turkey and freedom for Middle East people from centuries of despotic rule.

British troops were also sent to northern Italy to help bolster the Italian fight against Austria, though these were men who could be ill-spared from the Western Front. The widespread French Army mutinies of 1917 had caused British and Commonwealth troops to take on an even heavier burden of fighting there, and during the year they had fought great battles, including those of Arras (which included the capture of Vimy Ridge), Messines and Third Ypres. It was these troops who eventually halted the spectacular German advance which started in March 1918 and drove the German forces back to the line which they held when the Armistice was signed on 11th November 1918.

On that day the Emperor of Austria-Hungary abdicated, as had Kaiser Wilhelm a few days before.

By then revolution had broken out in Germany and the High Seas Fleet mutinied at Kiel. However, later stories about the collapse of German civilian morale 'stabbing Germany's soldiers in the back' simply do not bear close examination. The principal reason for the defeat of Germany was the tenacity and dogged courage of the British and Commonwealth troops and their astonishing advance in the last 100 days of the war. The USA declared war on Germany in April 1917 but did not have an effective army in France until over a year later. In time, US General John J. Pershing commanded over one and a half million troops whose presence was of enormous help to Allied morale. When their opportunity finally came Americans were able to demonstrate their valour in battle in the Meuse-Argonne, where they suffered 100,000 casualties during four weeks' fighting. Other battles were ahead for the Americans during the closing three months of the war, in which they lost a total of over 50,000 either killed or who died of wounds.

Although the focus of the war was mainly on enormous land battles, a word must be said about sea power and aerial combat. Virtually all sea operations against Germany – convoys, naval battles, sinking U-Boats and other actions – were carried out by the Royal Navy and British Commonwealth vessels. Without the maintenance of sea communication and supply no effective war could have been fought on the European continent, except possibly by France alone – with poor prospects of victory.

A key factor in the Allies' success in the Naval War was the convoy system, previously used a century earlier during the Napoleonic Wars. Nevertheless German submarines were effective and the crisis was reached in April 1917, by which time over 5,000 Allied and neutral vessels had been sunk by U-Boats. From then on, thanks to the Navy's efficient anti-submarine measures, matters improved and the menace decreased steadily.

The British and German surface fleets fought four major sea battles, at Coronel, Falklands, Dogger Bank and Jutland. The First Lord of the Admiralty, Winston Churchill, remarked that, unlike the Army, the Royal Navy 'could have lost the war in an afternoon' had it been defeated. It never was. Ships flying the White Ensign fought commerce raiders in the Indian

Ocean, hunted submarines in the Gulf of St Lawrence and rammed destroyers alongside the mole at Zeebrugge. The enormous endeavours of more than four years' sea warfare are not well remembered as nothing remains to mark them, and interest tends to focus on the major land battles, whose general locations are still marked by military cemeteries.

One aspect of the war which has come to be considered 'glamorous' is that of aerial combat. On both sides aircraft observed for artillery, and machine-gunned, bombed and gassed enemy troops. The Royal Flying Corps started the war as an unknown adjunct to the Army. After mixed fortunes it was built into a fighting force of men from every country in the British Empire.

The RFC devised techniques of aerial observation, photo-reconnaissance and ground support, offering the Army advantages which were not always quickly recognized. The Corps also fought in the skies over Britain during frequent German air-raids by airships and bombers which killed over 1,200 civilians. By the end of the war it was the world's most powerful and efficient air force with pilots capable of holding their own against their German counterparts. Flying without parachutes in flimsy machines called for great mettle and skill, but many hundreds of aircrew died, and No Man's Land was littered with crashed aircraft.

When the Armistice finally came, there was an underlying sadness to the celebrations. In the end, Belgium had been freed and honour satisfied but at unimaginable cost – the immolation of an entire generation of young men. Because the 1914–1918 War was so widespread, Commonwealth military cemeteries and memorials are to be found around the globe. However, the greatest concentration lies in northern France and Belgium. Indeed along the 70 or so miles of the BEF's section of the Western Front, a visitor to a war cemetery will, as often as not, be able to see a second, and sometimes third, such site from where he or she is standing.

{ 3 }

Munich and its aftermath

It's Tommy this, an' Tommy that, an 'Chuck
him out the brute!'
But it's 'Saviour of 'is country' when the
guns begin to shoot

Rudyard Kipling (1865–1936),
'Tommy'.

I T MAY BE THAT THE FIRST REAL SHOTS OF THE 1939–1945 War were fired twenty years earlier, on 21st June 1919. That day British sentries tried, mainly ineffectively, to prevent the scuttling of the interned German fleet at its mooring at Scapa Flow, Scotland. The first figurative shots were those fired during the Peace Conference which had started earlier that year in Paris. Papers were signed at Versailles on 28th June 1919, detailing the exactions from Germany and Austria for causing the 1914–1918 War. The figurative shots were the more dangerous, as they were the most telling, and far and away the most wounding.

Under the terms of the new Treaty of Versailles Germany was forced to accept territorial changes. Among these were the return of Alsace-Lorraine to France, (it had been taken from the latter after her defeat in the Franco-Prussian War of 1870); the separation of East Prussia from Prussia by the newly-formed Polish 'Corridor' to provide that state's only access to the Baltic Sea; the loss of territories in Posen and Silesia in the east; and the relinquishment of all her overseas colonies. In addition Germany lost her navy, her army was reduced to 100,000 men – a tiny fraction of its wartime size – and she was landed with enormous bills for reparations.

An objective reaction to all this may be difficult. But the stipulations of Versailles in 1919 did not show the wisdom displayed after the 1939–1945 War, when Churchill coined 'In victory, magnanimity' as part of the theme in his *The Second World War*. Instead, Versailles left a Germany seething with resentment and near total revolution. The country's economy was in ruins and shortly afterwards fell prey to runaway inflation. All these were factors in the development of one of the worst large-scale diseases ever to endanger the human race – National Socialism, or Nazism.

Adolf Hitler was an Austrian who had served in the German Army as a private soldier and junior NCO and was four times decorated for bravery in the field. He joined the emergent Nazi party in the early 1920's as, like many

12

Germans (but especially the Nazis), he had an overpowering desire for revenge. Hitler had particularly obsessive ideas about *Lebensraum* (living space), which was to be obtained by the conquering of neighbouring states, the amalgamation into Germany of all Germanic populations, the colonization of grain-growing areas like the Ukraine, and the control of European industry. He also believed that the Jews were largely the cause of Germany's ills and that they would make excellent scapegoats when such were required. His views on Versailles reflected those of nearly all Germans: it had been a shameful humiliation and disaster for Germany.

The fragile relations between France and Germany were worsened by the occupation of the Ruhr by French and Belgian troops on 11th January 1923 in a largely vain attempt to force Germany to pay its quota of reparations. The French occupation was condemned by Britain and the USA and aroused passive resistance among the Ruhr workers. The French received little benefit from their occupation but kept their troops there for over two years, rather than lose face.

Nevertheless, Germany's international standing, influence, and wealth progressed steadily, none of which helped the Nazi party. However, its opportunity came with the great economic world slump of 1930. During that period the Nazis won a spectacular success at the polls, with the aid of colossal propaganda financed by Ruhr industrialists, to whom Hitler had promised protection from Communism and suppression of the labour unions. Hitler skilfully exploited the despair created by the slump's mass unemployment and the residual national inferiority complex dating from Versailles. By the early 1930s the Nazi Party was an important element in German political life and, on 30th January 1933, President Paul von Hindenburg, the Head of State, appointed Hitler Chancellor (Prime Minister) and the infamous *Drittes Reich* (Third Empire) began.

When von Hindenburg died on 2nd August 1934, Hitler grabbed the opportunity to declare that the offices of President and Chancellor were united in him as *Führer* (Leader), and made the Army take a personal oath of allegiance to him. Hitler also held a controlled plebiscite to obtain confirmation (and demonstrate the 'legality') of his action – the first in a series of pseudo-referenda and a good example of his deviousness and cunning.

Hitler's greatest success in Germany was the ending of unemployment. This was achieved by creating work through rapid rearmament and large projects, such as the construction of the *Autobahns* (motorways). In September 1935 he felt strong enough to enact the Nuremberg laws against the Jews, who were conveniently useful as recipients of any required blame, and who had been subject to persecution for some time. Meanwhile in March 1935 Hitler announced the commencement in October of compulsory military service. By this time he had obtained a very good measure of political support from many on the right in Western European politics – not least in Britain – who saw the Nazi government as a buffer against Communism. In addition to this Hitler was undoubtedly helped by

American isolationism: the United States had not joined the League of Nations, the precursor of the United Nations Organization.

The era of appeasement had begun. In 1936 Hitler ordered his military forces to reoccupy the demilitarized Rhineland. At this time a demonstration of will by either Britain or France, or both, using force if necessary, would surely have halted his progress and aims. But there was none and, equally surely, this was the 'green light' to Hitler and gave him clear ideas on how to deal in future with Germany's former victors.

In the same year the German leader formed the Rome-Berlin Axis with Benito Mussolini, *Duce* (Leader) of Fascist Italy. This established political collaboration between the two countries which was to be cemented during the Italian occupation of Abyssinia (now Ethiopia). The Western powers made disapproving noises and began sanctions in protest against this invasion but took no military steps; further note of this supine attitude was taken by both the Axis dictators. The year 1936 also saw Hitler give extensive military support to General Francisco Franco; his anti-democratic civil war in Spain provided a splendid active-service training ground for German land and air forces.

In the years since Hitler's appointment as Chancellor, the Nazis had established a total grip over Germany by intimidation, murder, kidnapping and internment in concentration camps. Nothing was too devious or dreadful provided it furthered Hitler's aim to have total control of the country. Examples of his henchmen's handiwork included the murder of Engelbert Dollfuss, the Austrian Chancellor, on 25th July 1934, and the purge of the previous month, in which Hitler's rival Röhm and hundreds of influential Nazis were murdered by the already dreaded SS, the *Führer's* bodyguard and so-called elite troops.

After the occupation of Austria on 12th March 1938 and its annexation by the Reich, Hitler's next step was the annexation, on 30th October 1938, of the Sudetenland – a region of Czechoslovakia that contained a majority of ethnic Germans. This move followed the infamous Munich Agreement, concluded on 29th September 1938 between Britain, France, Germany and Italy (and in particular between Adolf Hitler and Neville Chamberlain, the British Prime Minister).

The Agreement was the consummation of the policy of appeasement, and the word 'Munich' became a synonym for 'surrender' from that day. It had produced another 'scrap of paper': the treaty waved happily on 30th September 1938 by Chamberlain on his return to Britain. It gave the world – so the British Prime Minister thought and declared – 'peace for our time – peace with honour'.

Few people in high office can have been so deluded, either before or since, but Chamberlain and countless others really thought that Hitler's territorial ambitions would be satisfied by having easily and bloodlessly acquired the Sudentenland. That this was not the case was proved six months later on 15th March 1939, when Hitler annexed the Czech territories of Bohemia and Moravia and declared them a German 'protectorate'. Some days later he annexed the territory of Memel – lost by Germany in 1918 – from Lithuania on the eastern coast of the Baltic Sea.

Now at last it became obvious to all that further dealings with such a man and further concessions were pointless – or rather, dangerous. It was realized that Hitler was contemptuous of conciliation and disregarded agreements. He might have understood firmness and action by democratic neighbours, but he had encountered no such opposition, and now demanded the return of the Polish Corridor, and the port of Danzig (now Gdansk) on the former's outlet to the Baltic. Danzig was a Free City under Polish suzerainty.

When Britain gave a guarantee to Poland at this time, Hitler sensed that things were not going entirely to plan and obtained a pact of friendship with the Soviet Union on 23rd August 1939. By including secret clauses on a future fourth partition of Poland, he believed that Germany's fear of war on two fronts had been eliminated. On 1st September 1939 Forster, the Nazi leader in Danzig, proclaimed the reunion of that city with Germany. This was at once confirmed by Hitler, who simultaneously ordered the invasion of Poland, an action which led directly to the outbreak of the 1939–1945 War (the Second World War).

Britain's reaction to the entry of German troops into Poland was to send an ultimatum demanding their withdrawal and stating that if no such undertaking were received by 1100 on Sunday 3rd September, the two countries would be at war. In the event no such undertaking was received and Britain and Germany therefore went to war. France, which also had an agreement with Poland, followed suit that afternoon and Canada and other Commonwealth countries declared war within the week.

The Soviet Union, who had agreed not to interfere with Germany when she attacked Poland, invaded that country a few days later, acquiring the eastern half. From 1941 onwards the USSR was to pay dearly for having a treaty with Nazi Germany that enabled the latter to start the war, but in view of the outcome in 1945 and subsequent events, she may well feel that it was all worthwhile.

So far as the Commonwealth was concerned, it was clear that there could be no peace or security so long as one ruthless and massively armed country which intimidated and engulfed others was on the loose. The British Empire was totally united in its belief that, no matter what the cost ('blood, toil, tears and sweat' as Churchill put it in 1940) the job, the defeat of the Nazis, had to be finished. And so 21 years after the 'war to end all wars' finished, war began again.

{ 4 }

Japan – her move to the 1939–1945 War

When you go home
Tell them of us and say
For your tomorrow
We gave our today

Text on the 2nd British Division's
Memorial at Kohima War Cemetery,
Assam (now Nagaland), India.

JAPAN, WHOSE EMERGENCE INTO THE MODERN WORLD had started in the late 1860s, was the only advanced industrial country outside Europe and North America between the two World Wars. Despite this, Japan had remained feudal in outlook, and the 'warrior classes' were still in control in the 1930s. She suffered from no inferiority complex about Europeans or other white races, as she had convincingly defeated the Russians in the war of 1904–1905. She had been Britain's ally since 1902, and in 1914 had captured Tsingtao and Shantung, the German concessions in China, and groups of German colonial islands in the Pacific. These gains were confirmed at Versailles in 1919, leaving Japan the dominant power in the Western Pacific.

But mere groups of islands were insufficient for these proud people and Japan began to feel she had more in common with Germany (who had no overseas possessions) and Italy (who had few) than with the other Powers.

In 1915 she attempted to control China and was prevented by American protest; from then on the United States was viewed as the Japanese Navy's prime potential enemy. But despite the naval view, the Army still saw China (as it had since the Sino-Japanese War at the end of the nineteenth century) as its main objective and Russia as the power which might thwart its continental designs.

In 1921 Britain was concerned about expansionist Japan and, acting under some American pressure, declined to renew the alliance of 1902, and in 1924 the United States excluded Asiatics as immigrants. Both these actions caused the Japanese deep offence. More affront was given by Britain's announcement that she would build a naval base at Singapore, correctly interpreted by the Japanese as a check on their ambitions.

16

The 'moderate' Japanese Government now came under pressure from their own countrymen, who particularly remembered that by the Treaty of Washington of 1921 the Japanese, American and British fleets were restricted to the ratio 3:5:5 respectively and that in 1922 their government had signed the Nine-Power Treaty guaranteeing the integrity of China. All these factors were damaging to the moderates, whose position was further weakened by the world economic crisis which started in 1929 and which hit Japan particularly hard. The militarists found it easier now to say that 'expansion' was the solution to Japan's problems.

This expansion started in September 1931 with the quick occupation of Manchuria. This was achieved under bogus claims that Japanese troops guarding the South Manchurian Railway under treaty right were being attacked by the Chinese. Manchuria was renamed Manchukuo, and became a puppet state of Japan. The occupation was not recognized by the League of Nations or the United States, and the Japanese left the League in 1933. Three years later she joined Germany and Italy in the Anti-Comintern Pact.

Japan invaded North China proper on 7th July 1937, after a suspicious, and probably trumped-up, incident with the Chinese at the Marco Polo bridge over the River Hun near Peking. These shots were possibly the first of the 1939–1945 War (if those fired at Scapa Flow to try to prevent the scuttling of the German High Seas Fleet are discounted).

The struggle in China continued for the next two years, against opposition by Chiang Kai-Shek, by which time the Japanese realized that they were suffering from over-confidence engendered by the war of 1904–1905 and tried to rectify the matter. Despite these efforts over-confidence was their downfall in August 1939, when in the Nomonhan region of Manchuria the Russians trapped a Japanese force of 15,000 and 11,000 of them were lost. That month the sudden news of the Nazi-Soviet Pact caused a revulsion against the militarists and the liberal Japanese Government returned to power. They remained there, however, only until Germany's success in western Europe in June 1940; in July a pro-Axis government under Prince Konoye was put into power by the Army.

The Army now started to expand more vigorously in China, and at the end of September Japan signed the Tripartite Pact with Germany and Italy. By so doing they opposed any country that came into the war on the Allies' side, which obviously included the United States. In April 1941 Japan signed a neutrality pact with the Soviet Union, which allowed the former greater flexibility to expand in China, but did little to reduce her suspicions of Soviet designs.

On 24th July the Japanese put pressure on the Vichy French Government to let them take over French Indo-China, provoking – two days later – the freezing by the Americans of all Japanese assets. The British and Dutch quickly took similar action. The upshot for Japan was that trade, particularly in oil, was stopped.

Japan imported nearly 90 per cent of her oil and had then a three-year stock at normal levels of consumption. But maintaining normal levels of consumption did not include furthering the war in China. For this to be possible another source of supply had to be found and the only likely candidate was the Dutch East Indies – provided that the wells could be captured before they were destroyed. Additionally the acquisition of the region would – if Malaya were included – put Japan in control of most of the world's production of tin and rubber, and at the same time deny these vital commodities to her actual or potential enemies.

The Japanese were faced with the choice of abandoning their expansionist ambitions or fighting against great odds. On 6th August, they tried unsuccessfully to persuade the Americans to lift the embargo. Furthermore later that month the Americans declared that they would hold all the Philippines in any war and continued to reinforce the archipelago despite the Japanese requests to desist.

A change of direction in Japan now became inevitable and in October 1941 Prince Konoye's government was replaced by that of General Hideki Tojo. Factors were weighed – the most important being that oil stocks were down by a quarter since April – and the decision to go to war was taken on 25th November. Even then Admiral Isoruku Yamamoto, who had been ordered to attack Pearl Harbour, was told that the assault would be cancelled if negotiations in Washington were successful.

On paper, the Allied and Japanese navies in the Pacific were of roughly equal strength, but the Japanese were much stronger in aircraft carriers, the crucial ships. In addition the Japanese ships were generally more modern and the Japanese Navy had none of the language difficulties which beset the Allies. Japan probably had more troops – though apparently not enough to carry out the enormous offensive operations that had been planned – and her control of sea and air meant that she could arrange local superiority of numbers. To this numerical advantage was added the Japanese Army's greater experience in amphibious landings, jungle warfare and night attacks; and the fact that it had taken part in a recent and lengthy campaign.

The Japanese Air Force was powerful and more than a match for those of the Allies both in numbers and in the quality of its aircraft. Their superb Zero fighters could fly from Formosa to the Philippines and back, thereby safely releasing the carriers with their aeroplanes for the attack on Pearl Harbour. Japan's merchant navy was small for an island nation with virtually no natural resources, but this vital defect would only show in the later years of the war.

The Japanese went to war with the odds in their favour provided that the war was not one of long duration – a reminder of Nazi Germany and her *Blitzkriegs* (lightning wars) – and provided that the American battle fleet was put out of action, as it was intended to be, at Pearl Harbour. The Americans, for their part, had broken the Japanese codes and knew all that was being said by Tokyo to the Japanese Ambassador. But prudently the Japanese did not tell him of the times and points of attack, and so the Americans were caught off-guard at Pearl Harbour.

Japanese strategy was both defensive and offensive, in the objective to secure oil to enable her to conquer China, who herself would be shut off from supplies. Japan was well aware of the far greater strength (present and, more especially, latent) of the United States, but had observed with satisfaction all that had been achieved by the numerically smaller German armies against the Allies in Europe and, in particular, against the USSR. Furthermore, the Soviets were under far too much pressure defending themselves to be able to do anything active against the Japanese. It seemed to Japan that, after successful attacks on Pearl Harbour, Hong Kong, Malaya and the Philippines, she would be well on the way to establishing a defensive ring from the Aleutians in the north round to Burma in the south. It was believed confidently in Tokyo that once the United States had been unable to break this ring, it would be accepted as containing what they called 'The Greater East Asia Co-prosperity Sphere'. Again, a reminder of Nazi Germany and her plan to shut out the East (i.e. the USSR) from Archangel to Astrakhan.

The Japanese attacks on 7th Deccember 1941 went almost according to plan and Japan achieved most of what she initially wanted. There was one area where she did not succeed, however, and it was in fact possibly to cost her the war. The American fleet at Pearl Harbour was the battle fleet (i.e. gunned ships) and that fleet was very successfully dealt with. It did not include the American aircraft carriers which were away at sea and unharmed. Just six months later, on 4th June 1942, these very aircraft carriers were to cripple Japan's own aircraft carrier fleet at the Battle of Midway, which started Japan on the inexorable slide to defeat.

This in no way diminishes the gallant fighting by the Commonwealth forces, against great odds in appalling climatic conditions and with insufficient food and weapons. They fought valiantly in Hong Kong, Malaya, Singapore, Burma, Thailand and Papua New Guinea. The American victory at Midway stopped the Japanese; subsequent fighting on land and sea and in the air by Commonwealth, American, Dutch and other Allied forces expelled them and sent them back whence they had come.

Fortunately, no costly amphibious attack on mainland Japan was necessary, as the atom bombs dropped by the Americans on Hiroshima and Nagasaki showed the Japanese that they could not win against such a powerful weapon. No doubt the A-bomb gave the Japanese an opportunity to admit defeat without so much loss of face – an opportunity which they would not have had had only conventional weapons and assaults been employed. Casualties on both sides, terrible enough as they were, would surely have been far greater had fighting through the length and breadth of Japan against a determined enemy been required.

{ 5 }

How the 1939–1945 War was fought

Go tell, the Spartans
Thou who passest by,
That here obedient to
Their laws we lie

Simonides (c. 556–468 BC).

THOUGH MANY NOW BELIEVE THAT THE 1914–1918 WAR could perhaps have been avoided, there were entirely unavoidable reasons for the 1939–1945 War. It was a crusade against the evil and totalitarian regimes which then existed in Germany, Italy and Japan. It was waged by the Allied nations as a struggle for freedom. It was a necessary war, which simply had to be fought to the finish.

Once again Britain and France were allied against Germany, with the Dominions of Canada, Australia, New Zealand and South Africa once more being quick to declare their support in a common cause, as did India and other parts of the British Empire. But the world that went back to war in 1939 had long lost its innocence, buried in Flanders' mud and millions of military graves. There was none of the early fraternization that had occurred between British and German soldiers on Christmas Day in 1914. Instead, there was from the start a feeling among the Allies that an unpleasant job had to be finished once and for all, and the sooner the better, using virtually any method – brute force, air attacks, propaganda, clandestine and guerrilla warfare – almost anything to rid Europe of the Nazi and Fascist systems.

Conscription was already in force in Britain before war began and therefore less emphasis was placed on voluntary enlistments. Still, many did volunteer, particularly for the more glamorous 'teeth arms', such as the infantry, the artillery, armoured units, aircrew and submarines. Whereas people in 1914 expected the war to be 'over by Christmas', there was little confidence in 1939 that this conflict would be finished in a matter of months and the British Government planned for a war of at least three years' duration.

France had evidently not learned all the lessons of the previous conflict, particularly that of the Schlieffen Plan. Aware of Germany's aggressive intentions, the French had constructed the Maginot Line, but its massive

20

defences ended at the Belgian border, leaving a clearly vulnerable gap. Nearby, the BEF took up positions on sadly familiar ground in northern France (not being allowed by the Belgians to take up positions in their country), amidst the cemeteries of the last war. Here they settled down with their ally to face Germany throughout an uneventful winter, since dubbed the 'phoney war' (but not by those who were there).

In May 1940 Germany struck with a series of *Blitzkrieg* attacks, entering through the tempting gap that had been guarded only by the declared neutrality of Belgium and the Netherlands. Both small countries surrendered within days, crushed by overwhelming military force. German formations dashed across Flanders, occupying the area of the old 1914–1918 War battlefields, separating the French and British armies and threatening Paris within days.

The British force was pushed back, turning to make a fighting stand at the French port of Dunkirk. There then occurred the most amazing mass military evacuation in history. In nine days over 200,000 British and 130,000 French troops were rescued by hundreds of ships of the Royal Navy and small craft manned largely by English civilian volunteers. When the BEF returned to England, it had left behind most of its equipment in France so that in the summer of 1940 the only fully equipped formation available in England was a single Canadian division, which had arrived too late to go to France.

After the evacuation the remaining French armies collapsed and France capitulated on 22nd June 1940. Italy declared war on her and, in the Far East, Japan later also took advantage, occupying her Asian colonies, while making agreeable noises to her two Axis partners in Europe.

In a way these rapid global events set the pace of the 1939–1945 War, which was to be a conflict of constant movement, with little of the static face-to-face attrition of 1914–1918. The war involved scores of nations; it ranged over every continent and sea, costing more than 15 million military dead and probably far in excess of that number in civilian lives.

Once France had fallen, the Germans turned their attention to the destruction of the Royal Air Force (RAF) as a precursor to their proposed invasion of Britain by sea (Operation 'Sealion'). But the *Luftwaffe* (the German Air Force) was defeated over south-east England by determined men flying Hawker Hurricanes and Supermarine Spitfires, armed with the then unusual armament of eight machine guns, and much helped by efficient radar. The Germans then turned to aerial bombardment of specific targets and built-up areas, and the 'Blitz' and subsequent bombing campaigns lasted months. Coventry, Plymouth, Liverpool, Manchester, Glasgow, Belfast and many other towns were bombed, but the main attacks were on London, where 20,000 people died. It was a form of warfare that Germany would later dearly regret having initiated.

Frustrated by the refusal of Britain (personified by Churchill) to capitulate, Hitler turned once again to continental Europe, which he now ruled from Norway to the Balkans. His target this time was the Soviet

Union. Despite having not resolved his struggle with the British Empire, Hitler launched Operation 'Barbarossa' on 22nd June 1941, sending his armies into Soviet-occupied Poland and across Stalin's border. The German Army, with Finnish, Romanian, Hungarian and Italian contingents, put three million men into the Soviet Union along a 2,000 mile front.

At first the population was inclined to welcome the invaders as liberators from Stalin's rule, but Nazi oppression ruined this illusion. Instead *Einsatzgruppen* (special action squads) came in the wake of the armies and enforced an official policy of extermination of certain sections of *Untermenschen* (lesser breeds). The USSR suffered most grievously of all during the war, from both this merciless treatment of Slav and Jewish civilians and the enormous land battles which were fought losing seven million soldiers and well over that number of civilians. As a result of Nazi cruelty and destruction, a partisan war with no quarter given developed, from which the ordinary German troops also suffered.

Great battles were worsened by Russia's harsh winters, with casualty rates every bit as high as those of the 1914–1918 War. The invasion of Russia was to prove ultimately the most disastrous campaign of all for Germany and immediately the fighting in the West became less intense. However, the middle period of the war did not go well for Britain and the Commonwealth. After initially defeating Italian attempts to occupy North Africa and Greece, British, Australian and New Zealand forces fell back in the face of German onslaughts there. However, the fighting in Greece may well have delayed the start of 'Barbarossa' by a few weeks, thereby bringing closer the bitter weather of the Russian winter, much to the Soviets' great advantage.

In the Far East, Japan attacked Pearl Harbour on 7th December 1941 and brought the United States into the war; Germany declared war on the United States shortly after. The Japanese had staggering success, overrunning most of the Pacific within a few months, conquering virtually all the British, Dutch and American possessions in the region. Even Australia was threatened and subjected to air raids on its northern town of Darwin. Most of Burma fell next, with Japanese soldiers pushing on towards India. All these advances were marked by extreme cruelty on the part of the Japanese whose *Bushido* code held that captured enemies were undeserving of decent treatment. Time and again captured Allied troops, nurses and civilians were abused, tortured or murdered on 'death marches' and in primitive work camps.

The Royal Navy initially suffered severe setbacks in the Pacific, losing capital and other ships to Japanese air attacks off the Malayan coast and elsewhere, whereas earlier it had enjoyed much success against German naval forces and had bottled up Germany's surface fleet in port. But it was the old enemy, the U-Boat, which gave the Navy its greatest trial.

During the war over 1,100 U-Boats roved the world's oceans, concentrating mainly in the North Atlantic across which stretched vital supply lines from North America. It was the setting for a desperate, unending battle; millions of tons of Allied shipping went down in torpedo attacks and tens of thousands of merchant seamen were lost. On the other side well over 700 U-Boats were sunk and the Allies eventually won the Battle of the Atlantic.

The 1939–1945 War saw the raising of Commando units – army and naval personnel specially trained as raiders. Although uniformed troops, they could expect short shrift from the Nazis after Hitler issued his 'Commando Order' directing them to be shot on capture. The German innovation of parachute troops was taken up by Britain, whose airborne regiments fought in several battles. Other raiding forces flourished, most of them originating during operations in North Africa's Western Desert, but some being used throughout the rest of the war. These units included the Long Range Desert Group, the Special Air Service and the unofficially (and improbably) named 'Popski's Private Army'.

Most of the British Army in Britain, and the Canadian divisions reinforcing it, spent the mid-war years training in preparation for the expected invasion of the European continent – a period of waiting totally unlike the ceaseless land battles which marked the previous conflict. However, raiding attacks were kept up against German coastal installations, highlighted by the Dieppe Raid-in-Force, which was carried out to test invasion tactics. The practical knowledge gained by this raid would later be of enormous help in planning how to breach the walls of Hitler's 'Fortress Europe'.

Meanwhile fighting continued in North Africa. The British Eighth Army – including Anzac, South African and Indian troops – tussled back and forth with General Rommel's *Afrika Korps*, which came perilously close to the Suez Canal. In Burma the British 'Forgotten' Fourteenth Army – with British, Indian, and East and West African soldiers – fought to push back the Japanese from India's border in what eventually proved to be the war's longest single campaign, lasting three and a half years.

However, Britain's most potent attacks were now starting to come from the air; the Royal Air Force was being built up into a mighty weapon. By May 1945 it comprised more than 9,000 aircraft and over a million personnel, including the Women's Auxiliary Air Force (WAAF). The RAF used Vickers Wellington, Short Stirling and Handley-Page Halifax bombers and – most effective of all – the four-engined Avro Lancaster heavy bomber and the twin-engined de Havilland Mosquito. Having suffered very high casualties in daylight raids early in the war (the USAAF lost over 8,000 four-engined bombers in such raids), the RAF decided to concentrate on night bombing, with Pathfinder aircraft going ahead to mark targets with flares, and the main (bomber) force following.

Although production centres and military establishments were original-ly the main targets in Germany, Bomber Command turned to area bombing attacks; the precedent for this was set by the *Luftwaffe*. The RAF bombed Nazi Germany heavily, sometimes night after night, occasionally using over 1,000 aircraft at a time. The industrial Ruhr, naval bases, and cities such as

Berlin, Hamburg and Cologne took the brunt, but anti-bomber defences exacted a bloody price and RAF Bomber Command lost over 7,000 aircraft with about 50,000 men killed; another 8,000 died in accidents. Because of the nature of their duties, RAF casualties fell in every theatre of war, many with no known graves and some whose remains continue to be found to this day.

The end of 1942 proved a favourable turning-point for the Allies. In October, General Sir Bernard Montgomery's Eighth Army defeated General Erwin Rommel's *Afrika Korps* at the Battle of El Alamein in Egypt, driving it back through Libya and into Tunisia. Within a few weeks the Russians had a great triumph against the Germans at Stalingrad (now Volgograd) and the Americans defeated the Japanese at Guadalcanal in the Pacific. That November, Anglo-American forces landed in Algeria, helping to hasten the expulsion of German troops from North Africa by moving to meet the westward-bound Eighth Army in Tunisia.

In June 1943 Allied troops set foot in Europe again, when a combined Canadian, British and American force invaded Sicily. On 3rd September they crossed to the Italian mainland and Italy's forces surrendered (later to re-enter the war on the Allied side). But German armies continued to resist strongly, using the country's mountain ranges and innumerable rivers to contest every inch of ground. Twice the Allies tried to hasten their advance by making amphibious landings behind enemy lines, forming large bridgeheads at Salerno and Anzio; both were expensive in casualties but ultimately successful.

A slow struggle continued for possession of Italy, the Americans taking the west-coast route and the British and Commonwealth troops – generally – the Adriatic side. Along with them marched a truly international force of Frenchmen, Poles, Palestinians and even a battalion of Brazilian infantry. It was to be a further year and a half before victory was won there; not until Mussolini had been shot by his own people and tens of thousands of Allied servicemen had died.

Most operations in the South Pacific theatre were waged by the United States, supported by Australian and New Zealand forces. The USA conducted a war of 'island-hopping', making amphibious assaults to regain control of Japanese-occupied territory in a vast war-zone, from the Solomon Islands to Iwo Jima and Okinawa. This far-flung American offensive was based on a strategy aimed at occupying islands for use as bases for the aerial bombardment of Japan and as staging-areas for the projected invasion of Japan itself.

In addition to heavy Army casualties, over 20,000 US Marines died during this three-year campaign against a fanatically brave enemy. Many sailors also died aboard ships attacked by *kamikaze* (divine wind) suicide-pilots, who crashed their explosives-laden aircraft onto vessels of the US Navy and of the British Commonwealth fleet which helped support the Okinawa assault.

The first Axis capital to fall was Rome, captured on 4th June 1944.

This great event was somewhat overshadowed two days later, on 6th June, when D-Day of Operation 'Overlord', the long-awaited invasion, dawned over the Normandy coast. A huge armada of 4,000 ships landed 130,000 troops that first day and the Allies established a firm beach-head at a cost of 'only' 9,000 casualties, many fewer than had been expected. With Montgomery in command of 21st Army Group, the Commonwealth-US ground forces, the British Second Army (which included the 3rd Canadian Division) landed opposite the inland cities of Caen and Bayeux to the east and the US First Army between the Cherbourg Peninsula and St Laurent on the west.

The enemy units counter-attacked with characteristic determination, but the Allies landed over 300,000 men within a week, despite unseasonable gales, and made steady progress inland. While the Americans attacked towards Cherbourg, the British and Canadians headed for Caen. Here Montgomery clashed once more with Rommel, his old adversary from the desert war. Rommel had many SS *Panzer* (tank) divisions in position and the subsequent fighting for Caen was hard. Canadian and British troops took heavy losses but captured the city on 9th July, opening the way for the pursuit of the enemy as they gradually retreated northwards.

At this time Britain became the victim of a new form of 'Blitz', as Hitler launched an aerial campaign, using unmanned missiles. Their name, *Vergeltungswaffen* (revenge weapons), made it clear that they were designed entirely for the destruction of civilian targets. The V1 flying bomb became known as the 'doodle bug' or 'buzz-bomb' from the sound of its engine; it carried a one-ton high-explosive warhead and was aimed against London and south-east England, where it killed over 6,000 people in a few months.

V1s were launched from the French coast until their sites were cleared by the Canadians in September. By then, however, a new phase in London's ordeal had begun, as on 8th September *Luftwaffe* troops in the Netherlands launched the first V2, a high-altitude rocket, also with a one-ton warhead. During a bombardment that continued into the new year, in excess of 1,000 of these V2s exploded in England, causing much loss of life, though the worst suffering was in Antwerp, where 14,000 people were killed.

Paris was liberated on 25th August, a symbolic day for the free world which raised high hopes of a swift final victory. But that was not to be, as the Germans withdrew into Belgium and the Netherlands with no sign of slackening their resolve. They opened the dykes of the extensive drainage works throughout the Netherlands to cause flooding – to act as an efficient military barrier – while positioning themselves along the Scheldt Estuary to deny Allied shipping use of the port of Antwerp. This ensured that supplies still had to be brought to the front from Normandy, hundreds of miles away. But eventually Antwerp was captured and reopened to become the Allies' main seaport.

As winter approached the Allies attempted to breach the formidable barrier blocking entry into Germany: the Siegfried Line. On 17th September a large airborne army of British, Polish and American formations attempted to outflank the German defences. They landed by parachute and glider behind the River Rhine with the task of holding the bridges at Grave, Nijmegen and Arnhem until joined by a corps coming up from the south. The Germans quickly moved heavy reinforcements into the area, held off the relief force and encircled the airborne troops at Arnhem. The Allied attempt ended in failure after a nine-day battle and the British 1st Airborne Division was virtually destroyed.

During the autumn of 1944 the Allies had penetrated Germany, but found that the enemy had one last surprise. In December the Germans attacked through the Ardennes Forest in Belgium against thinly held American lines. The so-called 'Battle of the Bulge', which followed, caused heavy losses (including another SS massacre at Malmedy), but the German forces were contained and pushed back before year's end. It was Hitler's last major effort as the vast armies of the Soviet Union were now deep into Germany, comparatively near Berlin. However, the Allies still had much fierce fighting ahead of them in Europe, including crossing the Rhine.

By the early months of 1945, the lack of front line reinforcements was a severe problem. It was bad enough for British units, with few fresh young troops available through conscription or released from other theatres. For the Canadians it was even worse: they had no conscription for overseas service; they relied on volunteers for replenishment. Without enough reinforcements, their wounded men had to be repeatedly returned from hospital to active service.

The Soviets were fighting in the streets of Berlin in April (where resistance was so fierce that there were over 400,000 casualties) and on the 30th of that month Adolph Hitler committed suicide in his underground bunker. The advance into Germany was marked by the liberation of numerous concentration camps – Belsen, Buchenwald, Auschwitz and a score of other infamous places. In these the Nazis had killed over six million people, particularly Jews, Gypsies, Slavs and political prisoners, in a programme of deliberate human extermination probably unequalled in history.

On 7th May 1945 Germany's surrender of all armed forces was signed. The German war was over, but it did leave the armies of the Soviet Union in possession of the capitals of middle Europe. Next day the free world celebrated 'VE Day'. For all that, there was still the war with Japan to be finished, though most of its conquered territory had been freed by then.

In Burma, Mandalay and Rangoon were retaken by the British Fourteenth Army, led by General Sir William Slim. Soon after, the Australians landed in Borneo and cleared Papua New Guinea; US General Douglas MacArthur led the Americans to liberate the Philippines. Once Okinawa was taken, Tokyo was within easy striking distance and aerial bombardment of the Japanese home islands by American bombers caused widespread destruction.

The Allies were well aware of the high cost in military and civilian casualties that would certainly be the result of an invasion of Japan. In July the Potsdam Declaration by the USA, Britain and China warned Japan of her 'utter destruction' should she refuse to surrender unconditionally. But Japan refused and warned darkly of the probable fate of the many thousands of Allied prisoners-of-war in captivity there should the land of Nippon be invaded.

On 6th August 1945 the first atom bomb to be used in 'anger' was dropped on Hiroshima from an American Superfortress. The mushroom cloud that arose that morning was the dreadful outcome of the conflict unleashed by Hitler six years before; mankind would ever after live in fear of nuclear war. This most destructive of all weapons had more explosive power than 20,000 tons of TNT and was over 2,000 times more powerful than the largest bomb so far used. It caused very heavy casualties, yet Japan still made no move to surrender, even fighting a strong naval engagement. So a second atomic bomb was dropped at Nagasaki on 9th August, with even more dreadful effect. It forced the Japanese to discuss capitulation and a delegation met MacArthur on the battleship USS *Missouri* in Tokyo Bay. Japan signed the surrender documents, formally ending the 1939–1945 War on 2nd September 1945 – six years and a day after it began.

After the joyous celebrations of 'VJ Day' were over, the world applied itself to the grim task of clearing up and taking stock. The cost of the Second World War of the twentieth century was appalling in human terms: at least 15 million military deaths worldwide, plus double that in civilian fatalities. Over seven million Russian soldiers died; over three million German; over two million Chinese; and two million Japanese. The United States lost nearly 300,000 servicemen. And this time the British Commonwealth had sacrificed over 600,000 lives to freedom's cause. As before, they would be duly honoured in death and the unique organization founded by Sir Fabian Ware once more took up the task of keeping faith with the Commonwealth's war dead.

{ 6 }

Great Britain and the Commonwealth

Why are young men told to look in ancient history
for examples of heroism, when their own countrymen
furnish such lessons?

Sir William Napier (1785–1860).

T HIS CHAPTER CONTAINS A VERY BRIEF HISTORY OF THE
armed forces of Great Britain, Canada, Australia, New Zealand,
Newfoundland, South Africa and India in the 1914–1918 and
1939–1945 Wars. For those who wish to study particular campaigns or other
aspects more thoroughly, detailed accounts are in print. The Cemetery
Registers' Introductions (in the Register Boxes in the larger War Graves
Commission sites) give a useful short history of actions in that area and
country, as do the Commission's Historical Notices. It is hoped that by the
1990s the latter will be in position in about half of the Commission's war
cemeteries and memorials.

Our purpose here is to provide visitors to war cemeteries or memorials
with an outline of where and when their countrymen fought and died.
Because of restrictions on space we have not included some Commonwealth
countries: Nigeria, Northern and Southern Rhodesia (now Zambia and
Zimbabwe), the British West Indies, and many other territories which were
at the time British colonies and which made vital and loyal contributions.
We offer apologies if we offend anyone by any such omission.

United Kingdom

Of the Commonwealth countries, the United Kingdom played the major
role in the 1914–1918 and 1939–1945 Wars because of the size of her
population and her direct involvement as a European Power. In all she lost
nearly 1,300,000 service personnel: 888,000 and 384,000 in each conflict
respectively. In addition over 66,000 civilians were killed, mainly as a result
of air raids (including over 1,000 in the 1914–1918 War), long-range
artillery over the Strait of Dover, V1 flying bombs and V2 rockets.

The Royal Navy went into action immediately in 1914, sustaining its first battle casualties at sea on 6th August. It soon began to suffer severe losses, primarily from German U-Boats. Perhaps even more seriously, the Mercantile Marine's losses from submarine attacks were enormous. This for a while threatened Britain's survival, for without the Mercantile Marine and the supplies it brought the war could not be won. The eventual success of the convoy system of protecting merchant ships eased the situation. By Armistice Day 1918 25,000 Royal Navy sailors and 10,000 merchant seamen had died at sea.

The most important single naval engagement was the Battle of Jutland, off the Danish coast on 31st May 1916, between the British Grand Fleet, and the German High Seas Fleet. The Royal Navy lost 14 ships and with them over 6,000 sailors; the Germans 11 ships and 2,500 sailors. Although perhaps a tactical victory for Germany, it was a strategic success for the RN, in that it discouraged the German fleet from venturing out again and established British naval supremacy for the rest of the war.

The British Expeditionary Force was fighting in France by the third week of August 1914. Casualties in the Retreat from Mons, the subsequent Battle of the Marne and the First Battle of Ypres were such that the original BEF ceased to exist. But reinforced by Regulars and Territorials, and later by conscripts, the British Army fought through every major battle, including Loos, 'Second' Ypres, the Somme (where it suffered 60,000 casualties in a single day – 1st July 1916), Messines, 'Third' Ypres, Arras, Cambrai, the Somme again in 1918 and the final drive to victory. British soldiers also fought in other campaigns of varying length and cost in manpower: on the Gallipoli Peninsula (25,000 dead); in Macedonia (10,000 dead); in Mesopotamia (18,000 dead); and in the Middle East, Africa and elsewhere. In many cases they were helped by troops of at least one Commonwealth country.

The Royal Flying Corps and Royal Naval Air Service (RNAS) were British arms, though they included a large minority of Commonwealth airmen. At first the German Air Force was often in control of the skies; later the position was reversed. The RFC's top-scoring 'ace' was Major Edward Mannock, with 73 confirmed aerial victories, only seven fewer than the 80 recorded by the famed German 'Red Baron' Manfred von Richthofen, shot down by Canadian fighter pilot Captain A.R. Brown, or Australian small-arms fire, on 12th March 1918. The RFC and RNAS were merged into a separate new service, the Royal Air Force, on 1st April 1918. It ended the war with nearly 300,000 personnel and 20,000 aircraft, the most powerful air force in the world.

On 3rd September 1939, less than 21 years after the previous conflict had ended, the United Kingdom once more went to war with Germany. The Royal Air Force and Royal Navy were involved almost at once, hunting U-Boats and attacking enemy naval targets. The Navy suffered early disasters, beginning with the sinking of the aircraft carrier HMS *Courageous* at sea, while the battleship HMS *Royal Oak* was torpedoed in the anchorage at Scapa Flow, Scotland. But successes were to follow. In December 1939 three cruisers disabled the German 'pocket' battleship *Graf Spee* in the Battle of the River Plate and the ship was scuttled off Montevideo, Uruguay. Other successful naval engagements followed at Matapan (south of Greece) and North Cape (north of Norway), and in 1941 the RN sank the German battleship *Bismarck* though the battle cruiser HMS *Hood* was lost in this action. Meanwhile aircraft of the Fleet Air Arm wrecked much of the Italian fleet at Taranto Harbour in November 1940; no doubt the Japanese noted this exploit.

Profiting from its experiences in the 1914–1918 War, the Navy at once used the convoy system for merchant ships. This helped ensure that, despite inevitable merchant losses, troops and adequate supplies of food and war material continued to reach Britain. The RN defeated the main U-Boat threat in mid-1943, aided by RAF Coastal Command and ships and aircraft from Canada. It had performed a remarkable rescue operation in evacuating the British Expeditionary Force from Dunkirk, France, in the summer of 1940, and later supported the Army in various invasion landings in North Africa, Sicily, Italy, Normandy and the Far East.

Events went badly for the Army at first, being expelled from Norway and France in rapid succession in mid-1940, though it fared better in Ethiopia and Somaliland, where it defeated the Italian forces. Setbacks in the Far East were even worse, as Japan occupied Malaya, Singapore, the East Indies and Burma. The Army was in action in the Far East from December 1941, trying to prevent the Japanese advance. In Burma, the Fourteenth Army's jungle struggle lasted for nearly four years and cost 20,000 British and Indian lives; a further 18,000 Commonwealth troops died in Singapore and Malaya. In North Africa, advancing from Libya into Egypt, Germany's *Afrika Korps* came threateningly close to the Suez Canal. However, victory at the decisive Battle of El Alamein in October 1942 enabled Britain eventually to drive the Germans from North Africa in May 1943. Ahead lay the slow but ultimately succesful campaigns in Sicily and Italy.

In what Churchill immortalized as Britain's 'finest hour', Royal Air Force Fighter Command won the Battle of Britain during August and September 1940; denying the *Luftwaffe* superiority in the air over Britain. The RAF later went on the offensive, launching bombing raids against Germany and operating in a tactical ground support role. How much the bombing offensive contributed to the shortening of the war is open to question. But what is certain is that the aircrews showed devotion to duty and over 50,000 of them died.

British servicemen fought on virtually every battlefield, from the Arctic to the tropics, in deserts and mountains, often side by side with Commonwealth comrades. The Merchant Navy carried out its unglamorous but essential task in even more hazardous conditions than had prevailed during the previous war at sea, at a cost of over 25,000 lives.

Canada

About 110,000 Canadians died in the 1914–1918 and 1939–1945 Wars (65,000 and 45,000 respectively); some were interred in Canada, but the vast majority lie buried abroad.

Canadian infantrymen were on the Western Front in January 1915 and in March the 1st Canadian Division took part in the Battle of Neuve Chapelle. In April Canadians fought in the Second Battle of Ypres, where they were subjected to the Germans' first use of gas.

When the 2nd Division arrived in France, the Canadian Corps was formed, later expanded by the addition of the 3rd Division. From April to August 1916 the corps fought in the defence of Ypres, until it moved to fight in the Battle of the Somme. On 9th April 1917 it captured Vimy Ridge, which had withstood all attacks for two years. Though this victory cost the Canadian Corps 10,000 casualties, it was certainly a great military success, and ensured that Vimy Ridge would later be chosen as the site of Canada's National Memorial.

Canadian soldiers met with success in August 1917, taking Hill 70, north of Arras. After being transferred to the Ypres front, the Canadians took the previously impregnable objective of Passchendaele on 6th November 1917 suffering 15,000 casualties in the process. In March 1918 cavalry and motorized machine-gun units of the Canadian Corps helped hold the line at Amiens, when the Germans launched their last big offensive. Then the Canadians formed the spearhead of the thrust between Hourges and Villers-Bretonneux, afterwards returning to the Arras area.

On 2nd September 1918, seven Canadians earned the Victoria Cross in exceptionally fierce fighting. The corps attacked across the Canal du Nord, forcing the Germans back to the Hindenburg Line, which was broken on the 27th of that month. On 9th October they took Cambrai. During the period between mid-August to mid-October, the Canadians had suffered over 30,000 casualties killed, wounded, or captured.

As events soon proved, Canadians excelled in aerial combat. In providing many members of the Royal Flying Corps, the Royal Naval Air Service and later the Royal Air Force, Canada made a great contribution in this field. More than 23,000 Canadian airmen served with British Forces and over 1,500 died. The Commonwealth's highest scoring airman to survive the war was a Canadian: Lieutenant Colonel W.A. Bishop VC, with 72 victories.

Canadian naval participation in the 1914–1918 War was limited, as its newly formed navy possessed only two old cruisers. However, many thousands went to serve with the Royal Navy. Fleets of Canadian trawlers and small craft carried out mine-sweeping and anti-submarine operations in coastal waters.

Canada entered the 1939–1945 War on 10th September 1939. Within two months the first contingents of Canadian troops arrived in the United Kingdom to supplement the BEF. Forestalled by the evacuation of the

British Army from Dunkirk and the Channel ports, Canada's role became one of defence of the British Isles. Far across the globe a small force of Canadians arrived in Hong Kong in time to meet the Japanese invasion, and fought with the British, Indian and Hong Kong forces in defence of the colony until the surrender on Christmas Day 1941.

On 19th August 1942 troops of the Canadian 2nd Division formed the bulk of the Dieppe Raid. Of the 5,000 Canadians who took part, only about 2,000 returned to England: nearly 1,000 had been killed and 2,000 taken prisoner. A further 500 Canadians lost their lives when they landed in Sicily as part of the Eighth Army on 10th July 1943.

On 3rd September a combined Canadian, British and American force made the first full-scale invasion of mainland Europe, attacking on the 'toe' of Italy and reaching Naples on 1st October. Canadian troops fought at Ortona and Monte Cassino and in May 1944 took part in the costly, but successful, attack on the Hitler line: the first major operation by a Canadian corps in the 1939–1945 War. The battle northwards through Italy continued to the war's end and ultimately cost the lives of nearly 6,000 Canadians.

Landing in Normandy on 6th June 1944 as part of the Allied invasion force, the Canadians played an important role in the battle to take Caen. They then advanced along the French seacoast to the Pas-de-Calais and took Dieppe on 1st September. Canadians fought with British soldiers in the freeing of the Scheldt Estuary and success here enabled the first Allied convoy to arrive in Antwerp in November 1944.

Some Canadian units played a prominent part in the liberation of the Netherlands while others went on to participate in the Battle of Germany. In February 1945 the Canadian First Army attacked in the Reichswald Forest, and helped drive the Germans back across the Rhine; the German forces surrendered to General Montgomery on Lüneburg Heath on 5th May 1945. From D-Day to VE Day 12,500 Canadians died.

During the 1939–1945 War the Royal Canadian Navy (RCN) grew to a strength of nearly 100,000 personnel and nearly 400 vessels. Their main duty was to act as convoy escorts across the Atlantic, in the Mediterranean and to Murmansk in the USSR. They also hunted submarines, and supported amphibious landings in Sicily, Italy and Normandy. In all the RCN lost nearly 2,000 sailors.

Although a major task of the Royal Canadian Air Force (RCAF) based at home was the hunting of U-Boats in the North Atlantic, its most important area of operations was Europe, where 48 Canadian squadrons served. The scale of their contribution was recognized on 1st January 1943 by the formation of No. 6 Group, an RCAF formation within Bomber Command. Canadian airmen fought in the Battle of Britain, North Africa, Italy and the Normandy invasion. About 17,000 died, the great majority while serving with Bomber Command.

Australia

Australia lost 102,000 men in the 1914–1918 and 1939–1945 Wars (62,000 and over 40,000 respectively).

Her first act of war in 1914 was to destroy German wireless stations at Rabaul and Yap, and to occupy New Guinea and the islands of New Britain, New Ireland and Bougainville; casualties during these operations were, happily, light.

The Australian Imperial Force (AIF), joined by two brigades from New Zealand, sailed for Britain in November 1914. En route through the Indian Ocean the escorting cruiser, HMAS *Sydney*, left the convoy to take part in a battle with the German cruiser *Emden*, running it aground on the Cocos Islands. Throughout the war the Royal Australian Navy (RAN) assisted with convoy protection and undertook other duties on every ocean.

The AIF was diverted to Egypt, where it was formed into a contingent named the Australian and New Zealand Army Corps (ANZAC), which landed with British and French troops on the Gallipoli Peninsula in April 1915. Australians took part in the fighting until their evacuation in December 1915.

Australians were also sent to France, where the 1st Anzac Corps arrived in April 1916 less two mounted divisions which remained in the Middle East as part of the Egyptian Expeditionary Force to fight the Turks. Australian troops took part in the First Battle of the Somme – taking the key objective of Pozières, though with heavy losses – and in many subsequent battles, including Messines and 'Third' Ypres (Passchendaele).

Australia's Middle East contingent helped drive Turkish forces from the Sinai and had a hand in the invasion of Palestine in 1917. In December 1917 they were with the British General Sir Edmund Allenby when he entered Jerusalem to take its surrender. The following year Australians helped in the capture of Damascus, which virtually ended the war in the Middle East.

For the last year of the war, all Australian divisions on the Western Front were brought together in the Australian Corps, which saw action at Arras, Polygon Wood, Mont St. Quentin, and took part in the breaching of the Hindenburg Line and the final advance to victory. Perhaps the corps' most famous engagement was at Villers-Bretonneux, in April 1918, where the Australian National Memorial now stands. After 30 months on the Western Front Australian dead totalled 47,000.

Australian air squadrons were part of the Royal Flying Corps until 1917, when they formed the Australian Flying Corps. Australian pilots were in combat in Mesopotamia and Palestine from the start of these campaigns and were prominent in the air war over the Western Front.

In the 1939–1945 War Australia's involvement extended over an even wider area. As in the 1914–1918 War the first AIF divisions intended for France were diverted for Middle East service. They and the New Zealanders fought with the British to defend the Suez Canal against the Italian threat from Libya. By February 1941 they had driven back the Italians beyond Benghazi. Meanwhile Australian warships were active with the British Mediterranean Fleet, taking part in the sea battles off Matapan and Taranto.

German forces arrived in North Africa in March 1941 and pushed the Allies back beyond the Egyptian frontier. The Australians were in the fighting at Tobruk in April 1941 and held out during the 14-month siege which followed. Australian troops also played a part in General Montgomery's breakthrough at El Alamein; in all some 4,000 Australians lost their lives during the North African campaigns.

An Australian Division moved to Greece in April 1941, where it merged with the 2nd New Zealand Division to revive the Anzac Corps. However, the corps was in the end forced to withdraw, carrying on the fight in Crete, which in turn had to be evacuated. Australians also took part in the Syrian campaign against the Vichy French, who were defeated after a five-week campaign ending in July 1941.

Soon after Japan entered the war an Australian force of 1,400 was overwhelmed on the island of New Britain. A similar fate met their garrisons on Timor and Ambon, and at Lae and Salamana in New Guinea. In early 1942 initial success by the Australians in Malaya was followed by heavy losses, and thousands of Australians were taken prisoner at Singapore. Many of these died in imprisonment in what is now Indonesia, and while working as labourers on the Burma-Siam railway. Australian casualties as a result of the Malayan Campaign included nearly 7,000 dead.

In Europe Australian casualties were almost all in the Royal Australian Air Force (RAAF), mainly while flying with RAF Bomber Command. RAAF airmen also flew against the Japanese, launching their first raids from airfields in Australia and gradually moving up the Pacific island chain. For her part, Japan carried out air raids against Darwin, Northern Territory, where over 200 Australian civilians lost their lives.

Throughout the war, the RAN was in action against both Germany and Japan and lost about 1,500 sailors. In one incident three Japanese submarines entered Sydney Harbour and sank a depot ship killing 20 seamen.

The Australians succeeded in holding Papua and helped check the Japanese advance through the south-west Pacific islands aimed at invading the island continent itself. From late 1942 onwards many Australian divisions took part in the Allied island-hopping campaign which gradually pushed back the enemy across the Pacific. In 1945 Australian forces landed in Borneo and adjacent islands and overcame the Japanese there. More than 14,000 Australians laid down their lives in the Pacific.

New Zealand

New Zealand lost over 30,000 men in the 1914–1918 and 1939–1945 Wars (18,000 and 12,000 respectively).

It could be said that New Zealand troops were the first Allied forces to occupy enemy territory in the 1914–1918 War, when they secured German Samoa immediately after the outbreak of hostilities. In October 1914 the New Zealand Expeditionary Force (NZEF) sailed for Europe but was diverted and landed in Egypt, where it helped repulse the Turkish attack on the Suez Canal in April 1915. On 25th April 1915 the New Zealand force landed south of Suvla Bay on the Gallipoli Peninsula – near the Australians – where they fought until evacuated in December 1915.

The New Zealand force was reorganized in Egypt and amalgamated with the Australians to form the Australian and New Zealand Army Corps, which took part in the successful battles against Turkish forces in Egypt and Palestine. New Zealand infantry went to France in April 1916 and fought in the First Battle of the Somme. They were at the Battle of Flers-Courcelette and Morval, fighting for 23 consecutive days and advancing more than two miles; over 1,500 were killed or died of wounds.

New Zealand soldiers also fought at Messines, Belgium, in June 1917 and in the Third Battle of Ypres in October 1917. They were at the capture of Bapaume in August 1918, and took part in the breaching of the Masnières line and in the attack which led to the surrender of the fortress of Le Quesnoy, France, on 4th November 1918.

New Zealanders also played an active role at sea and in the air during the 1914–1918 War and several hundred served with the Royal Flying Corps, the Royal Naval Air Service and the Royal Air Force.

At the outbreak of war in 1939 New Zealand dispatched its Expeditionary Force, advance echelons of which arrived in Egypt in February 1940. New Zealand Army units helped in the destruction of the Italian Army in Libya and Cyrenaica and when German forces invaded Greece in April 1941, New Zealanders fought a series of rearguard actions before withdrawing. Some went to Crete, where they inflicted casualties on the German airborne troops. After six days of heavy fighting, the surviving defenders withdrew to Egypt, leaving behind many dead and prisoners of war.

After service in Egypt and Syria New Zealanders were continuously in the field in North Africa until the campaign ended with the surrender of axis forces in Tunisia in May 1943. Captain Charles Upham of the New Zealand infantry received a VC for gallantry in Crete in May 1941 and a Bar in the Western Desert in July 1942 and survived – the only 'double VC' of the 1939–1945 War.

Moving to Italy in September 1943 New Zealand troops were engaged there almost continuously until the end of the war. They took part in the Battles of the River Sangro and Monte Cassino. Despite many losses they advanced to Florence, fought at the Gothic Line and helped to capture Trieste in April 1945.

In the Pacific theatre New Zealanders carried out island operations against the Japanese, including the capture of Vella Lavella, Treasury Island and the Green Islands.

The Royal New Zealand Navy (RNZN) was established early in the war, and HMNZS *Achilles* took part in the Battle of the River Plate. Among the many actions carried out by New Zealand minesweepers in tropical waters was the sinking of the more heavily armed Japanese submarine *I-1* by *Moa* and *Kiwi* off Guadalcanal in January 1943.

In 1939 the Royal New Zealand Air Force (RNZAF) had a strength of nearly 1,200 (all ranks). However, so effective was its expansion programme, that by June 1944 the RNZAF had reached a peak strength of nearly 42,000, with 15 squadrons of bombers, fighters and transport aircraft. These saw service throughout the South Pacific theatre of war. In addition almost 11,000 New Zealanders were attached to the Royal Air Force and served in almost every war zone; many of them flew with RAF Bomber Command in Europe.

Newfoundland

During the two World Wars Newfoundland was still politically a separate Dominion, becoming a Canadian province only in 1949. Within two months of war being declared in August 1914 she formed the Newfoundland Regiment, while over 2,000 Newfoundlanders joined the Royal Navy and served in British warships all over the world.

The Newfoundland Regiment was first deployed in the Middle East, taking part in the Gallipoli Peninsula fighting, where 43 Newfoundlanders were killed. The unit was later transferred to the Western Front, where on the first day of the Battle of the Somme – 1st July 1916 – it was among the units which were worst hit, sustaining about 700 casualties. Its contribution is marked by the Caribou Memorial to the Royal Newfoundland Regiment, which stands in Beaumont Hamel Memorial Park, the site of the line along which its attack started. The regiment went on to fight in the Third Battle of Ypres (Passchendaele) in 1917.

In 1939 Newfoundlanders served in the British armed forces. Some of these went to form two regiments of the Royal Artillery, which fought in North Africa and Italy; and in the Normandy invasion and in battles for north-west Europe. Newfoundlanders also served in the Royal Navy, the Royal Canadian Navy, and in the Merchant Navy. And there were Newfoundlanders in the RAF who formed their own night-fighter squadron. Over 900 Newfoundlanders lost their lives during the 1939–1945 War.

South Africa

The support of the Union of South Africa (now the Republic of South Africa – South Africa withdrew from the Commonwealth in 1961) in the 1914–1918 and 1939–1945 Wars was of great importance. Because of that country's command of the South Atlantic and its borders (in 1914) with German colonies in Africa it was well placed to influence events. Significantly, the rest of the world noted that South Africa declared her support in 1914 with enthusiasm, despite the fact that part of her population had been at war with Britain only a decade or so before in the Boer War. Those who consequently rebelled against this decision were put down by the South Africans themselves.

In 1914 the first task of the South African forces was to deny the enemy the use of its seaports in German South-West Africa (now Namibia), by taking Swakopmund and Luderitz Bay. The capital, Windhoek, was occupied next, on 12th May 1915, and the rest of the enemy forces in the territory surrendered on 9th July 1915.

Later that year 6,000 South African troops arrived in Britain to start training. From there they went to Egypt to help combat the invasion by Turkish-allied Senussi tribes, and defeated them at Hazalin in January 1916. The South African Brigade disembarked at Marseilles on 23rd April to enter the European theatre of war. The brigade saw its first action in France during the Battle of the Somme and perhaps its greatest trial was at the engagement at Delville Wood, most of which the South Africans captured on 15th July 1916 at a cost of nearly 2,400 men. This battle later established Delville Wood as the site of their National Memorial.

The brigade remained on the Somme and in October 1916 was involved in the Battle of Warlencourt. It later fought on the Arras front and in the Third Battle of Ypres. In April 1918 it helped stem the German offensive and played an important role in the Battle of the Lys and to the north of Le Câteau. There the Brigade crossed the River Selle, its final objective, on 19th October 1918.

Meanwhile South Africans were fighting in German East Africa (now Tanzania), where they steadily forced the Germans and their African levies to retreat southwards. In October 1917 a four-day action at Nyango resulted in the Union troops driving a wedge between the enemy positions, one of which surrendered on 28th November. The other German force escaped into Portuguese East Africa (now Mozambique) and, under the command of General Paul von Lettow-Vorbeck, continued to fight so courageously and skilfully that the campaign continued right up to the end of the war. This column of German colonial troops surrendered on 25th November 1918.

During the 1914–1918 War the Union of South Africa had no navy or air force of their own, but many South Africans enlisted in the Royal Navy, the RFC and the RAF.

On 4th September 1939 in a parliamentary debate, the Herzog government tabled a motion for neutrality in the conflict which had just broken out in Europe. However, an amendment moved by General J.C. Smuts (an opponent of Britain in the South African War), and carried comfortably, ensured that the Union of South Africa entered the 1939–1945 War on 6th September 1939, just three days after Britain.

South African troops moved into Abyssinia (now Ethiopia) to support British forces fighting the Italians and in January 1941 they helped take Mogadishu and marched in the entry into Addis Ababa on 6th April of that year. They continued to take part in operations in Somaliland until fighting ceased in East Africa the following November.

The main body of Union forces was with the British Eighth Army in Egypt, where they helped in the attempt to relieve the besieged garrison at Tobruk. Later, South African forces fought in the four-day Battle of Sidi Rezegh and reached Benghazi. Early in 1942 they suffered heavily in the German attack which led to the surrender of Tobruk on 21st June; 10,000 South Africans were taken prisoner. After the Eighth Army victory at El Alamein, most of the remnants of the South African land forces returned home.

In April 1943 a call for army volunteers to fight outside Africa brought the South African Armoured Division to Italy. Two months later this formation became involved in the pursuit to the River Arno. Union soldiers fought throughout the rest of the Italian campaign alongside British and other Commonwealth troops, until the German surrender in April 1945.

No South African navy existed at the start of the 1939–1945 War; the Royal Navy guarded the Union's coasts and shipping. However, by September 1940 South African warships had arrived in the Mediterranean for the hazardous 'Tobruk run' and stayed there for the next four years. Later the South African Naval Force took part in the invasion of French North Africa, and served in the Indian Ocean and with the Allied Pacific Fleet.

The South African Air Force (SAAF) saw service against the Italians in East Africa, particularly during the Abyssinian campaign. SAAF aircraft then joined the Desert Air Force in North Africa in late 1941 and provided air support at Tobruk and El Alamein.

South African losses numbered more than 21,000 dead in the 1914–1918 and 1939–1945 Wars (9,300 and 11,900 respectively). Thus it is a sad but proud fact that South Africa and India were the only two Commonwealth countries that lost more men dead in the Second World War than in the First.

India

In the 1914–1918 and 1939–1945 Wars the forces of India played a major role. (India was one country until partitioned on 15th August 1947, to form modern India and Pakistan; the latter was later further partitioned into Pakistan and Bangladesh.) Vast numbers of Indians served and they were militarily very effective. 159,000 laid down their lives (72,000 and 87,000 respectively) – the second highest casualty figure among the Commonwealth Forces. Although India was under British rule, there was no conscription of Indians. However, no sooner had the Viceroy announced in 1914 the commencement of hostilities with Germany than 58 Indian princes of native states declared their personal support for the war, and hundreds of thousands of Indians volunteered. The strength of the Indian Army rose to one million.

The Indian Army went into action for the first time in the war in August 1914, against the German colonies in China. Indian troops arrived on the Western Front as early as 20th October 1914, and they were in action that month at Wytschaete, near Ypres, where a sepoy won the first Indian VC of the war. They fought at Neuve-Chapelle in March 1915 (their most famous battle on the Western Front and now the site of their National Memorial) and later around Gevinchy. By the end of that year there had been over 7,000 Indian casualties.

The Indian Corps fought against the Germans at Ypres, Festubert and Loos, but their real enemy was the harsh climate of Flanders and northern France. This caused much illness and consequently the corps was withdrawn from the Western Front in December 1915 for service in the Middle East where Indian troops formed the major part of the forces which fought against Turkey in Mesopotamia, Egypt and Palestine. They had sustained 21,000 casualties, including 6,000 dead.

The Indian Cavalry Corps remained in action in France until the spring of 1918, while the Indian Labour Corps rendered valuable assistance to frontline units. The Indian Army also fought the Germans and their local *Askari* troops in East Africa.

In the 1939–1945 War the Indian Army formed the largest volunteer army the world has ever seen: over two and a half million men. Once again it was represented in the early operations and a company of the Royal Indian Army Service Corps was part of the BEF in the 1940 campaign in France, which culminated in the evacuation from Dunkirk. Indian troops were in action in the Western Desert campaigns, the Middle East, in Eritrea and Abyssinia (now Ethiopia), in Greece and throughout the entire Italian campaign.

But it was in the Far East war against the Japanese that the Indian Army played its greatest part, from the vain defence of Hong Kong and Singapore and other early setbacks, through years of combat in the jungles of Burma to the final victory in 1945. Indians also played an important part in checking the invasion of their own country at the Battles of Imphal and Kohima, which led to Japan's first retreat. Of the nearly 40,000 Commonwealth servicemen who died in the fighting in Burma, considerably more than half were Indian.

The Royal Indian Navy (RIN) also greatly expanded during the 1939–1945 War – to 28,000 men. Its ships took part in actions in the Red Sea, the Indian and Atlantic Oceans and the Mediterranean Sea, as well as supporting combined operations off the coasts of Sicily and Burma. In both the wars large numbers of Indian seamen served in the merchant navies of India, Britain and other Commonwealth countries.

The Royal Indian Air Force (RIAF) was mainly a tactical air force and supported army operations throughout the Burma campaign; it also operated anti-submarine patrols over the Indian Ocean. RIAF officers also served as aircrew with the Royal Air Force in the Far East and other theatres, and some flew in Europe with Bomber Command.

War was brought to India's doorstep in 1939–1945 and many more (15,000 more) Indians died than during the earlier conflict. Every man who served in the Indian armed forces was a volunteer and enlisted as a matter of honour.

PART II

The Commission's
establishment, responsibilites
and business

{ 7 }

Sir Fabian Ware and the founding of the Imperial War Graves Commission, 1914–1918

*In the course of my pilgrimage, I have many
times asked myself whether there can be more
potent advocates of peace upon earth, through
the years to come, than this massed multitude
of silent witnesses to the desolation of war*

King George V (1865–1936), Terlincthun Cemetery, 1922.

THE COMMONWEALTH WAR GRAVES COMMISSION IS responsible for maintaining cemeteries and memorials for one and three-quarter million war dead in 140 countries and territories. The maintenance of the sites is an awesome task, but the building of these cemeteries and memorials was even more so. Rudyard Kipling termed it: 'The biggest single bit of work since any of the Pharaohs – and they only worked in their own country!'

What was the genesis of this giant undertaking? It is part of the truly amazing story of the achievement of one man – Fabian Ware – who largely brought about the whole enterprise. There are many human beings who have made their mark in history, but none other has left such a profound and lasting memorial to mankind's sacrifice on behalf of democracy as has this remarkable Englishman.

When war broke out in 1914 Fabian Ware was 45 years old. At the time a special commissioner to the Rio Tinto Mining Company, he had recently been editor of *The Morning Post,* with a successful previous career as a senior educational administrator in South Africa. Too old to be accepted for Army duty, Fabian Ware nevertheless contrived quickly to get to the front lines, reaching Lille in France as commander of the Mobile Unit, British Red Cross Society.

This unit was a collection of gallant amateurs, driving civilian cars, whose often self-appointed job was to collect wounded men and stragglers. Officially, they were there under the direction of the Joint War

43

Committee of the British Red Cross Society and the Order of St John of Jerusalem. In September 1914 Lord Kitchener had suggested that the committee send a mobile unit to search for missing soldiers along the line of the retreat between the Rivers Aisne and Ourcq. During the First Battle of Ypres the unit was first attached to the French I Cavalry Corps, and later to the French X Corps behind Arras, proving its worth by transporting many wounded from combat to the hospitals.

As Ware went about his duties, he began to note the names of British war dead and the locations of their graves. His personal pursuit of this is interesting in that there was no previous Army policy of noting and maintaining grave sites. Certainly, there were very few marked graves of, say, the Battle of Waterloo or the Crimean War. Some graves of the South African (Boer) War at the turn of the century had been marked, but with little permanence.

Although Army regulations called for the clearance of battlefields and proper disposal of the dead, the chaotic conditions, sheer weight of casualties, and lack of system prevented it from being done at all effectively. At this time, dead servicemen's graves were marked with wooden crosses after burial by their comrades, but no set official record was kept. Ware observed that as military units moved from area to area, details of the dead men's whereabouts would very probably soon be lost – particularly in the case of those cemeteries near the front lines.

As commander of the Mobile Unit, Ware negotiated the supply of more ambulances and rations from the Red Cross Society in London, and pursued a policy of preventing his unit from becoming part of the Army Medical Corps. In October 1914 a visit to him by a Lieutenant Colonel Stewart, a Red Cross advisor, led to the first formal extension of the Mobile Unit's work to include the noting of graves to help the Red Cross in tracing the 'missing'. Thus, for the first time, the registration of graves now began to take place; sites were furnished with permanent markers and received maintenance.

The innovation was brought to the sympathetic attention of General Sir Nevil Macready, Adjutant-General of the British Expeditionary Force. He was concerned by growing public demand at home that the war graves should not be neglected, and he also well remembered the widespread distress caused by neglect of British graves in the recent South African War. Ware was able to convince Macready that an organization should be established to ensure proper marking and recording of graves, and that his unit was the right one for this sadly growing task. Macready advised the Commander-in-Chief, Sir John French, to obtain War Office approval for the creation of a graves registration organization as an integral part of the Army in the field. So, on 2nd March 1915, Ware's unit was officially charged with this work under the new title of 'Graves Registration Commission'.

It is interesting to note that later that month appreciation was expressed by the then General Douglas Haig, a corps commander and later to be commander of the British and Commonwealth Armies. Haig reported the following to the War Office:

> 'It is fully recognized that the work of the organization is of purely sentimental value, and that it does not directly contribute to the successful termination of the war. It has, however, an extraordinary moral value to the troops as well as to the relatives and friends of the dead at home . . . Further, on the termination of hostilities, the nation will demand an account from the government as to the steps which have been taken to mark and classify the burial places of the dead . . .'

Although still part of the Red Cross, the Commission was attached to the Adjutant-General's office, with some members being given 'local' rank: Ware became a temporary major. However, with some 27,000 registrations being made during 1915, it became evident to him that the Commission should leave the Red Cross and become an integral part of the Army; this happened on General Macready's recommendation to the War Office on 6th September 1915.

As the front settled into a 'static line' position, the burials became more concentrated, rather than scattered as they had been during the war movement in 1914. Available land in existing civilian cemeteries for the burial of war dead was fast running out and it was left to the bilingual Major Ware to negotiate with the French authorities. Partly as a result of these discussions the French decreed a *sepulture perpetuelle* for Allied and French troops in communal burial grounds. In 1916 these new procedures were effected, allowing for each army to select cemetery sites and, after completing stringent formalities with the French authorities, to acquire the necessary land. The basic principle of the right to the use of these lands in perpetuity was formulated.

Ware's abilities continued to show, not least when he prevailed upon the Adjutant-General to order equality of treatment for the fallen. In keeping with public opinion, an order of April 1915 established equality of treatment after an equality of sacrifice. The order forbade exhumations for repatriation, on the grounds of hygiene and 'on account of the difficulties of treating impartially the claims advanced by persons of different social standing'. In this way two of the Commission's most important principles were established – equality of treatment and no repatriation.

Around this time, bereaved families were requesting photographs of the graves of their loved ones. Most of the landscape was war-torn and very bleak, a dreary sight, which the Commission attempted to improve with grass and a few simple flowers. Ware took the view that since next of kin could not look after the graves, an official service should do so. He was also becoming concerned about the permanent care of the graves after the Army left at the end of the war. He was very worried that if no official body was authorized to care for the graves, some commercial organization might step in, with perhaps more interest in financial returns than in sympathetic treatment of the cemeteries.

In January 1916 Ware saw the establishment of the National Committee for the Care of Soldiers' Graves, with the Prince of Wales as president, and himself as a member. At the same time the British Treasury agreed to meet the cost of the upkeep of the graves, little knowing the eventual extent of the work and enormous expense it would entail.

Ware's thinking had been prescient. By now many other theatres of war had opened up, far removed from France and Belgium, which greatly increased the need for graves registration. Soldiers of the United Kingdom were dying on many distant fields of battle, being buried alongside comrades from Canada, Australia, New Zealand, South Africa, Newfoundland, India and every British colony. Thus Ware's direction was needed in Macedonia, Gallipoli, Mesopotamia, Africa and elsewhere. To manage these wider responsibilities, Ware was promoted to temporary lieutenant colonel and appointed Director-General of the newly created Directorate of Graves Registration and Enquiries. His office was moved to London in May 1916, he was provided with a staff of some 700, and he set to work there, unaware that the worst killing was still ahead.

Many graves were marked 'unknown', a source of deep concern to Ware, as he knew the next of kin would have no 'place of remembrance' for the dead loved ones. He introduced a new form of double identity disc made of compressed fibre, which greatly helped in the identification of the fallen in battles to come. (These discs were also worn in the 1939–1945 War.) Added to this was the skill of the men in Graves Registration Units, who developed methods of identifying many who in the early months of the war would have remained unknown.

The policy of providing whenever possible a marked grave for every 'unknown' was also one of the Commission's principles. It did not matter that there was no name to accompany the remains and a single grave was normally provided. This is most impressive, for up to 50 per cent of the dead in Belgium were unknown and some 40 per cent in France, something which is only too evident in some cemeteries. At Cabaret Rouge near Arras, for example, nearly 5,000 of the 7,500 headstones are marked 'Known Unto God'. In certain other sites the proportion is much higher.

As the number of burials grew, so the work of Ware's unit increased tremendously. Being a man of foresight, he formulated plans to have the National Committee for the Care of Soldiers' Graves become a permanent organization under Royal Charter, with its own funds and staff, and overseen by Britain's Secretary of State for War and commissioners from Britain and each of the Dominions. A brief but stormy fight developed with the Office of Works, whose responsibilities covered looking after Government buildings and park maintenance worldwide. Their staff also looked after some military and dependents' graves on foreign soil, and felt that they were the rightful department to take on the task of maintenance of the 1914–1918 War graves.

Ware was finally able to convince the authorities that the immensity of the job was beyond the scope of experience of the Office of Works. He found strong support in his argument from the Prince of Wales, who had demonstrated much interest in Ware's project from the very beginning. A popular figure with the frontline troops, whom he visited often, the Prince felt strongly that Lieutenant Colonel Ware's work was essential as a tangible tribute to the Empire's fallen. King George V had also paid keen personal attention to the enterprise and in 1917 made Ware a Companion of the Order of St Michael and St George (CMG) in recognition of his aims and dedication; other awards and knighthoods were to follow.

The Prince of Wales sent a minute to the Imperial War Conference, with his endorsement of Ware's memorandum that proposed the creation of 'an Imperial organization to care for and maintain in perpetuity the graves of those who have fallen in the War, to acquire land for the purpose of cemeteries and to erect permanent memorials in the cemeteries and elsewhere'. The Imperial War Conference examined Ware's memorandum and draft charter clause by clause and, with a few amendments, it was unanimously approved. On 13th April 1917 a resolution recommending its adoption was moved by Canada's Prime Minister, Sir Robert Borden. A Royal Charter was granted on 21st May 1917, establishing the Imperial War Graves Commission, with HRH the Prince of Wales as its first president, and Brigadier General Fabian Ware as vice-chairman.

Thus the bonds of Empire were strengthened through this unique organization – the first of its kind to be charged with the care of all the war dead of a nation. As the war drew to a close there were some 600,000 burials registered. In many cases the cemeteries were unkind to the eye and, because of static trench warfare, many of the early sites were not very appealing to visitors. But at least there was a record of where many of the fallen had their final resting places.

The Armistice of 11th November 1918 found the Commission with a list of 500,000 missing, almost equalling the figure for those having a known grave. The total cost of sacrifice was appallingly high – over a million British and Commonweath dead. One attempt made to give reality to such figures asked the public to picture a million men marching past the Cenotaph in Whitehall, London:

'Imagine them moving in one continuous column, four abreast. As the head of that column reaches the Cenotaph, the last four men would be at Durham. In Canada, that column would stretch across the land from Quebec to Ottawa; in Australia, from Melbourne to Canberra; in South Africa, from Bloemfontein to Pretoria; in New Zealand, from Christchurch to Wellington; in Newfoundland, from coast to coast of the island; and in India, from Lahore to Delhi. It would take these million men eighty-four hours, or three and a half days, to march past the Cenotaph in London.'

With so many dead, it would be a while before the families of the missing saw their loved ones' names carved in stone or cast in bronze, for no memorials to the missing were erected for some years. But built they would be. The headstones were erected much more quickly.

Thus in peace time began the efforts of Major General Sir Fabian Arthur Goulstone Ware KCVO KBE CB CMG Chevalier Légion d'Honneur, Croix de Guerre to build each cemetery and memorial with the dignity and beauty he visualized to commemorate the fallen properly and in perpetuity. For the rest of his long life, Sir Fabian Ware continued his dedicated work in the commemoration of the war dead. He was the founder of the Imperial War Graves Commission (later Commonwealth WGC) and served as its vice-chairman from 1917 until 1948, the year before his death on 28th April 1949 at the age of 80. He was buried at Holy Trinity Church Graveyard at Amberley in his beloved Gloucestershire. Tablets to his memory were erected in Gloucester Cathedral and Westminster Abbey. He was further granted the posthumous honour of having his grave marked by a standard Commission war-pattern headstone, to which he was – officially – not entitled.

{ 8 }

Planning and Construction

*There must be a beginning of any
great matter, but the continuing
unto the end until it be thoroughly
finished yields the true glory*

Sir Francis Drake (1540?–1596)

FORMAL PLANNING OF THE DESIGN AND CONSTRUCTION
of Commonwealth military cemeteries and memorials had started
while the seemingly endless war still raged. One result of the
Commission's first meeting in November 1917 was the invitation to Sir
Frederic Kenyon, then Director of the British Museum, to act as
Architectural Advisor. After visiting France and Belgium that winter, he
proposed that the design of the cemeteries be entrusted to young architects
who had served in the war, but that principal architects of note be appointed
to supervise and approve their work. This clear and simple solution was soon
adopted, and the work in France and Belgium entrusted to four principal
architects: Sir Edwin Lutyens, Reginald (later Sir Reginald) Blomfield,
Herbert (later Sir Herbert) Baker and Charles Holden. Sir Robert Lorimer
became the architect responsible for cemeteries in Egypt, Italy, Greece,
Germany and the United Kingdom; Sir John Burnet for those on the
Gallipoli Peninsula and in Palestine and Syria; and Major Edward Warren
for those in Iraq.

Much preliminary work on the construction of the cemeteries had been
carried out by the Army in the field by the time the Armistice was signed.
This was especially the case nearer the bases, where burials could be made in
an orderly way with plots, rows and individual graves. For obvious reasons,
the cemeteries nearer the front lines were less orderly, but the Commission
accepted fully that, whenever possible, war cemeteries which were 'secure'
in law (i.e. could not be disturbed by developers, road builders, etc.) and
maintainable should be left as such in perpetuity. It is interesting to read in
Ware's Introduction to the Sixth Annual Report of the Commission in
1926:

'. . . all the small cemeteries have not been moved into larger ones [for] several
reasons, of which only one need be given here. During the war certain authorized
sites were selected, some close to the trenches, where the dead could be buried,

49

and the soldiers were promised that, if they brought back their dead comrades to these, which they not infrequently did at the risk of their lives, they would rest there permanently undisturbed. This promise has been kept in all cases, except a few where the site originally selected has been found altogether unsuitable.'

The Western Front, where the great majority of the Commission's work had to be done, was still in a state of chaos and destruction, the like and extent of which had never been seen before. Many villages, such as Thiepval and Passchendaele for example, had disappeared from the face of the earth though they were still shown on maps. The boundaries of those cemeteries which had been in use on the front lines were often difficult to establish because of battle damage and individual graves were frequently obliterated.

Work on building the cemeteries began early in 1919, when the Commission sent out what were jocularly called 'Travelling Garden Parties' – mobile units to survey the sites and establish the blocks of rows and graves. These units travelled in trucks and were equipped with tents, tools, three-days' supply of food and water, and a supply of plants, seeds, and shrubs. Each team comprised a driver, a cook, a foreman, eight gardeners, 'and the inevitable small trench-found dog in charge of all'. They tackled what seemed a superhuman task, finding their way without roads or reliable maps through the battlefields' unbelievable mud, through featureless countryside dotted only with piles of rubble to mark long-destroyed villages.

Everywhere in this wilderness there were shellholes, mine craters, trenches and masses of barbed wire. The misery of manhandling trucks through miles of trackless mud, of working in winter gales, almost constant rain and driving sleet was made worse by the danger from live shells which lay all around. Pockets of still-lethal poison gas, and smoke from demolition parties touching off discarded ammunition added yet more difficulties. But despite such conditions, the survey parties managed to proceed fairly rapidly in selecting and roughing out the ground of the projected main battlefield cemeteries. The teams came back each week or so to headquarters, then set off again to other sectors, dropping off gardeners or registration officers where required.

There was a great shortage of even the most basic accommodation for the Commission's staff. This was made still worse by the return to the devastated areas and prior claim of farmers and their families and demobilized servicemen. This shortage of acceptable – or even bearable – accommodation, and conditions which were not far removed from primitive, did nothing to encourage the recruitment of staff to serve abroad. But it did perhaps help to weed out those who were not of the strongest character; who hoped for a 'soft' job; or for whom working for the Commission was not worthwhile despite the non-too-generous pay and living in the most battered piece of ground on earth.

Roads and bridges had been pulverized, which made the supply of rations, fuel, machinery and building material difficult. What there was could often be obtained only in the face of strong competition from the local population who, not unnaturally, felt they had first call. On top of all these difficulties was the knowledge that next of kin and old comrades might well soon decide to come to the Western Front to see the cemeteries and find them in poor state, with shell-pocked ground and broken or temporary markers. But this probably helped to concentrate minds and efforts and brought about the transformation of the hundreds of cemeteries from virtual contractors' sites into their present condition in a space of only a few years. There can be little doubt that those ex-servicemen who worked for the Commission in those early years had kept the toughness, tenacity and sense of humour which they had shown during the years of combat.

So the Commission set to at the end of the 1914–1918 War to turn generally muddy and bleak sites with wooden crosses into the places they are today – usually as close in appearance to gardens as they can be. The Commission obtained approval of certain basic principles to control the work of construction. These included the rulings that the memorials should be permanent, the headstones should be uniform and there should be no distinction made on account of military or civil rank.

One of the more pressing tasks was the concentration, usually into existing burial grounds, of the enormous number of bodies which were still in temporary graves, or which lay where they had died and had remained, until now, unfound. Immediately after the Armistice, the entire British front was divided into narrow sectors and combed repeatedly by 12-man parties of troops under a senior NCO in a systematic search for scattered graves. This work was later taken on by Commission personnel. In the 34 months between the Armistice and September 1921 over 200,000 bodies were recovered and buried and the official searching then ended. Nevertheless, by 1937 about 38,000 more bodies had been found by accident and, at that time, they were still being discovered at a rate of about 20 to 30 a week; about the same number are still being discovered annually in the late 1980s. The battlefields were exhaustively searched, each no fewer than on six occasions and some as often as 20 times.

The Commission set up its headquarters during the period of major construction in the château at Longuenesse near St Omer in northern France; it recruited gardeners, masons and other staff, but was frequently undermanned. The expansion of the Commission's work can be gauged by its financial expenditure: in the year ending March 1919 it spent £7,500, but 12 months later it had spent £250,000. Much of this money was spent on the old Western Front, most of it on wages.

Not all went smoothly in the Commission's early days. In December 1919, as the British House of Commons studied estimates, two points were tabled for Winston Churchill MP, Minister of War and ex-officio the chairman of the Commission. Thanks to a vociferous minority (many of whom had signed a petition to the Prince of Wales, which is still in the Commission's archives) he was asked to reconsider the shape of the Commission's grave marker (i.e. to approve the use of a cross rather than a headstone) and to instruct the Commission to pay greater regard to the wishes and feelings of the next of kin.

Had this latter request been accepted the principle of equality of treatment would surely have been lost. In the event a debate was arranged for 4th May 1920 in the House of Commons and Sir James Remnant rose to move a nominal reduction of £5 in the Commission's vote. The comparatively unknown MP for the City of Westminster, W. Burdett-Coutts, who had acquainted himself with the Commission's work and had agreed to speak, made an inspired speech, backing the Commission and its principle of equality of treatment. He quoted from a letter written by Rudyard Kipling, who had suffered the grievous blow of losing his only son and had no grave to visit. Kipling's letter ended with 'I wish some of the people who are making this trouble realized how much more fortunate they are to have a name on a headstone in a known place'.

The speech was very well received. Churchill closed the debate no doubt using his mastery of oratory, including in his address the phrase, '. . . there is no reason why, in periods as remote from our own as we ourselves are from the Tudors, the graveyards in France . . . shall not remain an abiding and supreme memorial . . .'. He appealed to the House to decide without dividing and Sir James Remnant asked leave to withdraw. The position of the Commission and its principles were secure. Three days after the Commission's meeting of 18th May 1920, Churchill wrote to Burdett-Coutts quoting the resolution passed at the meeting, part of which stated, 'It was largely due to his [Burdett-Coutts'] efforts . . . that the Commission are now in a position to carry on their work with the knowledge that they have the support and confidence of the public'.

Two dramatic features of the war cemeteries were the Cross of Sacrifice and the Stone of Remembrance. The former was designed by Blomfield and there are four sizes to suit the dimensions of the cemetery and the number of graves it contains. The Crosses range from just under 15 feet in height to just under 30 feet high and are considered to be among the best proportioned memorials of their kind. Close examination reveals that in plan they are not true octagons: the front-to-back measurement is slightly less than the side-to-side dimension.

The Cross stands on an octagonal block (weighing about two tons in the largest types), which rests on three steps. The two arms are in one piece and together measure about a third of the height of the Cross, measured from the base of the shaft; the shaft is also in one piece from the pedestal block to under the arms. The public's imagination was caught by the white stone – often Portland – against which the downward pointing bronze sword stands out, much as old arms and weapons against a wall.

The sword's symbolism is open to many interpretations. Some regard the sword itself, with its hilt, as being the Cross, and consider the stonework to be only a frame. To others, the sword symbolizes its position after the battle is over, or its offering up in sacrifice of those who died by the sword. There are probably nearly as many interpretations of the whole monument as there are contemplators.

It was originally the intention of the Commission that each architect should be free to design a special Cross of Sacrifice suitable in his view for the particular cemetery in which it was to stand, but general opinion so strongly favoured Blomfield's design that it has been used wherever possible. In certain places, Crosses of a different style have been erected to match the rugged surroundings and the cemetery walls. Examples of these may be found in the five war cemeteries on the Asiago Plateau in the foothills (but nevertheless at between 3,000 and 4,000 feet) of the Alps in Italy. In Macedonia too they are different, but the great majority of war cemeteries and plots of more than 40 burials contain a Cross of Sacrifice of Blomfield's design.

The minimum number of burials to qualify for a Cross is indeed usually 40, but there have been exceptions, of which two examples will suffice. There are 33 Commonwealth graves of the 1914–1918 and 1939–1945 Wars in the Falkland Islands, all scattered in one civil cemetery. Nevertheless, it was felt that this distant colony should have its own Cross and one was taken there between the wars – certainly the most southerly war graves' site in the world.

The second example is the so-called Royal Engineers Grave at Zillebeke, near Ypres, which covers an area of just over 100 square yards, so that the Cross completely dominates it. Commemorated by name on the base of the Cross are an officer, three NCOs, and eight men of, or attached to, the 177th Tunnelling Company, Royal Engineers. They still lie in tunnels under, or near, the site of the Cross. This is probably the smallest number of war dead anywhere to be accorded a Cross of Sacrifice.

While most Crosses are of Portland Stone, a fair number are made of the same stone as the nearby headstones. For example, those in Italy of the 1939–1945 War are all made of Botticino limestone. The highest Cross (an exception to the four standard sizes) in a Commission site is the centre piece of the Halifax Memorial in Nova Scotia, Canada. It is built of Canadian Standstead granite and stands on a granite podium about 10 feet high, giving an overall height of almost 40 feet. The largest blocks in the Cross itself weight about nine tons each. In the 1914–1918 cemetery registers the Cross of Sacrifice is referred to as the 'War Cross' so perhaps that was originally its official title. But the title 'Cross of Sacrifice' has attached itself to this great monument and the name of its originator has long since been lost.

The Stones of Remembrance are after a design by Lutyens and one is to be found in nearly all the large (containing over 400 war dead) cemeteries. (Brookwood Military Cemetery is an exception: it has two Crosses of Sacrifice and two Stones of Remembrance, perhaps because of its unusual 'U' shape.) It provides a handsome altar-like point of focus for, for example, ceremonies and one which is acceptable to all faiths. For this reason it is frequently the spot at which wreaths are laid since Christians, Jews, Muslims, Hindus, and non-believers all take it for what it is: a permanent memorial of dignity and beauty.

Both sides of each Stone bear the inscription: THEIR NAME LIVETH

FOR EVERMORE. The words were chosen by Kipling from the Bible (Ecclesiasticus Chapter 44, Verse 14) and the verse reads in full: 'Their bodies are buried in peace; but their name liveth for evermore'.

The dimensions of the Stones of Remembrance are such that they make them monuments as lasting as any work of man can be. Nevertheless, as they are usually of Portland stone, (those of the 1939–1945 War in Italy are of Botticino) they are liable to weathering. Each is a monolith, weighs ten tons, and is best described in Lutyens' own words:

> 'A great fair stone of fine proportions, 12 feet in length, lying raised upon three steps . . . all its horizontal surfaces and planes are spherical and parts of parallel spheres, 1,801 feet, 8 inches in diameter, and all its vertical lines converging upwards to a point some 1,801 feet, 8 inches, above the centre of these spheres.'

The Stones have so far been described as 'monolith', but this is not so in all cases: there are examples in Macedonia of Stones of Remembrance which comprise several large blocks fitted together. It was simply not possible to move single, 10-ton blocks of stone with the means available in the early 1920s, so several smaller pieces were necessary. Seen at a distance, the Stone looks like any of the other memorials – which indeed it is in its dimensions – but at close quarters the fitting stones are at once obvious, though not necessarily any less pleasing for that.

Portland stone was laid down millions of years ago under the sea bed, and so contains many fossils, especially of sea shells. These are frequently visible in all the Commission's stonework (including the headstones), but particularly so in the large mass of a Stone of Remembrance. Indeed it would be highly unusual to find a mass of Portland stone of that size with no fossils to be seen.

The aesthetic effect of the Cross and the Stone depends on their setting in relation to the varying levels of the cemetery and surrounding natural features. Each cemetery was therefore designed by a member of the Commission's staff *on the spot*, under the guidance of one of the principal architects, by whom the design was finally approved.

Stones form part of the furniture of the memorials to the missing and here, too, act as focal points for ceremonies, wreath-laying, or contemplation. The Stone is the central feature of the circular Indian Memorial at Neuve-Chapelle; a Stone stands under the great arch of the Thiepval Memorial; another is at the heart of the quadrilateral Runnymede Memorial to the Missing of the Air Forces of the 1939–1945 War; and South Africa erected a modified Stone in front of the memorial at Delville Wood in 1952.

The Commission had first intended that three of its principal architects – Baker, Blomfield and Lutyens – should each design one cemetery, to enable comparisons of style and such like to be made. In the event the three sites chosen were at Le Tréport, Forceville and Louvencourt, and Blomfield designed all three. Later, there was much ado about the great differences between estimates and tenders but, even when costs were high, the work had to go ahead.

It was generally agreed that the most successful was Forceville, though perhaps this was helped by the juxtaposition of the symmetrical cemetery and the unkempt civil burial ground. However, it was apparent that these cemeteries were simply too expensive (the estimate had been £10 per grave), and that steps to reduce costs had to be taken. For a start, it was agreed that the very expensive Stone of Remembrance could not be placed in the smaller cemeteries. It was also agreed that the Cross of Sacrifice would come in different sizes, in proportion to the size of the cemetery, and that the small cemeteries would not have elaborate entrance features.

There was much argument about costs and aesthetics but, in the end, the work was done within the original estimate of £10 per grave. The Commission and its contractors were able to improve on the first estimates by millions of pounds, partly owing to a favourable change in the exchange rates but mainly because of the savings that can be made by doing things on a large scale and by keeping a careful watch on expenditure. In fact, the headstones at £5 each were the most expensive items; deliveries of these between 1920 and 1923 went up from a few to over 4,000 a week. Whenever possible, rows of markers were set into concrete headstone beams, which lay invisible below the ground and kept the headstones upright and aligned, thus avoiding the usual untidyness of the individual headstones seen in civil cemeteries.

The amount of engineering work done by 1937 in France and Belgium alone is astonishing, as Ware's figures reveal. There were nearly 1,000 architecturally constructed cemeteries, surrounded by 50 miles of brick or stone walling; nearly 1,000 Crosses of Sacrifice and 560 Stones of Remembrance with many chapels, records buildings and shelters. There were the 600,000 headstones set in 250 miles of headstone beams and 18 larger memorials to the missing. A truly amazing effort when it is remembered that nothing of the sort had ever been done before.

Meanwhile the landscapers, horticulturists and gardeners were preparing their 'gardens' and taking care to avoid the depressing appearance of many cemeteries. From the start, the cemeteries were planted under the advice of Captain (later Sir) Arthur Hill, Director of the Royal Botanic Gardens at Kew. Trees and bushes were planted to avoid monotony and headstone flower borders laid out to counter any harshness caused by too many headstones. The paths were sown with grass, as were the spaces between the blocks and rows, which resulted in the whole giving a feeling of solace and peace, not of depression.

The gardeners and the Works men had their differences but that they ultimately agreed on the course to be followed is apparent from the cemeteries we see today. Their initial work included the planting of 63 miles of hedges, and the seeding to grass of 540 acres to produce turf resembling English lawns. In one year alone, over 1,300,000 plants were issued to the Commonwealth cemeteries in France and Belgium. There seems to be little doubt that the visitors find the results of the original landscapers' designs, and the endeavours of the present horticultural staff and gardeners, just as important and satisfying as the architects' and masons' stonework.

The Records Department of the Commission worked diligently to provide the cemetery and memorial registers and, in 1920, the Le Tréport and Forceville registers were published as Index No. FRANCE 1 and Index No. FRANCE 2 respectively. (There would eventually be nearly 2,000 indexes for France alone.) 'FRANCE 1' was in hard back, but 'FRANCE 2' already had the soft cover which has since become standard, thereby saving a great deal of money. The last entry in 'FRANCE 1' is the mention of an unknown British soldier. In 1922 Colonel H.F. Chettle, Director of Records, was able to identify him as Dexter, Private H., Royal Lancaster Regiment, who died of wounds on 27th April 1915. Was he perhaps the first longstanding 'unknown' to be positively identified?

During that year, 1922, construction of the cemeteries was going on apace, work on the commemoration of the missing by name on memorials was beginning, and sites were being sought and discussed. The first memorials to be completed were those to the missing of the Royal Navy, the choice of site being rather easier for those missing at sea than for those who were missing on the battlefields. Added to that, the three memorials at Chatham, Plymouth and Portsmouth were similar, which also helped. However, the Plymouth Memorial was made taller, probably to make it more visible from close inshore and from under the steep slopes to The Hoe, where it stands.

By the summer of 1926 the Commission had completed 13 memorials and preparations for others were at an advanced stage. At Port Tewfik, at the southern end of the Suez Canal, there was a stone memorial to 4,000 soldiers of the Indian Army, guarded by two handsome, crouching stone tigers. This was fated to be the only one of the Commission's memorials to be destroyed by war; this occurred in the fighting between Egypt and Israel in the 1960s.

Certain memorials have become special to particular Commonwealth countries: Vimy to the Canadians, Villers-Bretonneux to the Australians, Delville Wood to the South Africans, Neuve-Chapelle to the Indians, Thiepval to the British; the New Zealanders have their many memorials. But, perhaps the Menin Gate at Ypres holds something extra for all of them (except the New Zealanders, who did not wish it to include their names). It was their heroic joint effort which had kept Ypres a Commonwealth bastion and sally-port through the war. Its inauguration in 1927, the year of the Commission's tenth anniversary, marked the completion of most of the war cemeteries, though some of the large memorials (Vimy and Villers-Bretonneux) would not be completed until just before the start of the 1939–1945 War.

By 1937 the Commission had marked 750,000 graves and had commemorated 500,000 missing for which estimates of £10 million had been originally agreed. The actual expenditure was £8,150,000, nearly £2 million less, and much of this saving due to the careful watch kept on affairs by the Commission's Finance Committee. The committee was established in 1918 and still meets regularly to this day.

Who paid for the Commission's work? In accordance with a resolution of the Imperial War Conference of 1918, the cost was borne by the participating governments in proportion to the number of *graves* each required, which system is still used. The following table shows the proportions contributed by each Commonwealth country. The revised contributions reflect both subsequent political changes and the inclusion of the figures of the graves relating to the 1939–1945 War, which were added to those of 1914–1918 on 1st April 1963, and form a total.

Government	Percentage 1937	Percentage 1980s
United Kingdom	81.53	77.81
Canada	7.78	9.88
Australia	6.35	5.91
New Zealand	1.81	2.10
South Africa	1.14	2.07
India	1.02	2.23
British West Indies	0.23	–
Newfoundland	0.14	–
	100.00	100.00

In 1925 the Participating Governments agreed to contribute to an Imperial War Graves Endowment Fund of £5 million to provide money for permanent maintenance. The fund was completed in 1940. The United Kingdom, which had spread its contributions over a longer period than the other governments, donated an additional sum to enable the fund to provide an income of £218,000 a year, which was then estimated to be sufficient to preserve the agreed standard of maintenance.

Since the end of the 1939–1945 War, annual expenditure in respect of the 1914–1918 War alone has exceeded the income of the Endowment Fund. The excess and the whole of the amount required to meet costs in respect of the 1939–1945 War are provided by annual contributions from the Participating Governments, as shown above. Annual outgoings in the late 1980s are around £18 million. This is about £10 ($20) per commemoration, which in view of the high standard obtained by the Commission, and the number of countries in which it has to work, is good value for money. The Commission has a staff of around 1,300 worldwide.

{ 9 }

The 1939–1945 War sites
and reconstruction

No man is an Island, entire of itself . . .
any man's death diminishes me because I
am involved in Mankind; And therefore
never send to know for whom the bell tolls;
It tolls for thee

John Donne (1571?–1631).

THE PROBLEMS FACING THE COMMISSION AFTER THE end of the 1939–1945 War were perhaps less daunting than in 1919: it was now an experienced organization. Headstone production was now more efficient with machines being used more frequently in this operation. The system of commemoration of the missing by name on memorials had been accepted as the best that could be done for these particularly sad cases and was therefore followed again. And there were offices in some of the places abroad where fighting had taken place in both the 1914–1918 and 1939–1945 Wars.

All these factors, and the thankfully received mercy that numbers of dead were smaller, helped to make the task of the Commission arguably less difficult. Still, there were some difficulties following the 1939–1945 War which had been less evident after the earlier conflict. There was the fact that the war had spread worldwide, which meant transporting headstones and building materials over huge distances. Far more concentration of remains had to be carried out, as there could be no question of leaving either the small cemeteries built by the soldiers or scattered graves in places which were difficult to get to or separated by long distances, as subsequent maintenance would have been virtually impossible. This consideration applied to jungle and desert and Pacific Islands.

In addition to these problems there were extra climatic conditions to consider: tropical rains and great heat, and the cold of the Arctic. Also a worldwide organization needed to be set up to maintain the structures and care for the planting when the building work had been completed. Although the size of the task was not as great as it had been in the inter-war years, it still taxed those involved and required the same dedication as that shown by the staff of the Commission a score years earlier.

The cemeteries and memorials were cared for under almost normal Commission arrangements from the start of the second conflict in September 1939 until the overrunning of western Europe in May and June 1940. A few members of the Commission's gardening and maintenance staff, many of whom had French or Belgian wives and families, decided to remain despite the apparent dangers of their doing so. Perhaps some may have been influenced (as so many foreigners had been) by the thought that Britain would follow France and Belgium and surrender in a matter of weeks. In that case, 'home' (i.e. Belgium or France) would probably be preferable to Britain, which many had left many years earlier and which was now unfamiliar to them.

However, the majority – over 500 and including the office staff – were evacuated to Britain under contingency plans. Many of them were helped through the efforts of W.P.L. Arnott, of the Arras office, a major of the 1914–1918 War, and R. Haworth, a former captain, who was in charge in Belgium. During difficult journeys to the coast, the staff and their families competed on the choked roads with military movements and tens of thousands of French and Belgian refugees; they also came under air attack.

In the event almost all Commission personnel and dependents who chose to leave were embarked for the comparatively short, but dangerous, crossing of the Strait of Dover or the Channel. They arrived in England, virtually without baggage or money and were met by United Kingdom-based members of the Commission's staff. These helped the dispossessed refugees in their search for work and, for a limited period, their pay was made up by the Commission to the amount they had been receiving whilst in its employment.

Generally, finding work was not too difficult, as so many men had either already volunteered for the armed forces or had been called up. The Commission also helped as best it could to find accommodation for the men and their families, but in many cases this was more difficult than the finding of work. No new houses or flats were being built and there were few available: so many had been taken over by the authorities for servicemen.

Meanwhile some of the staff who remained on the Continent were taken prisoner and interned by the Germans; particularly those whose place of work lay in the path of the German advance, or who lived in remote areas where they could not be contacted in time, or whose loyalties were divided owing to their French or Belgian connections. The Commission sought and obtained information about these through the British Foreign Office and the Red Cross, and eventually exchanges were arranged. A party of them, returning on the Swedish SS *Drottingholm* – humorously known to the soldiers and staff as the 'Trotting Home' – were welcomed back by members of the Commission's staff, voluntary services and officials at Liverpool. They received the same assistance in finding jobs and accommodation as those who had escaped in 1940. Sadly a small number died either in internment or at home in France and Belgium.

As far as can be ascertained the Germans did not in any way damage the war cemeteries and memorials nor did they discourage local people from caring for the sites if they wished to do so. In some cases the Germans themselves arranged for some care to be given to the sites. They must have noted that the graves of their compatriots which happened to be in the Commission's cemeteries had been maintained in the same way as those of Commonwealth servicemen, and this may have had some bearing on their attitude. More probably, it was simply that they thought that the Commission had done a good job which was worth continuing, provided that it in no way impeded their war effort by using men, resources and supplies which could have been 'better' employed.

Nevertheless memorials were damaged – some severely. Examples are the Menin Gate (damaged mainly by small arms); the Neuve-Chapelle Memorial (by bombs and small arms); and the Villers-Bretonneux Memorial (by shelling). But, bearing in mind where these memorials stand – at the entrance to a city, on a crossroads and on a dominating hill respectively – it can be understood that they were used for cover or observation and were therefore liable to warlike damage, some of it probably inflicted by the Allies themselves. Some cemeteries were also damaged by tanks, shelling and fighting, but in no case did it appear deliberate.

When, in 1944, it became possible to start work again in France and Belgium, several of the Commission's old staff, or those who had found permanent work in the United Kingdom, decided not to return. Those who did go back found their cemeteries and memorials in states which ranged from good to totally overgrown, but, within a matter of some months, many of the latter were presentable again. Where repairs were necessary, these of course took longer to put right, but eventually the memorials and cemeteries were as fine as they had originally been. Any honourable scars which did not affect stability or inscriptions, and were not too unsightly, were left as silent witnesses of the later war.

Before the end of the 1939–1945 War, the graves' concentration units of the armed forces had been active all over the world in their enormous task of bringing to recognized permanent sites those who had been buried on the battlefield. As mentioned earlier there was to be far more 'concentration' of remains during and after the 1939–1945 than after the 1914–1918 War. The Commission designated architects of note to design new cemeteries and memorials. They included Edward (later Sir Edward) Maufe for the United Kingdom (who had been a Royal Artillery officer in the 1914–1918 War); Louis de Soissons for Italy; Philip Hepworth for France; Colin St Clair Oakes for the Far East; and Hubert (later Sir Hubert) Worthington for North Africa.

Assisted by the Commission's staff, both old and new, the architects set to with a will. Taking over the cemeteries from the services, they proceeded with the permanent marking of graves (i.e. with stones as opposed to wooden and steel crosses) and embellishment. The first Cross of Sacrifice in France was erected in the summer of 1948 in Chouain and the first cemetery, Dieppe Canadian, was completed in 1949. The architects obtained details on those with no known grave from the Records Department of the Commission and then designed the memorials to those casualties. The first of these to be unveiled were the 1939–1945 extensions to the 1914–1918 naval memorials and the last, inaugurated in 1961, was the Athens Memorial to the almost 3,000 who died in the Greek campaigns.

Nearly all the staff had been in the services; indeed, it was a requirement for employment with the Commission, unless the applicant had been unfit for service. (The ex-service requirement was waived in the 1960s.) Many went to places where the Commission already had offices and staff but, equally, others went to new areas, such as the middle and southern half of Italy, North Africa, Singapore and Burma. They had to contend with shortages of accommodation, supplies and, frequently, rations.

For many it was a lonely existence, as they were miles from fellow Britons. That hardship had not been suffered by their predecessors on the old Western Front battlefields, where hundreds of Britons were living close together (so many in fact that a British school was opened in Ypres). In some ways, their job was even more difficult than that of the earlier generation, but the Commission did all it could by way of pay, allowances, welfare and frequent visiting by Head Office officials to mitigate these difficulties. That the staff were, and are, of the same stuff as their predecessors is obvious by the state of the war cemeteries everywhere, be they in cool northern Germany, in warmer Italy or in the dry heat of El Alamein.

The last of the 'old' gardeners and staff who had served in the 1914–1918 War left the Commission's service on retirement in the early 1960s. Their successors, the ex-servicemen of the 1939–1945 War, had nearly all left by the mid-1980s. The staff changed, as did the methods of work and the tools and equipment they used. What has not changed much is the spirit of those working in the sites and their desire to make 'their' site or sites the best in the Commission. Many succeed, as there are, so to speak, very many 'best' sites among the Commission's cemeteries and memorials.

During the period of construction and after, offices were opened as, when and where necessary (for example, an office was opened in Naples, Italy, as early as May 1944). Many were temporary; others were later opened for what was seen, in 1960, as being the 'permanent' establishment of the Commission on its change from building cemeteries and memorials to maintaining them. But as with all organizations, it was found that changes had to be made following practical experience.

In the 1970s the organization of the Commission – Head Office, with regional offices below it, and with area offices below that – was rationalized by abolishing the middle tier and making the area offices work direct to Head Office. This resulted in a reduction of staff but meant that much more visiting and inspection had to be carried out by Head Office officials. The organization of the Commission is now (in outline only) the Head Office at Maidenhead; France Area with its office (the largest abroad) at Beaurains near Arras; Northern Europe Area with its office at Ieper (formerly Ypres) and responsible for Belgium, the Netherlands, Germany, Poland and

Scandinavia; United Kingdom Area with its office at Leamington Spa in Warwickshire, England; North Africa Area with its office at Heliopolis near Cairo; and Western Mediterranean Area with its office at Rome and responsible for Italy, Austria and Malta. The graves and memorials in the many countries which do not come under any of the Area offices mentioned are taken care of by Outer Area. For ease of liaison and administrative efficiency, Outer Area has its office in the same building in Maidenhead as Head Office.

There are many agency and similar offices, of which the most important and largest are the Canadian Agency in Ottawa, responsible for the war graves and memorials in Canada and the USA; the Office of Australian War Graves in Woden, Canberra, responsible for the memorials and graves in Australia and Papua New Guinea; and the South African Agency in Pretoria, responsible for the war graves in that country and Namibia.

The Commission, now over 70 years old, is set to proceed into the twenty-first century and into Churchill's 'periods as remote from our own as we ourselves are from the Tudors'. The cemeteries of the 1939–1945 War now look very much like those of the earlier conflict, with mature trees, grass swards and flowers. They may look the same, but there are differences. These may be in the cemeteries' surroundings, or in the closeness of the headstones. Many cemeteries of the 1914–1918 War are small, while most of the 1939–1945 War, not being battlefield cemeteries, are perhaps more neatly laid out. The similarities are striking but the differences, whatever they are, are such that a visitor instinctively knows if he is in a cemetery of the 1914–1918 War or in one of the later conflict.

The problems which face the present staff abroad are generally minor once the initial settling-in has been accomplished. Some have to learn the local language, even though English is quite often spoken or understood in most countries. If the man is accompanied by his family, the difficulties of education, local habits and customs, and other factors may weigh heavily. For example, should his children grow up feeling they are nationals of the country in which he works or should they be sent to boarding schools in the United Kingdom?

The problems are, in fact, largely the same as those which beset any expatriate family and most cope well. The Commission has a system of rotation so that families no longer need to spend the whole of their working lives in France or Belgium – something which was acceptable at one time, but not now. However, some stations are far from the beaten track and can create difficulties for that reason, especially so for the wife if she is English born, does not speak the local language, and is the only English-woman in the town or city. This can be very lonely and frustrating for her.

With worldwide air communications, any family requiring quick repatriation for, say, medical reasons, can usually be back in the United Kingdom in a matter of hours, or days at the most. The hardships endured by the earlier staff have largely gone, and pay and allowances are linked to those paid by the country's government or to local rates to ensure fair treatment.

As time goes on, more of the Commission's staff are recruited from the country in which they work, so that, for example, Japanese gardeners now tend Yokohama War Cemetery and Thai men and women tend the cemeteries in their country.

Working relationships between those on sites and in offices, and between Head Office and stations abroad, are generally good. However, even in the best organizations, not all goes smoothly all of the time, but difficulties are always ultimately resolved. The Commission offers jobs and careers and – as it has probably reduced the number of staff as much as it can without reducing its standards – job security for those who are loyal, adaptable and hardworking, and who have a feel for the work, is good. And so it should be, in an organization which has permanency and equality of treatment as two of its prime principles.

The result is that the Commission has built, and is custodian of, 2,500 constructed war cemeteries and plots and almost 200 memorials of all types. The ground area under the Commission's supervision is over 1,500 acres, of which over 1,000 are under 'fine' horticultural maintenance. Construction work for the 1914–1918 War was completed in 1938 and for the 1939–1945 War in 1961; since then the work has, in the main, been one of maintenance and keeping records. To do this, in about 140 countries and territories, requires a staff of around 1,400, of which most are gardeners and very many are nationals of the country in which they work. To meet the wishes of some of its members the organization changed its title in April 1960, becoming the Commonwealth War Graves Commission. Nothing else of moment was altered and its principles remain unaltered.

{10}

The principles and responsibilities of the Commission regarding the cemeteries

How sleep the brave, who sink to rest
By all their country's wishes blest

William Collins (1721–1759).
Ode written in 1746 following
the author's visit to his uncle's
regiment in Flanders not long
after the Battle of Fontenoy.

THE BASIC RESPONSIBILITIES OF THE COMMONWEALTH War Graves Commission consist of the permanent marking and maintenance of the graves of men and women of the forces of the Commonwealth, and of certain auxiliary and civilian organizations, who died in the 1914–1918 and 1939–1945 Wars. It is also responsible for the commemoration by name of all those whose graves are unknown or cannot be maintained, or whose remains were lost or buried at sea, or who were cremated. It also has the task of producing and updating records and registers of the war dead.

Basically, the Commission records the place of burial or commemoration of all members of the Commonwealth armed forces who died, *no matter where and no matter what the cause*, during the periods of the 1914–1918 and 1939–1945 Wars. For Commission purposes the period of the 1914–1918 War is 4th August 1914 to 31st August 1921, the former date being that of the declaration of war by the British Government, and the latter being the official end of the war, as opposed to the Armistice. For the 1939–1945 War the dates are 3rd September 1939 to 31st December 1947; the former date was once again that of the declaration of war by the British Government, and the latter the date agreed by the participating countries to produce a post-war period roughly equal to the time between the Armistice on 11th November 1918 and the official end of the 1914–1918 War (34 months). From VE day, 8th May 1945, to the chosen date, 31st December 1947, is in fact 32 months. The four dates given are inclusive.

64

But who is entitled to a war grave? In addition to those with an obvious right (i.e. the dead of the armed forces), the members of certain civilian organizations were entitled to 'war graves treatment', provided that they had died on duty or because of the increased risk brought about by the wars. These organizations included: the Mercantile Marine and other merchant navies, fishing fleets, war correspondents, the British Red Cross Society, the British Home Guard (originally, in 1940, known as the Local Defence Volunteers), the British National Fire Service, the Royal Air Force Ferry Command and several others.

A hypothetical example may help to illustrate some of the niceties involved in deciding on war graves treatment and the Commission's responsibility towards a civilian service. A terminally ill merchant seaman was being tended by a fit seaman on board a merchant ship which was attacked by an enemy aircraft. The sick seaman succumbed to his illness, and the fit one died of a bullet wound. In this case, the seaman who died of illness would not be entitled to war graves treatment but the other seaman, who died through the increased risk of war, would be so entitled. Had the ship been sunk, and both bodies lost, the name of the sick seaman who died would not appear on a Commission Merchant Navy Memorial, whereas that of his shot comrade would. If both bodies had been buried ashore, the grave of the one killed would be marked by a Commission headstone, the other by a headstone of a different, 'non-world-war grave' pattern.

The issue could become somewhat complicated when a serviceman died in his own country. In this case the next of kin had the choice of having the dead man buried either in a Commission war graves plot or in a family plot in a civil cemetery or churchyard. If they decided on a site other than a Commission plot, the next of kin retained ownership of the site and could decide on the type of marker. As it could be some time before the Commission's permanent marker was erected, the family frequently put up a permanent private memorial. The Commission is very limited in what it can do in the case of such graves as the next of kin might not welcome maintenance of the grave by Commission staff, for example. The Commission does regard these burials as war graves, but it is well aware that there can be problems in maintaining them and that it does not have the same control over them as it has over war graves in its own sites in the home countries and overseas.

These privately owned (and frequently privately marked) war graves are inspected by the Commission's staff. If the marker is found to have deteriorated, the Commission offers to replace it with a standard Commission headstone, at its own expense. Next of kin frequently accept this offer, as not only is a new headstone supplied, but maintenance then becomes the Commission's responsibility for all time. Should the next of kin's successor opt for a new headstone, the Commission's records will need to be altered, though no alteration of the cemetery register will be required as the type of marker is not mentioned.

Private graves which are privately marked and contain not only the war burial – who may or may not be on the marker – but also members of the family are now visited only to ensure adequacy of commemoration. These graves are deemed 'not within the Commission's control'. However, the war casualty is recorded in the Commission's registers so that a would-be visitor can still find the shared grave.

While deciding who is entitled to a war grave can be somewhat difficult, the policy of permanence is entirely straightforward: all the governments of the then British Empire collectively pledged the permanence of graves and memorials at the Imperial Conference in 1918. In the past, headstones and memorials that had any degree of permanence had been rare and reserved for a few exalted beings; the Commission was dealing with vast numbers of men, most of them ordinary private soldiers.

The Commission also subscribed to the principle of individual commemoration. Each man who died had been an individual, and whenever possible each of the war dead was to be commemorated individually. This rule has been adhered to: where a burial is identified, his name is engraved on the grave marker; where a serviceman has no known grave, his name is inscribed on a memorial.

The notion of uniformity of sacrifice was naturally and properly extended to uniformity of markers, which differed only in the details inscribed. It was also thought that markers of a uniform shape would be more appropriate to cemeteries for the uniformed services than the many different designs – good and bad – found in civil burial grounds. The Commission also decided that no distinction should be made on account of military or civil rank, race or creed. Of course, there were, and there still remain, differences in marking in the countries where the next of kin were allowed to choose the place of burial and the type of marker to be placed over a war grave, when the latter was not in a Commission plot.

The Commission's headstone (which is under copyright) was suggested by a committee of artists which included D.S. MacColl, Keeper of the Wallace Collection, London; Charles (later Sir Charles) Holmes, Director of the National Gallery, London; and MacDonald Gill, an authority on the lettering of inscriptions. The inscribed marker above an identified grave is the standard form of permanent commemoration provided by the Commission. Sometimes the provision of such a marker is not possible, and commemoration is made on a memorial or marker of some other form. This can be the case when the grave is not in a Commission plot, and it is usually because it is already marked by a privately owned memorial; it is a privately owned grave and permission to erect a Commission memorial has been withheld; the burial is in a 'common' grave; or the grave is unmaintainable.

There are variations on the uniform markers, however. In the Far East, a semi-recumbent bronze plaque is often found, while in Macedonia, a semi-recumbent stone is used; a different semi-recumbent stone is used on the Gallipoli Peninsula. Certain 'ad hoc' markers are also found, such as in Nassau in the Bahamas, or in the privately-owned cemetery at Schiermonnikoog, an island off the Netherlands' coast.

For those who died in service but not in either world war (in Cyprus or in the Falklands, for example) the standard headstone is usually erected but with a square cut in both 'shoulders' to identify a 'non-world-war grave'. Such marking is permitted by the Commission's Charters, provided that all expenses – initial and running – are met by the government concerned, and not out of the Commission's funds. These graves or plots are usually close to, or comparatively near, Commission war graves.

The standard headstone stands two feet eight inches high. Many considerations prompted Ware to press to have this stone, rather than a cross, accepted as the standard marker, the most important being that it allowed the details of the fallen to be shown. Atop the stone is an emblem, normally the badge of the regiment or service for British or Indian forces; the Maple Leaf for Canadians; the badge of the Australian Imperial Force for Australians*; the Fern Leaf for New Zealanders; the Springbok for South Africans; and the Caribou for Newfoundlanders. Although these are regimental or national symbols, they nonetheless impress on the visitor that Commonwealth servicemen and servicewomen from countries around the world fought and died together. Some 1,500 different national, regimental and departmental corps badges are inscribed on the headstones.

Below the emblem is the service or regimental number – usually omitted for officers. The serviceman's rank is given, initials (occasionally the first names, if requested by the next of kin), surname and the official abbreviation of any British decorations (with bars). Immediately below this is the name of the service or regiment, followed by the date of death, and age if known. The religious emblem (cross, Star of David, for example) features beneath this information, but is omitted if the next of kin so wish. Some headstones have a narrow (Latin) cross; others a broad one – the decision of the government, service or regiment, taken with the agreement with the Commission.

When the Commission got in touch with the next of kin to check the details it intended to inscribe on the headstone, it invited them to provide a personal inscription of up to 60 letters. (But not in the case of New Zealand war dead, as its government decided that their headstones should have no personal inscription. There are, however, a few exceptions – in Courcelles-au-Bois Cemetery, France, for example.) These are often poignant, expressing as they do the family's feelings of grief and loss:

L. CPL. H.G. CROSS
'FINE SON, WHOSE FATHER
WAS KILLED AT ARRAS 1918'
PRIVATE L.W. DWANEY
AGE 18
'HE WENT TO WAR
SO YOUNG A LAD'

Some are in a different vein: the headstone in Brookwood Military Cemetery marking the grave (XXI A 11) of Pilot Officer Ken Farnes RAF

---

* But the RCAF, and RAAF, have their Air Force badge.

(VR), a famous cricketer, reads:

'HE DIED AS HE LIVED – PLAYING THE GAME'*

Where the dead man (there are no women's graves in this category) has been awarded the Victoria Cross or the George Cross the decoration appears as an abbreviation after the name as mentioned earlier; in addition a much enlarged facsimile of the VC or GC is engraved on the headstone instead of the usual religious emblem. There is one war grave which is the last resting place of a serviceman who had been awarded the Victoria Cross twice (ie VC and Bar); in this case two slightly smaller VC facsimiles have been carved on the marker.

Perhaps the most surprising feature of the cemeteries, particularly of those in Belgium, France and Gallipoli from the 1914–1918 War, is the large number of dead who have remained unidentified. Over 204,000 dead of the 1914–1918 and 1939–1945 Wars who are buried in the Commission's cemeteries and plots are unidentified by name. Of these, a large proportion are totally unidentified (i.e. not even their nationality within the Commonwealth is known). They are, of course, commemorated on the memorials to the missing. The Commission inscribes all that it knows about the man. One might read for example that he was:

A L Cpl Australian Imperial Force; or
A Captain Canadian Infantry; or
A Serjeant Royal Field Artillery 24th June 1917; or
A Sergeant Pilot, RNZAF

But a distressingly high proportion are totally unidentified and the Commission uses two formulas for their headstones' inscriptions. For the 1914–1918 War (at the time when the headstones were erected it was almost always known as 'The Great War') the inscription reads:

A Soldier [or Sailor or Airman] of the Great War (cross) Known Unto God; and for the 1939–1945 War: A Soldier [or Sailor or Airman] of the 1939–1945 War (cross) Known Unto God.

The phrase Known Unto God was chosen by Rudyard Kipling and appears on all headstones marking the graves of those unidentified by name.

The work of identifying each burial accurately was difficult and did not go smoothly. In a number of instances, one will read at the top of a marker such wording as 'Buried Near This Spot', which means that there is a group of graves in the immediate area, but there is uncertainty as to who is buried in which. Other such formulas include 'Buried In This Cemetery', 'Buried Elsewhere In This Cemetery' and 'Known To Be Buried In This Cemetery'.

These inscriptions are particularly common on headstones on the Gallipoli Peninsula and in the Western Front cemeteries of the 1914–1918 War. At Maple Copse Cemetery near Ypres, most of the markers bear the

* Another famous cricketer, Captain Hedley Verity, Green Howards, is buried in Caserta War Cemetery, Italy (6.E.15); cricketers may remember that this Yorkshire spin bowler once took 17 wickets in a day.

latter inscription. The cemetery originally contained the marked graves of 142 Canadians from the Battle for Mount Sorrel in 1916, as well as those of 114 British soldiers, but was subsequently destroyed by artillery. Ware and his colleagues knew at least where the original cemetery had been and the names of the men buried there, even if they did not know the exact grave in which each was buried. Hence when the cemetery was reconstructed, 230 of the 256 headstones bore the inscription 'Known To Be Buried In This Cemetery'.

A headstone with the superscription 'Believed To Be' was erected on a grave when the Commission was reasonably, but not absolutely, certain of the identity of the remains. It is a testimonial to their caring attitude and their desire for accuracy that no attempt was ever made to deceive the visitor: if they were not sure, they said so. However, it is interesting to note that the superscription was omitted if the next of kin so wished – a thoughtful gesture on the part of the Commission.

When a grave was totally lost, for example, through battle, a 'Kipling Memorial' was erected with wording to that effect. To this was added, at Kipling's suggestion, the inscription, 'Their glory shall not be blotted out' (Ecclesiasticus 44, Verse 13). This type of headstone was normally erected in a Commission cemetery, as near as convenient to the original site. Where six or more burials, headstones without any superscription were grouped around or alongside a small stone memorial, which bore the explanatory inscription for all. These were known in the Commission as Duhallow Blocks, because the first such memorials were erected in Duhallow ADS [Advanced Dressing Station] Cemetery, Ypres. (Duhallow was the name of an Irish hunt.)

If one is walking around a local civil cemetery in England, one may see headstones bearing superscriptions such as 'Buried In Reading Road Cemetery'. This means that the war dead lies in a cemetery elsewhere in the town or village, but the plot has been deemed unmaintainable as a war grave. In these circumstances the remains are not disturbed, but the commemorative stone is erected in an accessible place. There are instances when the war dead lies in a cemetery in another town; the town's name is simply added to the inscription.

Although these so-called 'Special Memorial Headstones' have not been erected over graves, for record and statistical purposes they are considered by the Commission to be such. The names of the dead are in the registers of the cemeteries where the headstones stand, with a mention that these are 'special memorials'. There is no reference to them on the memorials to the missing.

It was sometimes necessary to mark more than one burial with a single headstone. Such plots are classified by the Commission as 'joint' or 'collective' graves. Joint graves contain no more than two burials and can take a number of forms. A single grave may contain the intermingled remains of two war dead and be marked by a single headstone commemorating both burials. As there are more details to be inscribed on the marker, certain modifications have to be made to the standard procedure. For example, if the men were from different regiments, their badges are so inscribed as to be conjoined and if necessary the religious emblem is omitted.

A joint grave may also take the form of a single grave, dug to extra depth, which contains two separately identifiable war dead, and which is marked by a single headstone commemorating both burials. In some cases, there are two adjoining grave spaces, each containing two war dead none of whose remains could be identified individually. A separate headstone marks each grave, but because it is not known for certain which of the dead lie in which grave, the four names are normally arranged in alphabetical order, two on each marker.

Graves which contain three or more war dead are designated collective graves. The forms that they take correspond exactly with those outlined for joint graves above, except in the number of dead they accommodate; they are often the last resting places for airmen of the 1939–1945 War.

The marking of collective graves varies according to the number of burials they contain and the space available: up to three names can be inscribed on a standard headstone. Where there are more than three deceased to be commemorated, two or more headstones are erected at the head of the grave, with the names arranged in alphabetical order. Where there is enough space, separate headstones are sometimes erected for all the deceased in the collective grave. These are placed at the head of the grave in alphabetical order of surname. If any of these markers is out of order, it is almost certain that that particular person was positively identified.

Trench graves are mostly found in 1914–1918 War cemeteries and almost always contain hospital dead rather than field losses. The dead were laid to rest side by side, shoulder to shoulder in a continuous trench (hence trench grave), dug specifically for that purpose. These plots are often marked by headstones set very close together and may resemble collective graves in appearance.

The number of war dead buried in a cemetery often far exceeds the number of separate graves. In extreme cases a cemetery may be a single collective grave; the so-called 'crater' cemeteries (where mine craters were used as burial places) are examples of this. In these circumstances the Commission erects a memorial wall at the side of the cemetery upon which the names of all the dead are inscribed. Two such cemeteries are Lichfield Crater, at Thélus, just north of Arras, which contains the remains of 52 Canadians who died on the first day of the Battle of Vimy, and Zivy Crater, in which 50 war dead lie buried.

The majority of headstones on the old Western Front were made of Portland stone, from the Portland quarries near Weymouth in southern England. However, other stone was used: for instance in Canada and Scotland markers were usually made of granite because it better withstands extremes of climate. Portland nevertheless remained, and still remains in the 1980s, by far the most common stone for Commission headstones in western Europe.

However, Portland is porous and not the longest-lasting of stones. Replacement headstones for Belgium, England, France, Germany, Italy and the Netherlands are now of Botticino limestone, which is quarried in Italy; it is impervious to damp and therefore lasts longer. At present about 2,000 headstones, out of a total of about 1,100,000, require replacement annually, but this figure may rise dramatically over the next few years as the more than half a million markers on the Western Front reach the end of their lives. Where replacement headstones are required for war graves in churchyards, note is taken of the predominant type of stone used both for the church itself and the civil markers; the new headstone is then, if possible, made of similar stone.

In churchyards and civil cemeteries a standard headstone may be erected on a privately owned grave, but as the Commission has only limited control over such plots, any new interment – of, say the widow of the war casualty – may result in the removal of the headstone and its replacement with a non-Commission marker. However, if the relatives prefer, the name of the newly buried person may be added to the original headstone, at the relatives' expense. It must be emphasized that this arrangement is only possible in the case of Commission markers on privately owned graves as no burial of next of kin or others is normally permitted in the Commission's cemeteries.

The manner in which the cremated dead are commemorated depends on the circumstances of cremation. In the participating countries, if the ashes were scattered at the crematorium the deceased is normally commemorated on a stone or bronze panel there and the name added to the cremation memorial register. If, however, the ashes were removed and buried in a grave in a cemetery, this is considered a burial and the name of the deceased is entered on the cemetery register, with no reference being made to cremation. For statistical purposes, the Commission classifies all cremations as burials and all crematoria as cemeteries. The Commission also considers those commemorated on cremation memorials as having been buried in the cemetery in which the cremation memorial is sited; again for statistical purposes. Under this system El Alamein War Cemetery, Egypt, is numerically the largest Commonwealth war cemetery of the 1939–1945 War. (If the names on cremation memorials are not included, Reichswald Forest War Cemetery in West Germany has this distinction.)

When formulating its policies, the Commission took great care to observe religious and cultural customs relating to the dead. Special efforts were also made to be as sensitive as possible to the next of kin's wishes, but without violating the principle of equality of treatment. There are no special graves for those with gallantry awards or for those related to politicians or prominent persons, though there are a few Commission plots which happen to contain officers only: some of these are at bases near military hospitals, where the dead from officers' wards were buried together for convenience's sake. Perhaps the Commission's principle or uniformity of sacrifice could be instructive for all of us.

{ 11 }

The principles and responsibilities of the Commission regarding the memorials

To save the world you asked this man to die;
Would this man, could he see you now, ask why?

W.H. Auden (1907–1973)
Epitaph for the Unknown Soldier.

THE COMMISSION'S CHARACTERISTIC MARKER IS ITS grave headstone, but it may well be that for some visitors the stones which make the greatest and most lasting impression are those of its memorials to the missing. The memorials built by the Commission were basically erected to produce 'wall space' large enough to receive the names of those who had died and had no known grave. They were not built as battle-exploit memorials to glorify aspects of the fighting, but some of them do indeed serve as national memorials in addition to being the place of commemoration of the war dead whose graves are unknown.

The seven 1914–1918 War memorials in Belgium bear over 102,000 names – almost exactly half of the 205,000 Commonwealth war dead at rest in that country. In France, 20 memorials bear nearly 220,000 names – two-fifths of the total dead there. Worldwide there are 85 memorials to the missing of the 1914–1918 War, and 42 relating to the 1939–1945 War. Together, they commemorate three quarters of a million Commonwealth men and women out of the total of one and three quarter million who died in both wars.

The policy of the Commission regarding memorials varied somewhat depending on the service being 'honoured'. The Naval Forces Memorials, commemorating naval and Royal Marine war dead, are sited at the manning ports of the participating countries. Each memorial commemorates by name all those from that manning port who died during the war periods and who have no other grave but the sea (i.e. who were lost or buried at sea) irrespective of the theatre of war or the ship in which they served. Those naval personnel who died on shore and have no known grave are

72

commemorated on special panels on the Naval Forces Memorials. These memorials do not include the names of those of the British 1914–1918 Royal Naval Division who have no known graves. As the division's units fought as infantry soldiers, the names of the missing were placed on the respective Land Forces Memorials.

The names of the dead are grouped on the memorials under the year in which they died. The war dead of the Royal Navy are listed first, followed by those of the other Commonwealth navies, country by country. Within each navy the names are arranged by rank in order of seniority. Each rank forms a heading, under which are listed, in alphabetical order, the surnames of the dead, each followed by full initials and the official abbreviated form of any British decorations held. Each panel is numbered to assist visitors in finding names: a panel number appears alongside each name in the memorial register, held at the site.

The Land Forces Memorials commemorate the war dead of the Commonwealth armies and other Commonwealth land forces. Each memorial pays tribute to those who lost their lives in a particular campaign, or in a particular theatre of war, within certain specified dates. The memorial may also honour troops who died while en route to a campaign, as long as they belonged to units which had been officially earmarked to take part in that campaign. Prisoners of war who died in captivity and have no known grave are commemorated on the memorial for the campaign in which they were taken out of battle, even if their deaths occurred elsewhere and outside the prescribed dates of the campaign.

The system of categorization used on the panels is different from that used on naval memorials in that there is no grouping by year; the names are grouped by commands and staff, regiments and departmental corps. The heading on the first panel will usually be 'Commands and Staff', followed by the names arranged once again by rank, starting with the most senior. Within each rank the surnames are listed in alphabetical order, once more with full initials and the official abbreviations of any decorations received. These panels will be followed by those which list the dead of the regiments and corps in order of seniority, which are laid out in exactly the same manner. The panels of the Land Forces Memorials are numbered – in the same way as the naval memorials – to aid the visitor in locating a particular name.

Where memorials commemorate more than one nationality – the Menin Gate at Ypres, for example – the names are grouped together by country, the dead of the British Army are cited first, followed by those of Canada, Australia, South Africa and India. Within each nationality the names are laid out in the same way as those of the British Army. An exception to this, in the case of an 'important' memorial (all memorials are important, but some are larger than others), is the Vimy Memorial, where the Canadian Government decided that names should be simply in alphabetical order by rank, irrespective of regiment and corps.

The Air Forces Memorials honour the war dead of the Commonwealth air forces, each memorial covering particular theatres of war. These memorials may be sited on their own or form part of a 'mixed-service' memorial. A large minority of those commemorated died from causes unconnected with flying: the airmen who were lost in the sinking of SS *Lancastria* in the evacuation of France in 1940, for example. The layout of the panels is generally similar to that of the naval memorials. The missing airmen of the 1914–1918 War are named on a special 'sub-memorial', which forms part of the Arras Memorial in France.

The Merchant Navy Memorials commemorate seamen of the Commonwealth merchant navies who lost their lives as a result of the increased risks brought about by war and who have no other grave but the sea. A number of merchant seaman who died during the wars and were buried at sea are not commemorated by the Commission, as their deaths did not come within the Commission's responsibilities. Merchant seamen who were serving in effect as Royal Navy sailors under the so-called 'T124' Agreement on board armed merchant cruisers, and have no grave but the sea, are commemorated on a special memorial at Liverpool, England.

On Merchant Navy Memorials the dead are generally listed under the name of their ship, beginning with the surname and initials of the master – if he died. He also has 'Master' entered against his name to show his appointment; the remainder of the names follow in alphabetical order without mention of rank or trade. Ship names are arranged alphabetically, each with its port of registration – whether or not it was sunk.

All memorials usually have certain important features in common. The abbreviation VC (Victoria Cross) normally precedes the surname (i.e. is to its left) instead of following the man's initials, which is the practice with other decorations. The intention, as in the case of the inscribed facsimile of the VC on a headstone, is to catch the visitor's eye. Those with similar ranks, names and initials (e.g. Pte Smith F.G.) have their service number added in full after their initials. These identical names and initials are listed in numerical order, so Pte Smith F.G., 28479 is listed above Pte Smith F.G., 29578.

There is no space on the panels for any personal inscriptions, so some of the 'individual' feel may be lost. But memorials were almost all unveiled at ceremonies with religious participation, whereas war cemeteries were not officially opened; the rationale is that separate and appropriate services would have been held at the time of burial, but this may well not have been the case in frontline cemeteries.

Each of the larger memorials has an 'Addendum' panel to which the names are added of those who were overlooked for various reasons: not infrequently because of the loss of regimental records during the fighting. Names are added as they become known and, as they are not included in the main lists, each casualty is given his full personal details with regiment or corps. However, if a recently notified war fatality was from, say, the Duke of Cornwall's Light Infantry (DCLI), and there is space enough for his name to be added to the foot of the DCLI list, then it is so appended, albeit out of alphabetical order.

War dead are still being found, and are buried in one of the Commission's 'open' cemeteries (except if the casualty is found in one of the metropolitan countries, where the next of kin may claim the remains for 'private' burial or cremation). If the casualty can be identified (unlikely in the case of sailors or soldiers, less so in the case of airmen in aircraft) the memorial register and Commission records are amended at once – as the man is no longer 'missing'.

However, the man's name remains on the memorial itself until such time as the panel requires replacement through wear and weathering. The name is then removed, the other names on that panel being rearranged to make the removal less obvious. The wisdom of this course of action becomes obvious when it is borne in mind that on memorials bearing tens of thousands of names, several hundred of the missing may be subsequently found and buried in war cemeteries: the excision of the names would leave the panels looking most ugly. For statistical purposes, the number of names actually inscribed is no longer necessarily the number of those commemorated on any given memorial. As each new casualty is found and identified, he ceases to be commemorated on the memorial, even though his name remains there until the panels are replaced.

While on the subject of the names on the memorials, it will be remembered that over 200,000 of the three-quarters of a million commemorated are buried in the Commission's sites as 'unknowns'. It therefore follows that a large number of those buried in, say, Tyne Cot Cemetery, Belgium, are commemorated on the Tyne Cot Memorial or perhaps the Menin Gate – or even perhaps, but less probably, on a more distant memorial, such as Ploegsteert.

Certain civil organizations, and civilian individuals such as accredited war correspondents and air ferry pilots, are entitled to war graves treatment in certain circumstances. If they died and have no known grave, they are entitled to have their names inscribed on the appropriate memorial to the missing. The names of foreign civilian 'followers', however, were often not fully known. Therefore, all that could be done to commemorate those listed as 'missing' was to give an estimated total. For example a 'notional' 10,000 are honoured on the Giza Memorial, Cairo, but no names are inscribed.

All the foregoing are memorials to those with no known grave, but there are also many 'alternative commemoration' memorials. The term 'alternative commemoration' is applied by the Commission when, for reasons beyond its control, it is no longer possible to mark or maintain a registered war grave and where exhumation and reburial in a Commission cemetery or plot is undesirable or impracticable. In such cases, where non-disturbance of the remains can be assured, arrangements are made for commemoration by alternative means, either by an 'unmaintainable graves' memorial (with several names) or a special memorial headstone or plaque. As the circumstances which lead to this action being taken differ enormously, the layout of the names on the new memorial is decided on an ad hoc basis. For statistical and record purposes, the place of burial becomes the site of the memorial, but a note of the whereabouts of the actual grave is always kept in the Commission's archives, lest it should be asked for, or circumstances change so much that the grave can once again be marked and maintained.

War cemeteries are closed to any new burials, even if the person to be buried has died of causes attributable to his war service or present day strife. Exception is made for remains which are found and known to be of servicemen who died in the war periods. Similarly no-one dying now, whose grave is unknown or who has been buried at sea, may have his name added to any of the Commission's memorials.

Visiting the memorials is especially poignant for the family and friends of the dead as they must live on never knowing where their loved one rests; for those who can visit a known and marked grave the experience may perhaps be a little less sharp.

{ 12 }

The business of the Commission

*They buried him among the Kings because he had done
good toward God and toward His House*

Inscribed on the tomb of the Bishop of Salisbury
at the behest of King Richard II in 1395 and one
of the texts on the Tomb of the Unknown
Warrior.

LIKE ANY OTHER ORGANIZATION THE COMMISSION HAS
its daily, seasonal and yearly business, plus its normal and long-term
plans and tasks. It has its staffing department, its accounts, pay, and
legal and welfare departments; a drawing office and a printing office; and
many other branches similar to those which may be found in a small
government ministry in almost any country.

It also has a department which deals with the many foreign
governments in whose countries the Commonwealth's war dead lie. This
department works closely with the British Foreign and Commonwealth
Office, and with the diplomatic representatives of the Commonwealth
countries, both in Britain and abroad. In this context, it is useful to
remember that the High Commissioners in London of Canada, Australia,
New Zealand and India, and the Ambassador for the Republic of South
Africa, are ex officio Members of the Commission, the governing body.

To summarize, it can be said that while the Commission is similar to a
small state department it does not work to that state alone, but to several.
And yet it has a large measure of independence, as there is nothing else like
it in the Commonwealth. Although the Commonwealth Secretariat has
some superficial similarity, it performs a different function.

This chapter is intended to outline some of the interesting cases
encountered and to give an idea of some of the problems that have faced,
and are facing, the Commission and what it has done, and is doing, about
them. These do not include problems of say, welfare, as they would be found
in any organization which has staff in many countries overseas. The cases
and problems covered here are largely those which the Commission's key
departments of Records, Works, and Horticulture have had to deal with or
which have been of particular interest to them.

These three departments produce much of what the public see, read
and think about the Commission. The Records Department keeps and
amends records and registers, memorial panel lists, and headstone inscrip-

tion details. Works keeps the more than a million markers and the hundreds of memorials maintained and repaired. The Horticultural Department keeps the cemeteries looking generally splendid, no matter what the local climate is like. The Commission's other departments are geared to produce the administrative support required by its vital 'operational' staff.

By far the majority of the Commission's staff are gardeners, and were it not for their dedication and eye for detail, the Commission's cemeteries would look like 'ordinary' cemeteries. (Their thoughtfulness includes such touches as growing a low 'anti-splash' plant in front of each headstone, high enough to prevent muddied rainwater splashing upwards onto the marker, and yet low enough not to obscure the personal inscription.)

The Works men are fewer in number than their gardening colleagues, but every bit as essential and dedicated. One only has to think of their 10-year job of refacing the Thiepval Memorial to recognize dedication to work. Here, in this very high and exposed site, all the bricks had weathered and had to be replaced by more durable engineering bricks, in often appalling weather and dangerously high off the ground. But most of the anecdotal pieces mentioned below concern the Records Department as, by its very nature, it has the most to do with the resolving of cases concerning the public.

Discovery of remains

Individual remains

The Commission does not search for remains; such operations were discontinued years ago. But from time to time remains are found by chance, such as the discovery at the end of 1981, at Derudeb, Sudan, of 25 British and Indian soldiers of the Indian Army who had died in an Italian air attack on their troop train on 19th January 1941. All were identified from the names on their previously lost graves at the scene of the attack and were reburied in Khartoum War Cemetery.

Also in 1981 there was the discovery – during the demolition of farm buildings in Ovillers-la-Boisselle, Somme, France – of the remains of 49 British soldiers (from five regiments) and two German soldiers of the 1914–1918 War; none could be identified by name. They were buried (the Germans included, with the Volksbund's agreement) in the Commission's 'open' cemetery at Terlincthun in northern France.

Three Australian soldiers of the 1914–1918 War were found in the late 1970s in a dugout in the side of a railway embankment on the Somme; they were named from their identity discs and also buried in Terlincthun. In the mid-1970s the unidentified remains of 25 Royal Navy sailors were recovered from the wreck of the HM Submarine *E24*, sunk by a mine off the German island of Heligoland in 1916 and raised during sea-channel clearing operations. They were buried in Hamburg (Ohlsdorf) Cemetery, Germany, but as the 25 were only a proportion of the crew, none could be positively identified.

When a discovery is made, however, it is usually of a single body during road-widening, well-digging, the preparation of foundations, or similar activity, most often on the old Western Front. Perhaps about 20 to 25 sets of remains are discovered in an average year. Very few are now identifiable, as the identity discs have been lost, and forensic tests (which are not generally made) would probably yield nothing after such a long time.

On finding the body of a Commonwealth serviceman in, say, Belgium, France or the Netherlands, the finder notifies the police who, after they have completed their formalities, tell the Commission's Area Office at Ieper or Beaurains. The remains are buried amid little publicity in an 'open' cemetery, in that country, and the grave is marked in the normal way. The Area Office notifies Head Office of the Commission at Maidenhead, Berkshire, and action is taken there by the Records Department to amend the records and registers as necessary.

The same basic procedure is followed if, for example, airmen of the Battle of Britain are found in Britain. These, however, can usually be identified as details of the aircraft and its pilot are not unduly difficult to trace. German airmen who died in the Battle of Britain and in raids over England are buried in the German Military Cemetery at Cannock Chase in Staffordshire.

In cases where the identification of remains is thought possible, the task is normally the responsibility of the civil and military authorities of the country in which they are found, helped by, say, the British Ministry of Defence. The Commission accepts such identification for the marking of their graves and the amendment of records and cemetery registers. Where war dead have been buried as unknowns in the Commission's sites, it is the Commission which decides whether or not additional information which seems to point to identification is sound enough either positively to identify the casualty or, as happens in some cases, to accept him as a 'believed to be' category burial.

Servicemen sometimes 'went missing' a long way from the battlefield. Four New Zealand airmen disappeared in the 1939–1945 War, when their aeroplane crashed in an isolated location in their homeland, and were not discovered until the 1970s. They were identified and buried in different places in accordance with the next of kins' wishes – the normal procedure for those dying in their home countries.

However, the authorities were unaware that these four airmen's places of burial were war graves and therefore did not notify the Commission. Thanks to a New Zealand official's chance remark at the Commission's Head Office, the matter became known and the necessary steps were taken to regularize the position. The four were at the time correctly commemorated by name on one or other of the New Zealand Provincial Memorials.

There is only one Commonwealth war grave in Venezuela, South America, that of Leading Airman P.H. Brade RN, age 18, in Caracas

Southern General Cemetery. He was in a naval aircraft flying from HMS *Goshawk* when it crashed in dense jungle on 16th November 1943. It is not clear what happened to the other crew members, but Brade was not discovered until the aeroplane was found by chance in the early 1970s. There being no Commission plot in the country, he was buried in a civil cemetery.

When the remains of servicemen who died in the 1914–1918 War are found and identified, no attempt to trace the next of kin is made by the Commission. There are two main, and good, reasons for this. First, any next of kin would now be very old indeed and the news of the discovery of the serviceman after over 70 years could be a severe shock; second, most of the next of kin addresses are now completely out of date. The Commission does not disturb next of kin by asking for up-to-date addresses but, of course, makes a note of them if they are volunteered or produced in ordinary correspondence.

The Commission or the Ministry of Defence do notify the next of kin of the discovery of any 1939–1945 War dead. However, these war dead are found – understandably – less often than the scores of thousands who disappeared in the glutinous mud and shell craters of the old Western Front. Notification will probably continue for the next 20 years or so, by which time the next of kin of that war, too, will be very old, and the practice may then cease. Even now, most addresses of the next of kin of 1939–1945 War dead are out of date, and more often than not the Commission's undelivered letter is returned by the Post Office.

At the time of writing, the most recent recovery of a war casualty of the 1939–1945 War was the discovery by members of the Bayeux Museum staff of the remains of Flight Sergeant Reginald Thursby RAF, still in his Hawker Typhoon aircraft, deep in Normandy soil. He had flown from his base near Bayeux on 9th August 1944, with others of No 198 Squadron, to attack ground targets, when he was hit by anti-aircraft shells and his aeroplane set ablaze. He radioed his commanding officer, Squadron Leader Yves Ezanno, to report that his aircraft was on fire and he was trying to return to base. Two minutes later he said he was baling out. That was the last that was heard of him and his name was correctly included among those inscribed on the Runnymede Memorial.

On 5th November 1985 Flight Sergeant Thursby was buried at St Charles de Percy War Cemetery in Normandy, an 'open' cemetery. His funeral was attended by, among others, his former CO, now General (Retired) Ezanno of the French Air Force, and Mrs Doreen Young, who was his fiancée at the time of his death.

It is interesting to note that in the last 10 or so years, about 10 aircrew entitled to war graves treatment have been found in England, and that only in a single case has the next of kin opted for burial in a site other than a Commission cemetery, normally Brookwood Military Cemetery. When it is borne in mind that next of kin may claim the body of a serviceman who died in his home country for private burial, it is gratifying to know that they see the Commission's cemeteries as the best, most secure and most fitting resting places for their loved ones.

Mixed remains

Where remains of Commonwealth and American servicemen were inter-mingled, those remains were, if they were predominantly Commonwealth, buried in the country in which they were found; if they were predominantly American, they were normally buried in the USA. An example is the case of Major General Orde Wingate DSO and two Bars, who was commanding the Chindits in Burma when the aircraft in which he was flying was shot down on 24th March 1944. The Americans on board outnumbered the British and so Major General Wingate is buried, with the others (among them war correspondents Stuart Emeny of the News Chronicle and Stanley Wills of the Daily Herald), in Arlington National Cemetery, Virginia, USA, Section 12, Collective Grave 288. Also in this cemetery is buried Field Marshal Sir John Dill, Chief of the Imperial General Staff 1940–1941, and Chief of the British Joint Staff Mission to the USA and Senior British Representative on the Combined Chiefs of Staff from 1941 until his death on 4th November 1944. His handsome equestrian statue in Arlington was erected by the Americans: 'unequal' treatment, but out of the Commission's hands.

Judicial executions

The Commission's duty is, among other things, to commemorate all those who died in the 1914–1918 and 1939–1945 Wars, irrespective of the cause, or place, of death. It follows that those Commonweath servicemen who were shot or hanged following sentence by courts martial or civil courts are entitled to war graves treatment, whether they were buried in a military cemetery or the prison yard, in Britain or elsewhere. There were very few of them if taken as a proportion of the total number of war dead, but nevertheless there were enough at over 340 executions in the 1914–1918 War and around 40 in the 1939–1945 War.

Executed servicemen buried in military cemeteries (the great majority) have standard Commission markers on their graves and there is normally nothing on the headstone, and never anything in the register, to indicate the casualty was executed. But if the next of kin wished to indicate that the man was judicially executed by a reference to the fact in the personal inscription, this was reluctantly agreed to by the Commission. One example will suffice: Private Albert Ingham, 18th Battalion, the Manchester Regiment, was executed on 1st December 1916 at the age of 24. He is buried in Bailleulmont Communal Cemetery in the Pas-de-Calais, France, Grave B12. His father asked to have the following personal inscription on the headstone and it will remain there for ever: 'Shot At Dawn. One Of The

First To Enlist'. The register entry says that Private Ingham 'Died of wounds', which is a kind way of not telling the whole truth.

Another soldier of the same regiment, who was executed on the same day and is buried nearby, has no unusual personal inscription and his register entry does not mention any cause of death. Among those who were executed were murderers, deserters and others. And sad though it may be, it must never be forgotten that one man's desertion or cowardice (no matter how awful the prevailing conditions) might have caused the deaths of a score others through their not receiving a vital message or ammunition, or their being surprised by the enemy.

Those who were convicted of a capital crime by a civil court – while on leave, for example – and executed were buried in unmarked graves within the prison's confines. This effectively prevented the Commission from carrying out its duty of marking the grave. Where this was the case, the man's name was inscribed on the memorial to the missing appropriate to the place where he was executed. This does not diminish the 'worth' or dignity of the memorial, any more than does the grave of an executed man that of a war cemetery. Although the behaviour of some of those who were killed in action was not exemplary away from the battlefield, it would be wrong, and quite impossible, to try to evaluate a man's worth or behaviour before deciding on the manner of his commemoration. It is perhaps appropriate here to mention that at one time the Victoria Cross could be forfeited for bad behaviour. King George V disagreed with this ruling and expressed the view on 20th July 1920 that there should be no more forfeitures and said that a man should always be allowed to wear his VC, even 'on the scaffold'. If that be so, why should any man be denied the right to have his name on a memorial or on a headstone? There were moves (not by the Commission) in the early 1980s to expunge the small number of names of executed British and Canadian soldiers commemorated on the Brookwood Memorial; these correctly came to nothing. Until the man committed the offence for which he was executed, he might have been a brave and splendid serviceman. He should be correctly honoured for that – and he is.

Deserters

A serviceman who died while a deserter (not as an absentee, but having been officially deemed a 'deserter' by a Court of Enquiry; that is someone who probably intended never to serve again) was not commemorated by the Commission. If, however, during his period of desertion he joined another service (which was sometimes the case) and died, the Commission did honour him. If he had been deemed a deserter and later found to have been killed in, say, an air raid while overstaying his leave, again he was commemorated by the Commission. If the serviceman was a deserter who was apprehended, tried, found guilty and executed, then he was likewise commemorated, as at the time of the trial and execution his desertion had obviously finished.

Requests from next of kin for the omission of names from memorials to the missing

There were a few such cases, and the reason for not wanting a name to be inscribed on a memorial is not clear, but probably political. After a request by the next of kin not to inscribe the names of two British seamen on the Tower Hill Memorial, London, the Commission decided that a wish by the next of kin could not override its duty under its Charters and that the names would be inscribed; and so they were.

Removal of War Cemeteries

It has already been made clear that the Commission has a fundamental interest in the permanence of a burial site and in the permanence and non-disturbance of the graves it contains. From time to time there are reasons of overriding public interest for the exhumation and transfer, perhaps to another cemetery, of the burials in a Commission site. Examples of such cases are where a valley is being flooded by the rising waters behind a new dam, which would result in the graves being submerged, or where the moving of, say, three burials would allow for the widening and making safer of a stretch of roadway, and where no other course is practicable.

Any proposal for the exhumation of remains coming from any source is minutely examined by the Commission, and permission is only granted for the exhumation and transfer to take place if all the necessary criteria are met. Reburial is almost always in a Commission site. Sometimes, if only one or two burials are involved, as in the second example above, reburial will be elsewhere in that site if there is space enough. Certainly there can be no repatriation, even if requested by next of kin, and reburial is invariably in the same country.

Great care is taken by the Commission that all decencies are observed; that there is the minimum of publicity; and that the new graves are re-marked (often with the original markers) as quickly as possible. If the actual work is not being carried out by the Commission itself, a member of the Commission's staff is always present at the sites of exhumation and reburial.

Sometimes local and other authorities eye the sites which, when they were established say, after the end of the 1914–1918 War, were in the countryside, but are now surrounded by the vastly expanded town or city. It would be easy and profitable for the authority if the Commission were to remove the remains to another site, to develop the land by building houses, opening a car park, or extending a university. But the Commission does not necessarily consider these to be overriding public necessities, and cases of this sort have been rejected over the years.

There have been perhaps about 10 requests in the last 20 years for the removal of Commonwealth cemeteries which have been successfully resisted by the Commission. In the same period there have been about the same number to which the Commission has reluctantly agreed. The sites in these cases generally contained far fewer burials – under 2,000 – than the cemeteries which it refused to remove. (The latter in total contained around 12,000 burials.) The cost of the work, which of course has a bearing on the matter, is normally met by the authority which requested the transfer of the site. These costs can be considerable as they cover such items as moving Crosses of Sacrifice and headstone beams, horticultural layout, exhumation and reburial.

Some authorities are particularly helpful to the Commission; a case in the Netherlands makes a good example. A motorway was being designed and its best line would have necessitated cutting off some of the frontage (but no graves) of both Bergen-op-Zoom War Cemetery, and the Canadian War Cemetery. The Commission requested that the matter be reconsidered, as it felt that the appearance and tranquility of both cemeteries would be adversely affected by the proposal, and that it was possible to alter the route. In the event, the authorities realigned the proposed motorway for some thousand yards (a shorter distance would have produced an unacceptably sharp curve) and neither cemetery is now affected at all.

Sometimes, only a Cross of Sacrifice or similar has to be moved. In such cases, the Commission does not resist to the same extent as it does when burials are concerned, providing that the scheme is aesthetically acceptable and that the authority pays for the work. One such case was at Dranoutre Churchyard in Belgium, where the Cross of Sacrifice was so sited near a road junction as to restrict the field of vision of drivers and other road users. At the request of the authority, the Cross was resited by them in the churchyard, which resulted in a clear view and a much safer junction.

Another case was the Cross in Brandhoek New Military Cemetery No 3 in Belgium, where a new road for fast traffic was scheduled to cut across a rear corner of the cemetery, close to which the Cross stood. The proposal was that the Cross should be moved to the other rear corner of the cemetery, but was complicated by the fact that six burials (including that of a German) would also have to be moved to vacant spaces in the cemetery.

The matter was considered carefully, particularly because of the exhumations required, with the Volksbund being consulted about the German grave. The upshot was that the Commission agreed to the whole proposal and the work was carried out, all costs being met by the authority. The cemetery has lost nothing aesthetically but, it must be admitted, is not as quiet as it was before, when the original main road was about 100 yards away.

Exhumations

In addition to requests from authorities for the transfer of cemeteries and graves, there are cases when the Commission itself decides to move burials to another site, and when the Commission is asked to do so by individuals. The following are examples of the types of cases which occur.

An isolated grave in a communal cemetery

The grave of a gunner of the Royal Artillery was the isolated one of the 26 scattered in several small plots in Bapaume Communal Cemetery, France – a civil cemetery. It was near the greenhouses and workshops of the cemetery and, at its head, was the storage tank for heating oil. It was difficult to make the grave look anything but what it was: not up to the Commission's standards and looking in a rather sorry state. Furthermore, the easiest access to the storage tank for the fuel pipe from the road tanker was across the grave; and that was where it was seen during an inspection.

The Commission began the process for deciding if a burial should be moved. Eventually the decision was reached that exhumation should take place and that the gunner should be moved into a nearby plot of six in the same communal cemetery. Generally, the Commission prefers such transfers to be into a plot or cemetery which is completely within its care. As the dead man was from the 1914–1918 War and as he was still in the same cemetery, it was decided that no attempt should be made to contact any next of kin, but all records and registers were amended.

A Canadian airman of the Jewish faith

A privately owned grave in a civil cemetery in South Wales contained the remains of an RCAF officer of the Jewish faith, who had died in the area in the 1939–1945 War. His brother, who was living in Canada, asked the Commission if the remains could be exhumed and repatriated. When the request was refused, the brother asked if the remains could be moved to the Canadian Plot in Brookwood Military Cemetery. His request was backed by medical evidence stating that such a move would help to alleviate the mental stress he had suffered for some time. The Commission, which in the event was not well placed as the grave was privately owned, agreed to the move, and the Canadian airman was reburied in the Canadian Plot. All costs were met by the brother, who was present at the reburial.

A British soldier of the Jewish faith

All but three of the 5,000 war burials in Singapore are in Kranji War Cemetery. One of those three was the only war grave in Singapore (Thomson Road) Jewish Cemetery, a civil burial ground. The local authorities decided that the cemetery should be cleared, and the Commission therefore agreed that the burial should be exhumed and moved into the cemetery at Kranji. As it happened, the local Jewish authorities were moving all the remains into another Jewish cemetery in Singapore and pressed hard for the war buiral to be re-interred there as well. As has been mentioned, the Commission normally insists that any remains which are exhumed are reburied in a site over which it has full control; but, after careful consideration, and knowing that the new site was secure and would be well maintained, the Commission agreed that the remains of this Jewish serviceman could be buried in the new Jewish site.

A British soldier of the 1939–1945 War buried in a war graves plot in a general cemetery

A British officer was killed in early 1945 and buried in a war graves plot in nearby Sittard *General* Cemetery, Netherlands, with another officer and 19 soldiers. After the war his father, feeling that he would much prefer his son's remains to be in Sittard *War* Cemetery, a couple of miles away, pressed the Commission strongly for his exhumation and reburial. Despite the fact that the father (who has since died) was a man of substance and made, as he saw it, a good case for the concentration, permission to move the son was turned down and his body remains in the plot. It seems sad, perhaps, that in the rare case where a next of kin asked for remains to be moved into a war cemetery, albeit from a war graves plot, permission was refused.

An RAF airman of the 1939–1945 War buried in a war graves plot of the 1914–1918 War

With the above case in mind, it is worth mentioning a later instance of which the outcome was 'happy'. Perhaps the passage of nearly a score years had softened some hard thinking.

A visitor to the Commonwealth Plot in Quievrain Communal Cemetery near Mons (Bergen) in Belgium was upset to find that his RAF airman brother, who had died in May 1940, was the only serviceman of that war buried there: all the other 40 dead were soldiers of the 1914–1918 War. He asked the Commission if, exceptionally, his brother could be exhumed from one of the Commission's own plots and buried in a cemetery of its choice, in which most of burials were of the 1939–1945 War and included airmen; his request was supported by his elderly mother's plea. This unusual request was considered and granted. The airman was exhumed and reburied in Adegem Canadian War Cemetery, Belgium, the 'open' cemetery for Commonwealth dead of the 1939–1945 War who are found in that country.

An RCAF airman in Britain

During the 1939–1945 War a military aircraft took off from Newquay, Cornwall, England, carrying around 12 people on a flight to North Africa. It crashed in the sea very shortly after take-off and everyone on board was killed. The bodies of all except the pilot, Flying Officer Arthur Douglas Gavel RCAF, were recovered and buried in various parts of Britain as, having died in the United Kingdom, the next of kin could chose the place of interment. Some weeks later an unidentifiable body was washed ashore, and the local authority decided that it was that of an unidentified merchant seaman, despite the fact that one airman had not been recovered. The Commission accepted this ruling and the grave was marked as that of an unknown seaman of the Merchant Navy.

In the early 1980s, thanks to the efforts of the Newquay Police, evidence was produced which made it seem extremely likely that the 'unknown seaman' was in fact Flying Officer Gavel, and the Commission was asked if an exhumation could be made to settle the matter. The Commission had long since carried out no exhumations for the sake of identification. However, it agreed to the proposal and, after the necessary legal formalities had been observed, the body was exhumed and examined by RAF pathologists, who had been provided with medical documentation from Canada. They established beyond doubt that the body was Gavel's.

Some days later the funeral of Flying Officer Gavel took place; he was reburied in the same grave in the Commission's Plot in Newquay. His reburial was accompanied by the normal religious service and an RAF Guard of Honour was present. His brother and sister-in-law of Swift Current, Saskatchewan, had travelled from Canada and were present to see the final chapter on Flying Officer Gavel closed on a fine summer day in 1984.

An isolated grave in Italy

Flight Lieutenant Donald Massingberd Leith-Hay-Clark RAF, seconded from the Lincolnshire Regiment of the British Army, was killed on 27th January 1944 and buried near the spot north of Rome where his aircraft had crashed. His father, Major N. Leith-Hay-Clark, was assured by the then owner of the land that the privately marked grave would be cared for for ever. For that reason he obtained Italian Government authority to prevent the Commission from moving his son's remains into a Commission war cemetery. It was most unusual in Italy for such an isolated grave to be allowed to remain where it was, then literally in a field, as the authorities were keen that the remains of all foreign servicemen of all nationalities should be buried in war cemeteries.

The grave was inspected by the Commission in the early 1980s and found to be in a dense thicket which had grown over and around it. The recumbent headstone, which covered the whole grave, was broken, and it was clear that building developments nearby might soon overwhelm the site. The matter was obviously urgent if the grave was simply not to be lost under the developer's debris or the ever growing and almost impenetrable thicket.

In view of Major Leith-Hay-Clark's strong objections to the body's being moved, the Commission tried at length to trace him or his wife to obtain permission for exhumation and transfer. In the event both the father and mother had died, but lawyers acting on their behalf and on behalf of two surviving nephews (Flight Lieutenant Leith-Hay-Clark's only brother had also been killed in the war) agreed that exhumation was the correct solution and would probably have been agreed to by the father, had he still be alive and faced with the present circumstances.

Flight Lieutenant Leith-Hay-Clark was reburied in Cassino War Cemetery, with a headstone bearing the linked badges of the Lincolnshire Regiment and the RAF. Exceptionally – as the parents would probably have liked, had they still been alive – it bears a superscription stating that he was originally buried at Casaletti de Santa Ruffina. He was buried next to Flying Officer J.D.P. Flannery, whose body was found by fishermen in the Mediterranean Sea, still in his Hawker Hurricane fighter, in the late 1970s. Had Flying Officer Flannery lived, he would have been the third baronet of that name. His mother attended his funeral.

Servicemen not recorded previously

From time to time next of kin or others enquire about the place of commemoration of a serviceman who died in one of the wars, and it turns out that the Commission has no record of the man. The matter is thoroughly investigated and it usually transpires that the Commission had not been advised of the death by the Ministry concerned; such cases almost always concern the 1914–1918 War and the writer knows of only one recent case from the 1939–1945 War.

Mention is made elsewhere in this book of the addition to the Halifax Memorial of the names of Canadian servicemen who died in Canada in the 1914–1918 War and whose places of burial are unknown. Two other examples, one from each war, may be of interest.

A daughter was sorting through her recently deceased mother's effects and came across two letters concerning her grandfather, who had been a gunner and had died in the 1914–1918 War. One letter was from the major commanding the battery (who had himself been killed shortly after on the Somme) to the dead man's wife, commiserating on the death in action of her husband, and the other was from the chaplain who had buried him in 'a cemetery near Loos, France'.

The daughter wrote to the Commission to ask in which cemetery her grandfather had been buried. It turned out that the Commission had no record of him. As is usual in such cases, the Records Department got in touch with the Ministry concerned, giving all the details which were in the two letters. It was established that the gunner was indeed entitled to war graves treatment, but for reasons unknown his death had not been reported to the Commission.

Usually such a casualty is added (as were the Canadians) to the 'Addendum' panel of the appropriate memorial, as it is almost always possible to establish where the man's unit was when he died even though his place of disappearance or burial cannot be established. In this case, it was known that he had been buried in 'a cemetery near Loos'; there are several in the vicinity. One of them, Fosse 7 Military Cemetery (Quality Street),

Mazingarbe, contains 130 burials, of which over 40 are from the Royal Artillery, 50 from Scottish regiments and, significantly, over 20 graves which are unnamed or have been destroyed by shell fire.

It seemed highly likely that the grandfather was buried in one of the latter 20, and the Commission offered to erect a special memorial headstone at the side of the cemetery bearing the superscription 'Believed To Be Buried In This Cemetery'. This was entirely acceptable to the granddaughter of the gunner and it was done. Had she not agreed, the appropriate step would have been the addition of his name to the Loos Memorial.

The second example concerns a sailor who had been discharged from the Royal Navy on medical grounds during the 1939–1945 War and had died within a few weeks. Later his brother wrote to the Commission and asked if he could be helped in the refurbishment of his brother's privately marked grave. The Commission had not been notified of the sailor's death but – as a serviceman is entitled to war graves treatment when he dies of causes brought about by his service career in the war periods, even if he has been discharged within these periods – the sailor brother's grave was deemed to be a war grave. With the brother's approval, a standard Commission headstone was erected in a cemetery in a Medway town in Kent, England, and the grave is, and will be, maintained in perpetuity. In the cases of the gunner and sailor all records and registers were amended.

The Tomb of the Unknown Warrior

The Cenotaph in Whitehall, London, was designed by Sir Edwin Lutyens and completed shortly after the 1914–1918 War; it was scheduled to be unveiled by King George V on Armistice Day 1920. However, in October of that year the Dean of Westminster, Herbert Edward Ryle, suggested to Buckingham Palace that there be a complement to the unveiling – that the body of an unidentified soldier be exhumed from the battlefields and reburied in Westminster Abbey, as an ambassador of the dead to the living.

The King had liked the idea of the Cenotaph, but was not initially keen on the exhumation of the soldier two years after the Armistice. However, the King later strongly supported the idea, influenced perhaps by Lloyd George, the Prime Minister, who was enthusiastic about the proposal.

To ensure that the warrior was unknown, the military authorities on the old Western Front were instructed to exhume six unidentified 'British' (in the old sense) soldiers; they might in fact have been sailors in the Royal Naval Division or airmen. On 9th November 1920 six working parties, commanded by subalterns, went to the six main battlefields – Aisne, Arras, Cambrai, Marne, Somme and Ypres – each to exhume the remains of one soldier buried in a grave marked 'Unknown'.

The six bodies were put in coffins (burial at the front was usually in a greatcoat or blanket, or nothing but the man's uniform) and taken to a hut near Ypres where they were received by a clergyman, the Reverend George

Kendall. A blindfolded officer went inside the hut and at random touched the coffin of the soldier who was to be laid among kings in Westminster Abbey. The body was brought across the Strait of Dover from Boulogne to Dover on HMS *Verdun*, the ship chosen to honour the French by reminding all of perhaps their finest hour in the war.

At the Abbey, where the congregation included many private mourners, 100 holders of the VC lined the nave. There was a brief service and the Unknown Warrior was lowered into his grave near the Great West Door. The grave was refilled with earth brought from the battlefields, and covered with a large stone slab with the laconic inscription: 'An Unknown Warrior'.

Later, a longer descriptive text was to be produced by the Dean as he thought – surely correctly – that in 50 years' time people would want to know who, or perhaps what, the Unknown Warrior was. The new black marble stone from Belgium was laid on the tomb in 1921. The most famous text on the stone, 'They buried him among the Kings because he had done good toward God and toward His house' was not, as the Dean thought, the original work of a north England priest. The text was actually over 500 years old, as King Richard II had, in 1395, had it inscribed on the tomb of his friend, the Bishop of Salisbury, who had also been buried in the Abbey.

Although it was the Dean of Westminster who wrote to the Palace about the proposal, the original idea had been that of the Reverend David Railton, the Vicar of Margate, Kent, England. He was a Padre in the war and had been much moved in 1916 by the sight of the grave of an unidentified soldier of the Black Watch in the garden of his billet. At the time he considered writing to Field Marshal Haig to suggest the repatriation of a symbolic 'unknown' but, instead, on his return to England in 1919 he wrote to the Dean who accepted the idea and in turn, wrote to the Palace.

The grave is unusual in several respects. It is probably the first such grave; the French 'Unknown Warrior' was buried on the same day under the Arc de Triomphe in Paris but the idea had been British. It is also unusual in that the body was repatriated. This was strictly against the Commission's rules, but surely an acceptable breaking of those rules, as the man was unknown and of immeasurable symbolic significance. In any case, so far as can be ascertained, the matter was largely dealt with by the Abbey and Palace authorities without the Commission's involvement, at least in England.

Lastly, it is unusual in that there is a Cemetery Register entry about the Unknown Warrior and, as has been seen, details about unidentified soldiers obviously cannot be included in the normal alphabetical lists of names. The entry reads:

'   Westminster Abbey
Near the west door of the Abbey, under a black
marble slab, is buried an unidentified
soldier whose body was brought from France*
and placed there, with all possible honour,
on the 11th November 1920.'

The grave is effectively not within the Commission's control as it is privately marked, owned and maintained. Despite this, it remains perhaps the best known and most visited war grave in the world.

In 1923 the then Duchess of York placed her wedding bouquet on the tomb. It was an appropriate gesture as her brother, Captain the Honourable Fergus Bowes-Lyon Black Watch, had been killed at Loos on 27th September 1915 and had no known grave. Who is to know that she was not laying the flowers on his grave? Her Royal Highness was later to become Queen and later Queen Mother.

The Gardeners' service at Westminster Abbey

In 1933 it was suggested by Frank Tyrrell, a member of the Commission's staff, that a small ceremony might be held in the Warrior's Chapel (now known as St George's Chapel) in Westminster Abbey on the evening before Armistice Day. The suggestion, welcomed by the Dean of Westminster, was that Commission gardeners should bring from France to the Abbey a wreath of flowers grown in the Commonwealth war cemeteries, hold a short service and lay the wreath at the base of the Tablet to the Million Dead (below which is the tablet to Sir Fabian Ware). The first ceremony took place on the evening of Friday 10th November 1933. The ceremony is still held, but now at noon on the Friday preceding Remembrance Sunday, when two or three gardeners from Belgium and France make, bring and lay a wreath and the Dean officiates. The Chapel is a few paces from the Tomb of the Unknown Warrior, and near to the 1939–1945 Civilian Roll of Honour, which is in volumes housed in a cabinet set against the west wall of the Abbey.

The treatment of stonework

The painting of inscriptions in stone

The Commission's practice is generally not to paint in inscriptions on headstones or memorials as, once done, it has to be repeated – a very time-consuming and therefore expensive exercise. Furthermore, it is felt that usually the inscriptions and badges look better without the addition of paint, legibility relying on the light and shade in the sharp incisions. Exceptions are often made in the case of granite headstones, where the inscriptions can be hard to read even when well cut. In this case black paint is normally used.

* But it could have been Belgium as Ypres was one of the places from which a body was brought.

The major exception to the rule is the Menin Gate Memorial, Ypres, where many of the names are within the memorial cloister and high up. Despite good letterwork, it was apparent that many of these could not be read easily and it was decided that it was essential that the inscriptions be painted in black. As the memorial bears 55,000 names, there are certainly well over half a million separate letters and figures and the cost of painting by hand would have been very large. The Commission hit on a splendid, and very much cheaper, solution. Briefly this entailed cleaning down the panels and sticking lining paper over them; scorching the paper with a blow lamp, which only burnt away the paper over the inscriptions as air was trapped beneath (elsewhere the paper merely browned but remained stuck to the stone); brushing the paper to get rid of charred pieces, so producing sharp edges; spray-painting the paper which acted like a stencil – the paint only reaching the panel where the paper had been burnt away; removing the paper with water jets. The result was well-painted, sharply defined inscriptions, achieved without the need for skilled operators, and the establishment of a system which could be used again when necessary. All the inscriptions, no matter how high up they are, can now be read by anyone with reasonable eyesight.

The inscriptions on some other memorials, of which Cassino and Athens are examples, have also been painted, but these, being small in comparison to the Menin Gate, were done by hand at no great trouble.

Unnaturally fast erosion of stonework

There have been cases of stonework eroding unnaturally fast, because of fumes and dust emanating from local factories and works. When necessary, the Commission has taken steps to make good the damage, to recover costs, and to receive the operators' assurance about the safety and purity of future emanations. All such cases have been satisfactorily dealt with. As a routine measure, the Commission uses a toxic wash, applied as a spray, to destroy unsightly growths on headstones: apart from the growths' disagreeable appearance, they hasten erosion. The wash also inhibits further growth and keeps the headstones looking clean and their inscriptions legible.

Ceremonies and visitors

The Commission does not now normally organize ceremonies to commemorate feats of arms or anniversaries, or similar; but probably thousands of ceremonies are held in the Commission's cemeteries or at its memorials every year. Some, of course, take place every year and examples which spring to mind are the ceremonies at the Merchant Navy Memorial, Tower Hill, London and Arnhem (Oosterbeek) War Cemetery, Netherlands.

Although it does not arrange these events, what the Commission does do is ensure that the site is at its usual high standard; give advice and

Above: The site of the Menin Gate Memorial, Ypres, Belgium before 1914—no 'gate' in the city's ramparts, but the roadway is guarded by two stone lions. The 'Cloth Hall's' tower is in the background.
Below: Commonwealth soldiers leaving Ypres for the front through the shelled roadway; the 'Cloth Hall' is nearly destroyed.

The Ypres (Menin Gate) Memorial. 1914–1918. Perhaps the best known of the Commission's memorials and a source of great pride to the citizens of Ieper, (Ypres) who daily close to motor traffic the main road which runs under the arch to enable the 'Last Post Ceremony' to be held. It commemorates over 50,000 soldiers of Britain, Canada, Australia, South Africa and India.

The Thiepval Memorial (adjoining Thiepval Anglo-French Cemetery), Somme, France. 1914–1918. The largest Commonwealth war memorial, commemorating over 70,000 Britons and 830 South Africans, most of whom died in the Battle of the Somme, July–November 1916, and have no known grave. In the general view, the crosses in the foreground mark 300 French burials; there are the same number of Commonwealth burials, marked by headstones, on the left. The second view is a close up of one of the piers and its name panels.

Maple Copse Cemetery, Zillebeke, Belgium. 1914–1918 'before' and 'after'. Note the 'odd' markers in the second photograph—no exhumations were carried out for purely 'tidying-up' reasons.

Tyne Cot Cemetery, Passchendaele, Belgium and the Tyne Cot Memorial (British and New Zealand), 1914–1918. The Cross of Sacrifice stands on a German bunker in the largest, with nearly 12,000 burials, Commonwealth War Cemetery. The Memorial commemorates 34,000 Britons and over 1,000 New Zealanders.

Bayeux War Cemetery, Calvados, France. 1939–1945. 'Before' (with temporary cross markers) and 'after' (with permanent headstone markers). This is the largest Commonwealth cemetery of over 20 in Normandy.

Sai Wan Bay War Cemetery, Hong Kong. 1939–1945. Before and after permanent construction. Note the single "non World War" headstone in the foreground with distinctive cuts in its 'shoulders'.

Wreaths at the Stone of Remembrance in Arnhem (Oosterbeek) War Cemetery, Netherlands. 1939–1945. The majority of the graves are of airborne soldiers who fought in the Battle of Arnhem, September 1944.

produce briefs if asked or if it thinks it necessary; and make such security arrangements as it thinks expedient, for example, to prevent visits by those who might wish to disrupt the ceremony. As the Commission is acting as 'groundkeeper', a member of the Commission's staff is present at some of the more 'important' of the ceremonies. But, with the best of wills, the Commission cannot be represented at all, as they are simply too numerous and widespread; and most of the annual ceremonies are naturally crowded on or around 11th November.

The millions of visitors to the cemeteries and memorials, and the participants in the ceremonies held there, are of course most welcome. One of the objects of the Commission's work is to have its sites in a condition such as gives peace, pleasure, consolation and solace to them. Visitors sometimes upset the staff (usually the gardeners) by unintentionally treading on and breaking down grass verges; by picking flowers; by occasional unseemly behaviour (the writer saw a model languishing on a Stone of Remembrance for fashion photographs); by having transistor radios playing; or by playing games, such as football. There are a variety of other misdeeds which are upsetting to the staff and, much more important, to other visitors.

One understandable source of irritation for the Commission's staff is to see entries in the 'Remarks' column of the Visitors' Book which say something along the lines of, 'Thank you, people of Country X, for looking after the graves'. The people of Country X normally do no such thing, though they may well turn up in force on special days and lay wreaths and flowers. The gardeners and Works staff do all the hard work, whether it is cold or hot, wet or dry, throughout the year. Being entirely human, they are not pleased to see the credit for their work being passed to those who come to the cemetery perhaps but once a year. The fact that the gardener or bricklayer may be a national of that country is beside the point: the gardeners and others see themselves first and foremost as members of the Commission's staff.

Although the Commission does not now organize ceremonies, it was very much involved in the original unveiling of the memorials to the missing. These events were complicated, and involved royalty or other VIPs, the participating countries, the host country, the armed forces of several countries and many other visitors. It is greatly to the Commission's credit that these ceremonies were so well organized that they invariably went well, were moving but not morbid, dignified but not unduly sad. Most important, they were of some help and consolation to the relatives of those who were missing, perhaps the most difficult war loss to bear.

Plaque markers

As has been seen, the Commission's standard marker is its two feet eight inches-high headstone, usually of Portland or Botticino limestone (the latter now being used for replacements for weathered Portland headstones) and granite, although other stones, such as Hopton Wood, Orton Scar and local stones, are sometimes used. A comparatively small proportion of the Commission's sites have plaques of bronze or stone. The following is a survey of these types of marker and where they are to be found.

Stone semi-recumbent plaques (Gallipoli plaques) are used in all the cemeteries on the Gallipoli Peninsula and in Haidar-Pasha (Istanbul) Cemetery and Chanak Consular Cemetery in Turkey, all of which are of the 1914–1918 War. They have no service badge.

Stone semi-recumbent plaques (Macedonia plaques), slightly different in layout from Gallipoli plaques, are used in the following cemeteries in Macedonia and elsewhere in Greece, all of which are of the 1914–1918 War. They have no service badge. (Other cemeteries in the area have headstones.)

Bralo British

Dedeagatch British (Alexandroupolis)

Doiran Military

East Mudros Military, Lemnos

Karasouli Military

Lahana Military

Portianos Military, West Mudros, Lemnos

Sarigol Military

Struma Military

Syra New British

Bronze semi-recumbent plaques are used in the following war cemeteries in the Far East, all of which are 1939–1945 War. They bear the service badge.

Bangladesh	: Chittagong and Maynamati (Comilla)
Burma	: Rangoon, Taukkyan (Rangoon) and Thanbyuzayat
India	: Digboi, Gauhati, Imphal and Imphal Indian, and Kohima
Indonesia	: Ambon and Djakarta
Japan	: Yokohama
Malaysia (Sabah)	: Labuan
New Caledonia	: Bourail
Papua New Guinea	: Lae, Rabaul (Bita Paka, New Britain)
Thailand	: Chungkai and Kanchanaburi

As mentioned elsewhere, there are some ad hoc markers, ranging from the Schiermonnikoog semi-recumbent stone plaques, bearing one name each, to the large recumbent stone plaques in Malta, with up to a dozen names.

Flags

Flags are not normally flown in Commission sites because of the difficulties this would cause. These would include firstly deciding in which of the 2,500 constructed sites flags should be flown; if the numbers of war dead were to be used as a criterion, then what should that number be? It would also have to be decided which flags should be flown – those of the countries mainly represented in the site (and if so what would constitute mainly) or those of the participating countries? Furthermore should the flag of the host country be flown, as a matter of courtesy, and, if there are foreign dead from yet other countries in the site should not the flags of these be flown as well? Once the flags were in place the matter would arise of who should raise them at sunrise and lower them at sunset. (Most of the cemeteries on the old Western Front are now maintained by Mobile Groups and it follows that few sites have their 'own' gardening staff.) There might be objections to flags dominating the Cross of Sacrifice or, say, a cremation memorial, and unfavourable reaction in a host country to the flag of a country of which it disapproves or with which it has poor or no diplomatic relations.

The passage of years has shown that the Commission was, and is, right in not flying flags in its cemeteries. Exceptions are, however, made in certain special cases, such as on the occasion of a ceremony marking an anniversary or where a memorial was designed to bear flag poles.

The Thiepval Memorial is such a case and it has a unique function for, as apart from commemorating the British missing of the Somme, it also honours their French Allies. It therefore has two poles on its summit, from which to fly the Union and French flags. For reasons of administration and safety (access to the summit is not easy), the flags are not flown during the colder months. The Canadian and French flags fly near the Vimy Memorial but this is a Canadian, not Commission, memorial.

Care of foreign war graves

The headstones marking foreign war graves in the Commission's cemeteries and plots vary in appearance with each country having its own design. The shape and the type and style of inscription were chosen by the country concerned in consultation with the Commission to ensure that the markers tone in well with those of the Commonwealth. For example, the French normally mark their Christian graves with crosses. This was accepted by the Commission, but the height of the cross was reduced to that of the nearby Commission headstones. French non-Christian graves are marked by headstones and their Jewish graves by the Star of David on an upright, both once again of the same height as the Commission's headstone. Foreign graves in Commission cemeteries where plaques are used are marked by similarly shaped plaques of bronze or stone.

The Commission cares for nearly 40,000 foreign war graves (both Allied and ex-enemy): nearly 22,000 of the 1914–1918 War and over 17,000 of the 1939–1945 War. Those countries which have 100 or more burials in the Commission's cemeteries are:

Country	Number of burials		
	1914–1918	1939–1945	Total
Austria	208	–	208
Belgium	335	315	650
Bulgaria	230	–	230
Czechoslovakia	–	216	216
France	5,805	856	6,661
Germany (with Austria 1939–1945)	13,186	6,746	19,932
Greece	124	337	461
Italy	17	874	891
Netherlands	–	3,759	3,759
Norway	9	213	222
Poland	–	3,981	3,981
Russia	462	57	519
Turkey	1,214	–	1,214
United States	63	74	137
	21,653	17,428	39,081

Note: These figures are subject to alteration in the rare event of a request for the repatriation of the remains being made to the Commission (referred to later), or the finding of German remains in the UK or intermingled with those of Commonwealth dead abroad.

There are also nearly 300 graves containing war dead from Brazil, China, Denmark, Ethiopia, Hungary, Japan, Portugal, Romania, Serbia (1914–1918), Transjordan, and Yugoslavia (1939–1945). (Serbia was an independent state in 1914–1918, but part of Yugoslavia in 1939–1945.)

The graves are maintained by the Commission free of charge to the countries concerned, with one exception – Germany – which is referred to later. Even though the cost of caring for these graves is not small, it was thought that the concessions made in the foreign countries, such as tax exemptions and free gifts of land, compensated well for the care of their graves in perpetuity.

While *maintenance* is free, replacement headstones are usually produced by the Commission at the cost of the foreign government, or by that government itself. Unlike the memorials to the Commonwealth missing, the Commission has no memorial to the missing of foreign countries.

German war graves number nearly 20,000, about half of all the foreign graves cared for by the Commission. They are from Greater Germany for the 1914–1918 War and Germany with Austria for the 1939–1945 War. The Federal Republic of Germany makes an annual contribution to the Commission through the Commission's office in Ieper. This is calculated to offset the cost to the Commission of caring for Commonwealth war graves in Germany (were the Commission not to carry out this duty, it would have to be done by the Germans), and to pay for the maintenance of the large number of German graves in the Commission's care. This payment has nothing at all to do with Germany being a former enemy – many of the other foreign war graves hold dead from former enemy countries – it is simply a reflection of the size and cost of the task carried out by the Commission for the Federal Republic.

The case concerning German war graves is, in any event, unique in that the Commission maintains the German Military Cemetery at Cannock Chase on behalf of the Volksbund. This cemetery (not to be confused with the nearby Cannock Chase War Cemetery, which happens to have a high proportion of German graves with those of the Commonwealth) contains about 5,000 graves of the 1914–1918 and 1939–1945 Wars, considerably more than half of which are from the latter conflict. In the early 1960s the German authorities decided that those German graves scattered throughout Britain which were not already in the Commission's cemeteries or plots should be concentrated into one site. Cannock Chase was chosen, one of the reasons being its similarity to Lüneburger Heide, the heathland in western Germany, much loved for its open and wild aspect.

This concentration was completed in the space of a few years, leaving about 1,000 burials in their original places of burial, alongside Commonwealth graves. The headstones, with up to four names on each, were chosen by the Volksbund and are of their own design, as there are no Commonwealth graves in the site. The cemetery was opened in the mid-1960s with a ceremony which was somewhat marred by the action of morons during the night before, when the headstones and flagstones were daubed with swastikas and slogans.

Those buried in the Military Cemetery range from a field marshal, Ernst Busch, Commander-in-Chief North-West Europe at the time of the surrender in 1945 and who died as a prisoner of war, to private soldiers who died as prisoners of war, airmen who died in crashes and sailors who were washed ashore. Internees, all of whom were accepted as qualifying for war graves treatment by the Germans, are also buried there. And in a special plot, there are the four collective graves of the airmen who died when their airships were brought down over England in the 1914–1918 War. Among these airmen was the airships' most famous commander, Kapitänleutnant Heinrich Mathy, whose widow visited the grave in the late 1970s. From time to time German airmen are still found, often from the Battle of Britain in 1940, and the Germans have in all cases readily agreed to their burial in this 'open' cemetery.

One of the German aircrew found in the mid-1970s was a fighter pilot who had been killed in the Battle of Britain; he was discovered by chance in south-east England, still in his aircraft. He had been nearly 40 at the time of his death, not young by any fighting man's standards. The airman was identified without difficulty by the Volksbund and a gold signet ring he was wearing was returned to his widow, who later visited his grave. In 1980, the German next of kin of another airman was so touched and pleased by the arrangements (which included an RAF Guard of Honour) made for his brother's funeral that he made a handsome donation to the Commission's funds.

But things do not always go quite right. A German fighter pilot was buried during the 1939–1945 War in Dunkirk Churchyard, Kent, not far from the wreckage of his aeroplane, which had embedded itself in the ground. When the Volksbund were carrying out their concentrations into Cannock Chase, his was one of the bodies buried there. About 10 years later an 'aeronautical archaeology' team was digging up the aircraft and found one of the airman's legs, which (understandably) had not originally been found in the tangled, buried wreckage.

A member of the Commission's staff (the writer) called on the undertaker who had been asked to deal with the matter and took the remains away, sealed in an oak casket, to be reunited with the rest of the burial in the grave at Cannock Chase. The journey, successfully accomplished in the end, was not without grim humour, as the leather carrying strap around the casket broke while the official was going down the stairs at Stafford railway station. The casket bounced to the bottom, but fortunately held shut. A helpful railway porter picked up the box and asked of the staff member, no doubt alluding to the casket's weight, 'What've you got there guv? A body?' Rarely, surely, can a chance remark by an innocent have been nearer the mark!

Cannock Chase War Cemetery – referred to earlier – was opened in the 1914–1918 War and contains the graves of New Zealanders who died in the area from wounds received on the Western Front or while training locally. In fact there are more German burials in this cemetery than New Zealanders but, as they lie next to each other, the headstones are of the pattern agreed between the Commission and the German authorities.

Some foreign governments are generous in their help towards the Commission. The Belgian, French, and Netherlands authorities carry out routine maintenance on many of the Commonwealth graves which are in isolated, scattered sites, at no cost to the Commission. The Polish authorities maintain the three Commission cemeteries in Poland free of charge, mindful no doubt that 4,000 Polish graves are cared for by the Commission.

The business generally works very well, and it is significant that there are but rarely requests from the foreign authorities for the exhumation of their graves, and such requests almost always arise from demands by the next of kin for the repatriation of the remains. If a formal request is made by the foreign war graves organization, the Commission cannot refuse, as what foreign governments decide to do is, correctly, their business. Of late, the only 'large-scale' exhumations after demands by next of kin were of around 35 Italians buried in Britain, all of whom were repatriated in the early 1980s. All arrangements were made, and the costs met, by the Italian authorities; the Commission's part was one of interested bystander. The headstones marking the former graves were removed in accordance with normal practice.

The Commission always makes it clear that all foreign war graves, ex-Allied or ex-enemy, are maintained in exactly the same way as those of the Commonwealth. For their part, the foreign governments are always the first to agree that this is no idle boast. In fact certain cemeteries begun by the Germans and containing graves of both sides (for example Hautrage and St Symphorien in Belgium) which were later taken on by the Commission are still maintained by the latter, entirely to the Germans' satisfaction.

Protection of immediate surroundings of sites

The Commission has always paid close attention to the problem of protecting the immediate surroundings of their war cemeteries and memorials from undesirable development. Discussions on this have taken place with many foreign authorities in Europe, and have almost always resulted in an understanding and acceptance of the Commission's wishes. Outside Europe, too, when sufficiently early warning of development plans has been obtained, the Commission has usually been able to remove or minimize any unpleasant effect.

Sometimes nothing can be done by the Commission, as when, for example, a previously pleasant suburban area becomes run down and unkempt. No matter how well the cemetery itself is maintained, its proximity to squalor will have a detrimental effect on it. In really bad cases of this sort, the Commission may be forced to carry out the removal of the burials to another war cemetery. An example in the early 1980s was the removal of a small number of war burials from a site in the Netherlands, where they had become an 'island' in the middle of a commercial plant nursery.

Vandalism and theft

The Commission's buildings, memorials, and markers are occasionally defaced with graffiti or daubings. These are so varied in message that any attempt to list the causes they espouse is pointless, though they are frequently political or religious. Examples of this vandalism are the spray-painting of slogans on the Plymouth Memorial and on the entrance gate pillars of the Runnymede Memorial, and the damage to the stones and fabric of the German Military Cemetery, Cannock Chase.

Abroad damage includes the breaking of headstones bearing the Star of David in Iraq (replacements in that country now bear no religious emblem). Similar damage was done to Jewish headstones in a Canadian war cemetery in Normandy (replacements for these do bear the Star). Further examples are the spraying of swastikas on headstones and the Cross of Sacrifice in a war cemetery in the Netherlands and the destruction of a row of markers in Germany by a drunken hooligan driving a tractor or similar vehicle. Among the unwitting vandals are those who went shooting in some of the cemeteries in Ploegsteert Wood in Belgium and peppered headstones – rather than their quarry, one imagines – with their shot.

Thefts of mowers and gardening equipment from cemetery toolsheds are frequent and steps are being taken to make forcible entry more difficult. Determined thieves often steal the bronze swords from Crosses of Sacrifice. These are now replaced by swords made of identical-looking fibreglass, but bronze plaque markers stolen in the Far East are still being replaced with bronze plaques.

The Commission's reaction to vandalism or theft is first to rectify the matter by cleaning, repair or replacement and then to hold any 'post mortem' afterwards. For example, headstones to replace those damaged by vandals are given priority over those which need replacement because of wear. They are often erected (in Europe) within about three weeks.

Accidental damage

Commission sites suffer a certain amount of accidental damage: for example, a contractor's lorry might strike a gatepost and the case of the discharge into the air of gases which affected stonework is mentioned elsewhere. Mining subsidence has caused problems at Cannock Chase and on another occasion, the heathland surrounding the German Military Cemetery caught fire and about 100 headstones were destroyed.

Then there are the so-called 'Acts of God', one of which was the striking by lightning, despite conductors, of the tower of the Australian Memorial at Villers-Bretonneux. Another was the flooding – to a depth of a good six feet – of Florence War Cemetery in Italy, when the River Arno broke its banks during torrential rain. In all cases, whether accident or 'Act of God' the damage is made good as soon as practicable and the costs recouped if possible.

The Commission and other countries

The Middle East

Some damage was done to the war cemeteries in the Suez Canal Zone in the Israeli-Egyptian conflicts of the 1960s and 1970s. The Indian Memorial at Port Tewfik, Egypt, was destroyed and later replaced by the Heliopolis (Port

Tewfik) Memorial. This is described elsewhere as is the killing of a Commission gardener in Suez War Memorial Cemetery in 1970. Commission supervisory staff were prevented from visiting any of the sites in the Canal Zone during these conflicts, but the Egyptian gardeners kept the cemeteries in fairly good shape. When at last the cemeteries could be inspected, there was general relief that they had been so well tended (in view of the war) by the dedicated locally employed staff.

The war between Iraq and Iran dragged on for eight years, so that the inspection and maintenance of sites in Iraq (difficult even before the war began) was very difficult and in some cases impossible. The graves in Iran are much easier to maintain, as they have all been concentrated into one site – Tehran War Cemetery in the British Embassy's residential compound at Gulhek, about six miles from Tehran. The Tehran Memorial is in this war cemetery.

The civil war in Lebanon has resulted in much damage to the Commission's sites, including scores of shattered headstones. Many of these have been replaced but, as in the case of Iraq, real restoration will not be possible until Lebanon is again at peace.

One of the results of the Turkish invasion of Cyprus in 1974 is that the 'Green Line' no-man's land separating Turk from Greek includes Nicosia War Cemetery and its adjoining Wayne's Keep Military Cemetery. The latter contains non-world-war graves and is cared for by the Commission on an agency basis. Access to the war cemetery by the Commission's staff is unpopular with the Greeks if Turkish staff are used, and vice versa. The Commission has been much helped by the British military authorities with regard to normal maintenance, but proper maintenance by staff will not be possible until a political solution to the situation has been found, something which may well be many years off.

Jerusalem War Cemetery on Mount Scopus (in which the Jerusalem Memorial is located) was in an Israeli enclave in Jordan in the 1960s and access was at one time virtually impossible for Commission staff. Arrangements were later improved, but remained unsatisfactory, as entry was limited to certain vehicle convoys passing through the city's Mandelbaum Gate. At one time the cemetery was nearly derelict but its condition was improved after access became easier. After the entry into East Jerusalem of Israeli forces in the 1967 War, admittance became easier still for the Commission's staff and the cemetery and memorial are now maintained to the same standards as those in Israel.

The 1986 troubles in South Yemen did not unduly affect the Commission's work, as it did not have staff stationed there. There are only two sites and the number of burials – 300 – comparatively small. The original Aden Memorial in that country was at Steamer Point, but some of its bronze name panels were stolen and all those named were therefore subsequently commemorated on the Heliopolis (Aden) Memorial, Egypt. As Steamer Point was one of the places where heavy fighting took place, the Commission may well feel satisfied by the previous resiting of the memorial.

The four war cemeteries in Libya are in the Commission's North Africa Area, whose office is at Heliopolis in Egypt. At the time of writing (late 1980s) the border between Egypt and Libya is closed; there is a break in diplomatic relations between Libya and Britain and the Area's officials have to make ad hoc arrangements to travel there to supervise work – at present going by a circuitous route, often via Athens and Tripoli. Despite these difficulties, the cemeteries are still maintained to as high a standard as possible – though probably not entirely to the Commission's satisfaction.

Malta

For some time the Government of Malta considered the idea of having the Commission combine its sites into one. The Commission, mindful of its policy of not disturbing remains except in cases of overriding public need, enlisted the help of the participating countries to resist the idea. This appears to have been successful, as nothing further has been heard of the idea for some time.

Albania, China and USSR

The Commission accepted many years ago that the graves of the 35 British soldiers and airmen and three Australian soldiers who were then believed buried at Tirana, Albania, were lost. Even if they had not been, events have since shown that they could not have been inspected or maintained. The 38 dead, all of the 1939–1945 War, were therefore commemorated in Phaleron War Cemetery, Athens, Greece, by the erection of individual standard headstones, bearing particulars, and grouped around a rectangular stone on which is inscribed the explanation, '. . . gave their lives in Albania and were buried in graves which cannot now be found'. One of these, Brigadier A.F.C. Nichols, was awarded the George Cross. Now, however, in the late 1980s, the Commission has some reason to believe that the burials may in fact have been made at Sarande (in Albania) and the matter is being investigated.

Seventy-two dead of the 1914–1918 and 1939–1945 Wars (51 British and 21 Indian) were buried in China; their approximate burial locations were known, but the actual graves were lost. After the establishment of a Communist regime in that country in 1949, it became obvious that there would be no further opportunity to find the graves or, if found, to maintain them properly. The war dead were therefore commemorated by name on the Sai Wan Bay Memorial, Hong Kong. As it happens, moves were made in the mid-1980s, in the improved political situation, to see if any of the China graves could be found, but without success.

The recording of the names of all those buried or commemorated in the USSR on the Brookwood (Russia) Memorial, Surrey, England, is described in the note on the memorial. The essential difference between the marked graves and memorial headstones in the USSR and those in Albania and

China is that some of the former can still be visited by Commission staff, albeit at irregular intervals; those in Albania and China, at present, cannot.

South Africa and Pakistan

South Africa became a republic on 31st May 1961 and withdrew from the Commonwealth. However, the participating countries felt that there were strong practical, historical and sentimental reasons for the continuance of her participation in the Commission's work and agreed, as did South Africa, that she should continue as a member of the Commission. The Crown confirmed this decision as Grantor of the Commission's Charters.

When Pakistan withdrew from the Commonwealth on 30th January 1970, she considered her position as a member of the Commission. In March 1972 she notified the latter that as a consequence of her withdrawal, she would cease to be a member of the Commission. The other member countries invited her to remain, quoting the precedent of South Africa, but Pakistan was adamant. Her contribution to the Commission's funds (1.07 per cent in 1970) is now covered by slightly bigger payments from the other participating countries.

The Falkland Islands

Mention has been made of the fact that the Commission may, within the terms of its Charters, accept work on an agency and repayment basis if it so wishes. At the time of writing (the late 1980s), work to the value of about £1 million is being carried out annually, much of it the care of battle-exploit memorials.

After the Falklands War of April–June 1982, the Commission accepted an invitation from the British Government to construct both a cemetery for those of the South Atlantic Task Force who had died and were to be permanently buried in the Falkland Islands, and a memorial naming those who were lost, or buried, at sea. In a departure from the policies adopted for the 1914–1918 and 1939–1945 Wars but in accordance with precedents (e.g. the Indonesian Confrontation), the Government had agreed that, if relatives so wished, the bodies of those killed in the Falklands War might be repatriated for permanent burial. Therefore, of the 255 who died, 64 were repatriated to Britain and one to Hong Kong. Of the remaining dead, 174 had no grave but the sea and 16 were permanently buried in the islands.

The site selected for the cemetery and memorial was at San Carlos, on the western beaches of East Falkland, where the troops had first come ashore. The non-world-war pattern headstones of Orton Scar (a darkish stone, chosen to tone in with the landscape) were made and inscribed at the Commission's workshops at Beaurains, France and the dedicatory and 174-name panels were made in the north of England. Headstones, panels, stores and equipment were shipped out in late 1982. The cemetery with its 14 graves (two of the 16 dead were left undisturbed where they had been buried) was prepared, and the surrounding oval stone wall and the memorial were constructed by the Commission's staff with the help of the Royal Engineers.

The cemetery and memorial were dedicated on 10th April 1983 in the presence of the relatives of all those buried or commemorated there. It was a remarkable agency job, all done well within a year of the end of hostilities, in a place 8,000 miles from Britain. Headstones were also erected over the two graves of the 16 who were buried in the Falklands but left undisturbed at the request of the next of kin. The cemetery is now maintained under arrangements made by the British authorities.

What was also remarkable was these these islands, so distant from Britain, should already contain 21 burials of the 1914–1918 War, and 12 of the 1939–1945 War, in small plots in Stanley (the capital) Cemetery. Some of those of the 1914–1918 War were from the Battle of the Falkland Islands, when ships of the Royal Navy under Admiral Sir Doveton Sturdee sank most of Admiral Graf von Spee's ships on 8th December 1914. The German ships had themselves previously sunk two of the British ships under Admiral Sir Christopher Cradock in the action off Coronel, on the west coast of Chile on 1st November 1914.

Some of the graves of the 1939–1945 War are of sailors and marines who were wounded during the Battle of the River Plate and who later died ashore. During this battle Royal Navy ships under Commodore Henry Harwood brought about the scuttling of a German 'pocket' battleship, coincidentally named *Admiral Graf Spee* on 13th December 1939.

Complaints about the funding of the Commission

As has been seen, the Commission carries out its worldwide task with only a small staff (around 1,300) at a late 1980s cost of around £18 million ($36 million). Yet there are still a number of carping voices which ask why so much (or any) money should be spent on the war dead. No argument or reasoning will ever persuade such people that what the Commission does is right, decent and honourable. The maintenance of war graves and memorials is the least that can be done in the memory of those who died to ensure that others – including the carpers – may live free and able to express their views, however distasteful. The amount spent annually by each of the participating governments is minute in comparison to annual national budgets.

Quite apart from the morality of caring for the graves of the war dead, future generations would surely be the poorer if the war graves of the 1914–1918 and 1939–1945 Wars were allowed to disappear, as the graves of men who fought earlier historic battles were allowed to disappear. How marvellous it would be now to be able to visit the marked graves of a few of the ordinary soldiers who died in the Battle of Hastings in 1066, as well as that of King Harold (who was killed and whose place of burial is known).

PART III

Interest and Reference

{ 13 }

Visiting the sites

All these were honoured in their generations
and were the glory of their time

Ecclesiasticus 44:7.

V ISITS TO THE CEMETERIES AND WAR GRAVES MAIN-
tained by the Commission have been popular for some time now.
There are organized tours of the 1914–1918 Western Front and
others that include 1939–1945 sites in Italy, Normandy and the Netherlands. For the individual wishing to visit such sites, travel agents may hold
information, or ex-servicemen's organisations such as the Royal British
Legion may be able to help (the address of the British Legion is given in
Appendix G at the back of this book).

The most convenient sites to visit are the Commission's cemeteries and
memorials for the Western Front of the 1914–1918 War, closely followed by
the sites commemorating the dead of the 1939–1945 War in northern
France (especially Normandy), Belgium, Germany and the Netherlands.
Sites in other countries are often so scattered (as in North Africa, for
example) that visiting more than one or two may prove impossible.

If you would like to visit the place of commemoration of any particular
serviceman but are unsure where it is, you should contact the Commonwealth War Graves Commission (addresses are given in Appendix G),
preferably some time before the journey. It is important to give the
Commission all the information you have on the casualty. At best, this will
include service number, rank, surname with forenames or initials, service,
regiment or departmental corps. Supply the date of death, if known; if not,
at least state whether the casualty died in the 1914–1918 or 1939–1945
War. Do not be discouraged from enquiring if you do not have the full
details – the Commission's tracers are very good, but an enquiry about
'Smith J. who died in the First World War' will not, with the best of good
will, get anywhere, as there are probably about 200 'Smiths J.'. There is no
charge for this sort of telephone or written enquiry, although, a charge may
be raised if you are enquiring about five or more casualties, or if you are not,
say, a near relative or an old comrade.

There are certain areas that cause difficulty. The Commission is
unwilling, for example, to produce the commemoration details of those war

107

dead listed on a village or town war memorial. The names on these memorials are often short of detail and therefore might well result in an incorrect 'trace' and the Commission does not have the staff for an exercise of this sort. Nor does the Commission normally produce lists of, say, all members of the Royal West Kent Regiment who are in given cemeteries, as the Commission's overall lists of the war dead are in alphabetical order of the surnames of the dead, no matter where they are buried. It is extremely time-consuming to scan the cemetery registers and pick out the individuals by their personal entries. The position in regard to the names of the war dead on Commission memorials is, however, simpler as the panel numbers relating to the missing of particular regiments and departmental corps are usually shown in the introduction to the memorial register.

In some areas, retired employees of the Commission are available as guides, and the nearest Commission office to the site may be able to assist in locating these individuals. A local guide is very valuable, particularly where a foreign language is spoken, to say nothing of the time saved in locating the places you wish to visit. A guide's knowledge of the area will generally provide some interesting background information on the events that took place, adding greatly to the interest of a trip. Do not expect the Commission's overseas staff to accompany you to the site you wish to visit, however – they have full-time jobs, and escorting visitors is not normally one of them.

When touring in north-west Europe, the Commission's green and white roadside direction signs can be seen when you reach the general area of the cemetery or memorial; and it is possible to do a great deal of visiting by using these and the Commission's Michelin maps. The Michelin maps numbers 51, 52 and 53 have been overprinted to show the sites of the Commission's war cemeteries and memorials in north-west Europe. The maps are the ordinary Michelin motoring maps, with added purple, numbered, circular spots. When read with their attached alphabetical key of cemetery and memorial names, these numbers enable you to find the site(s) you seek. Road systems are changing all the time, however, and the map may not show, for example, the latest motorway to be opened or its effect on other roads.

Map 51 covers the Ypres Salient in Belgium, and France as far south as Arras; map 52 covers the Somme south and west of Arras, and map 53 covers the Arras area and the Somme south and east of Arras. If your visit is to Normandy, buy Michelin map 54 from a book shop. There is no overprinted version of this map, although there are some 20 cemeteries there. Alternatively, a battlefield map can be bought from the museum at Arromanches, Normandy.

When in Europe, the place of commemoration of a particular casualty in Belgium, the Netherlands or Germany can be traced through the Commonwealth War Graves Commission's Northern Europe Area at Ieper (or Ypres) in Belgium – telephone enquiries should be made in Flemish or English. For France, the office to be contacted is at Beaurains near Arras, which is responsible for the war graves and memorials in France and the single site in Switzerland. Both these offices have good tracing facilities and should be able to find places of commemoration provided that the details are sufficiently complete. The full addresses of these offices are given in Appendix G.

For accommodation in northern France and Belgium, the Michelin Guide offers the best advice. Ieper (Ypres) is the most convenient base for visiting sites in Belgium, while Arras and Albert are well placed for the France 1914–1918 War sites. In Normandy, Caen offers the best base.

A car is obviously the best way to travel while visiting sites. The closest Channel ports to the United Kingdom are Ostend (Belgium) and Dunkirk (France) for Ieper, and Calais and Boulogne (France) for Arras and the Somme. If you are using public transport, the nearest airports for Ieper are Ostend (25 miles), Brussels (80 miles), or Lille in France (20 miles). Ieper has a railway sation. The nearest airports for Arras and the Somme are Lille (20 miles) and Paris Charles de Gaulle (80 miles). Arras is well served by rail. For Normandy, Le Havre or Cherbourg are probably the best ports, and there are flights from London to Dieppe, Caen, and Cherbourg. There are also numerous rail services to Caen.

From December to March, the weather may well be cold or wet, and the sites snowbound or foggy. The cemeteries will not look as attractive as they do in spring, summer, and autumn and daylight hours are short.

In addition, the site may be simply inaccessible during the winter months because of the waterlogged condition of the woodland tracks – the sites in the Ploegsteert woods are cases in point.

When you are visiting a *memorial*, your own private thoughts or memories are of greatest importance; but, apart from these, the following are of interest:

- the architecture and motifs, and juxtaposition with any cemetery in which the memorial is situated;
- the dedicatory inscriptions;
- the layout of the names by nationality, service, regiment, rank and name;
- the addition of the service number when two or more have the same rank, name and initials;
- the letters VC and GC (usually to the left of the surname);
- names followed by 'SERVED AS . . .'; and
- any honourable scars (wartime damage).

When visiting a *cemetery*, the main points of interest are:

- the architectural features (entrances, pavilions, seats, register boxes) depending on the size of the cemetery;

- the frequently disordered and 'higgledy-piggledy' look of the front-line cemeteries and the ordered look of the concentration sites; the latter sometimes having a disordered nucleus of original, front-line graves;

- the headstones with different badges, details, religious emblems and, in particular, personal inscriptions. There will be no personal inscription where no reply could be elicited from the next of kin, or if the next of kin was not known, could not be traced, or did not want one. Normally there will also be no personal inscription of any New Zealander's headstone (because of a decision by the New Zealand government);

- the headstones to those who 'SERVED AS . . .';

- the foreign forces' headstones, sometimes in a group, sometimes interspersed with those of the Commonwealth dead;

- the alphabetical order of surnames when headstones are set up over a collective grave (any one which appears to be out of order is the one positively identified);

- the equality of treatment;

- the single graves containing several burials;

- the nibs which hold the headstones upright in the beams; both should be below ground and invisible, but sometimes the nibs can be seen;

- the plot and row numbers inscribed on the sides of headstones at the ends of rows;

- the garden-like atmosphere;

- the headstone borders, with taller plants at the back of them (behind the headstones), in about every third row, to help break the harshness or monotony caused by too much stonework;

- the bushes at the ends of rows, often trimmed to a conical shape, the anti-splash plants and the roses (or other tall plants) placed *between* graves so as not to obscure inscriptions;

- the now-mature trees;

- the Cross of Sacrifice (usually in sites of over 40 burials) and the Stone of Remembrance (usually in sites of over 400 burials);

- the fossiled shells of prehistoric creatures on the grave markers where they are made of Portland stone;

- the different types of stone used for markers (in the late 1980s, Portland is still by far the most common);

- the surroundings of the cemetery (and pondering on whether the Commission has difficulty in protecting them from unseemly development); and

- the graves of VCs or GCs that may be identified by the facsimile decoration inscribed on the headstone instead of the religious emblem.

Information on the history of a site can be found in the register box at the entrance to the cemetery in all but the smallest sites. The register may be taken out and its introduction read. Some sites may have an etched steel historical notice that will be well worth reading.

Good behaviour is expected on the sites. Music or children playing football are not at all in keeping with these places. Nor is litter; and although there is no objection to picnics (many of the sites are deep in the country, far from town centres) all wrapping paper and rubbish should be removed. Visitors should also remember that there are no lavatories in the cemeteries or at the memorials.

Visitors may leave wreaths, sprays or cut flowers in cemeteries, on particular graves or at memorials – the wire in wreaths may, however, rust and stain stonework, so wreaths should be placed with care. Flowers will be removed by the staff when they look untidy. Nothing may be planted in the cemeteries.

Most of the cemeteries and memorials are always open. The few that close at sunset usually do so because there has been trouble with vandals or thieves. Some of the Commission's plots are in communal civil cemeteries, however, and while the plot is not closed, the civil cemetery may be closed at times decided by the local authority.

Sometimes visitors feel that they would like to make a donation to the Commission for the work it does. It is not necessary to do so, as the Commission is funded by the participating governments, but cheques, made payable to the Commonwealth War Graves Commission, may be sent to the Maidenhead address. The Commission places all such donations in its General Fund for the care of the war cemeteries and memorials. It cannot, in the interest of equality of treatment, earmark any amount for spending on a particular grave, cemetery or memorial.

If you wish to have a wreath laid on your behalf on a grave anywhere, write to the Commission at its Maidenhead address and ask for details. It will arrange for a Royal British Legion poppy wreath to be laid on the grave or at the memorial of your choice on any particular date, within reasonable limits. You will be asked to pay for the wreath, but any profit goes to the Royal British Legion, not to the Commission.

Please do sign the visitors' book at any of the Commission's sites. This book is usually kept in the register box. Doing so is good for staff morale, while the remarks in the book are carefully examined at the Commission's head office when the book is complete.

When visiting the Commission' sites in north-west Europe, there are several places and museums nearby that give a very clear idea of the conditions in which troops fought and died.

Belgium

Ypres (Ieper) War Museum in the Cloth Hall (the Cloth Hall was totally destroyed in the 1914–1918 War but faithfully rebuilt to the original plans).

Ypres Ramparts, into which is set the Menin Gate Memorial and on which lies Ramparts Cemetery (Lille Gate); the Lille Gate itself is largely original.

Hill 60. A large site containing mine and shell craters, pillboxes and battle exploit memorials. Perhaps the 'best' battlefield site in Belgium. Three miles south-east of Ieper.

Hill 62. Original trenches (not artificially preserved) and museum, very near to the Canadian Hill 62 Memorial and Sanctuary Wood Cemetery which contains the grave of Lieutenant Gilbert Talbot (of Talbot House, Toc H, fame). Three miles south-east of Ieper.

Pool of Peace, Spanbroekmolen (originally known as Lone Tree Crater and detonated on 7th June 1917 by the British on the opening day of the Battle of Messines). An enormous, flooded, mine crater, near the Commission's Lone Tree Cemetery. The Pool is owned and managed by Toc H and features a stone tablet (renovated in 1984) with an explanatory text. Six miles south of Ieper.

Toc H's original Everyman's Club in Poperinghe, founded in 1915 following a suggestion by Colonel Reginald Talbot. It was named Talbot House in memory of his brother, Lieutenant Gilbert Talbot. The initials 'TH' soon became 'Toc H', from signallers' phonetics, giving the name to the movement. The Reverend P.B. Clayton MC and Bar, became its first warden. Seven miles west of Ieper.

France

The Vimy Memorial and nearby shell and mine craters, trenches (artificially preserved with concrete 'sandbags'), tunnels and war cemeteries. Considered one of the architecturally finest memorials. Seven miles north of Arras.

The Mur des Fusillés (execution wall) Arras, near the Arras Memorial. The place in which alleged members of the resistance, saboteurs and hostages were shot by the Germans in the 1939–1945 War.

Newfoundland Park, Beaumont-Hamel. A large site containing shell craters, trenches (not artificially preserved), three war cemeteries and battle exploit memorials. Perhaps the 'best' Commonwealth battlefield site in France. About 18 miles south of Arras, near the Thiepval Memorial.

The Ulster Tower, a memorial to the 36th (Ulster) Division, containing a chapel and living quarters, sometimes occupied as living accommodation by a Commission gardener. The memorial is a replica of Helen's Tower in Ulster. Near the Thiepval Memorial.

The Lochnagar Crater, Ovillers-la-Boiselle. An enormous, dry mine crater (the largest of the Western Front), detonated by the British on the opening day of the Battle of the Somme, 1st July 1916. Privately-owned by an Englishman, but open to visitors. Twenty miles south of Arras.

The South African Museum in the grounds of the Delville Wood Memorial. Twenty miles south of Arras.

The Sir William Legatt Museum, run by a Franco-Australian Committee, at Villers-Bretonneux. Ten miles east of Amiens and near the Australian National Memorial.

The Arromanches Museum on the Normandy coast, near the point where the Mulberry Artificial Harbour's landing pier reached the shore in the landings of 1944.

Netherlands

The Overloon Museum. Perhaps the largest 1939–1945 War museum in the country. Four miles north of Venraij.

The Arnhem (Oosterbeek) Museum, the theme of which is the airborne landing of September 1944.

Few experiences are more rewarding than a visit to the old cemeteries, memorials and battlefields of the two world wars and Laurence Binyon's *We will remember them* will, perhaps, thereafter acquire a new significance.

{14}

The Cemeteries

I always say that, next to a battle lost,
the greatest misery is a battle gained

The Duke of Wellington (1769–1852).

T HERE ARE OVER 23,000 CEMETERIES worldwide which contain one or more Commonwealth war graves; of these 2,500 were constructed by the Commission. This chapter will examine 60 of these, chosen according to historical or other interest, size and location. The choice hopes to reflect the diversity of the Commission's plots. At the entrance to most cemeteries is a register that introduces the place and explains the background to the making of the cemetery. Examining these in detail can be very useful, informative and thought-provoking. For example in the Somme battle area there are two cemeteries only a short distance apart. Devonshire Cemetery contains 163 burials of the Devonshire Regiment, of whom 160 were killed as they left their trenches on 1st July 1916. They are buried virtually where they fell and one has to look at the high ground slightly to the east to see the advantage held by the enemy. A few yards down the road are 99 burials of the Gordon Highlanders who also died that day and are buried on the site of their last action.

The introduction to the cemetery register at the entrance to the Devonshire Cemetery runs as follows:

DEVONSHIRE CEMETERY, MAMETZ

GORDON CEMETERY, MAMETZ

Mametz is a village in the Department of the Somme, four miles east of Albert, with a station on the light railway from Albert to Peronne. It was within the German lines until the 1st July 1916, when it was captured by the 7th Division; and Mametz Wood, north-east of the village was taken on 7th July and the following days. The 7th Division erected a memorial in the village, and the 14th and 16th Royal Welch Fusiliers erected memorials in the wood to commemorate these engagements. (The 38th (Welsh) Division captured the wood again in August 1918.)

DEVONSHIRE CEMETERY
The 8th and 9th Battalions of the Devonshire Regiment, forming part of the 7th Division, attacked on the 1st July 1916 from a point on the south-west side of the Albert-Maricourt road, due south of Mametz village, by a plantation called Mansel Copse; and there, on the 4th July, they buried their dead in a portion of their old front line. In this place, subsequently called DEVONSHIRE CEMET-ERY, lie one officer of the 8th Devons who fell on the 28th June; three officers and 29 other ranks of the 8th and seven officers and 121 other ranks of the 9th Battalion, killed on the 1st July; and a serjeant and a driver of B/92nd Brigade RFA, killed later in the Somme battles. Ten men of the 9th Devons are unidentified. Devonshire Cemetery stands on the top of a high, steep bank, containing dug-outs, and it looks North and East to Mametz and Carnoy. It covers an area of 664 square yards. It is bounded by a brick wall and a thorn hedge, and on the north-east side by Mansel Copse; and it is planted with Irish yews. *

The Register records particulars of 163 War Graves.

GORDON CEMETERY
On the opposite side of the road a little nearer Maricourt, is another battle cemetery of the 1st July 1916. The 2nd Gordon Highlanders, also of the 7th Division, buried here in the British support trench six officers and 93 other ranks of their battalion; and three artillerymen, who fell on the 9th July, were buried beside them. Four of the Gordons and one artilleryman are unidentified.

Gordon Cemetery stands on the level of the road, and is separated from it by a light railway. It covers an area of 418 square yards. It is bounded by a low brick wall and a thorn hedge, and planted with thorn trees and standard roses. The headstones of the 93 non-commissioned officers and men are arranged in two semi-circles around the Cross.

The Register records particulars of 102 War Graves.

Many of the cemeteries contain the graves of holders of the Victoria Cross or George Cross. These graves are generally not mentioned in this chapter, as they are included in the section devoted to that subject. Unlike the Commission's memorials to the missing, the war cemeteries and plots were not inaugurated as it was felt that words of committal would have been said at the time of burial whereas that was clearly not the case with memorials.

In general, battlefield cemeteries – those in which burials were being made during the actual fighting – are often other than symmetric as there was no time for careful layouts and straight lines. Use was made of existing trenches, shell craters and the like and there was often danger to the burial party, which had to complete the task as quickly as decorum allowed. The resulting layout has been preserved to this day. The concentration cemeteries – new cemeteries built after the wars – are far more orderly. Burials were brought in from isolated, insecure or unmaintainable graves on the former battlefields and buried in a more regimented way. Some

---

*On 1st July 1986, the seventieth anniversary of the start of the Battle of the Somme, the Duke of Kent, President of the Commission, unveiled a memorial just outside the cemetery which reads "The Devonshires held this trench; the Devonshires hold it still."

cemeteries illustrate both battlefield and concentration burials. At Tyne Cot Cemetery, Passchendaele, for example, battle burials are to the rear of the Cross of Sacrifice and scattered in no particular order; concentration burials are to the front of the Cross and in strict blocks and rows.

The cemeteries will be described below under the name of the country in which they are situated, the countries following in alphabetical order, using the modern late 1980s name – e.g. Sri Lanka, as opposed to Ceylon. Following the section on United Kingdom are notes on Additional Cemeteries in very brief form (again in sections by countries) on those sites which are also well worth a visit.

The Commission's titles of war cemeteries do not include the definite article unless it is part of the place name used in the title. So we have Phaleron War Cemetery and Dieppe Canadian War Cemetery but The Hague Cemetery. A list of the cemeteries in this chapter, less 'Additional Cemeteries', is given at Appendix E.

Algeria

Le Petit Lac Cemetery, Oran

Oran is a port on the Mediterranean coast and was one of those chosen for the landing of American contingents of the Allied invasion of North Africa, Operation Torch, in November 1942. The naval force was British. The assault landings in the harbour were resisted by the Vichy French, with heavy Allied casualties, but the landings on either side of the port were successful.

Le Petit Lac Cemetery is on the south-east of Oran, over two miles from the centre, and the name is derived from a lake which was once in the area. The cemetery was originally a large war cemetery, formed early in 1945 by the Americans, for the burial of all Allied servicemen. After 1945 all but the Commonwealth burials ('Commonwealth' including foreigners who were serving in the Commonwealth forces) were removed, but in 1950 the French re-opened the cemetery as a French National Cemetery. The Common-wealth Plot is still in its original site about 200 yards from the entrance, and is hedged off from the main cemetery. It is a small cemetery, but is remarkable for the numbers of different nationalities buried in it. It contains nearly 200 British burials, 15 Canadian, five Australian and small numbers of New Zealand, South African, Indian, West African, Belgian, Nether-lands, Norwegian, Polish and Yugoslav.

Australia

Adelaide River War Cemetery, Northern Territory

This cemetery contains over 400 Australian and 25 British graves of the 1939–1945 War and is situated on the Stuart Highway about 70 miles south of Darwin. The headquarters of a base was established at Adelaide River town and the cemetery was used by military hospitals. Later, war graves from all except two cemeteries in the Northern Territory were brought into it, including those killed in the Japanese air-raid on the Naval Base at Darwin on 19th February 1942, when over 200 died.

The Northern Territory Memorial stands in the cemetery. It commemorates by name nearly 300 Australian soldiers, airmen, and seamen of the Merchant Navy who lost their lives in the Timor and northern Australian regions and waters, and have no known grave. Many of these belonged to 'Sparrow Force', a small body of Australian troops sent to Timor in December 1941 to support the Dutch against the Japanese invasion of the island.

Austria

Klagenfurt War Cemetery

Klagenfurt is the capital of Carinthia, and the war cemetery is about two miles west of the town. It is the only Commonwealth war cemetery in the country and was opened in June 1945 by the British occupying forces (British Troops Austria – BTA). They moved into it all (except one) of the Commonwealth burials scattered throughout the country, which included those of prisoners-of-war, airmen, and others who had died after the war while on garrison duties. It contains over 500 British burials, four Canadian, 30 Australian, 25 New Zealand, 20 South African and six Indian. There are also, in Klagenfurt (Annabichl) Cemetery, about two miles away, nearly 60 non-world-war burials of British servicemen who died during the occupation after the end of the 'war period' (31st December 1947). The British, and one German, graves in this cemetery are marked by non-war pattern granite markers, and are maintained by the Commission on an agency basis for the British authorities.

Belgium

Bedford House Cemetery, Zillebeke

The cemetery is about one and a half miles south of Ypres and comprises several enclosures that were originally separate cemeteries but now form one, some being divided from the others by an extensive water-filled moat. Bedford House was the name given by the Army to the Château Rosendal, the ruins of which are still clearly visible and which was used by field ambulances and brigade headquarters. A bridge erected over the moat by the Royal Engineers still stands and is in regular use by the gardeners and visitors; shell damage to its steelwork can still be seen. The cemetery contains over 4,500 British burials, 350 Canadian, 200 Australian, 30 New Zealand, 20 South African and 20 Indian. Seventy of the British graves are of soldiers of the BEF who died in the area in the fighting between 24th and 26th May 1940, and were moved into the war cemetery from their battlefield graves.

Dickebusch Old Military Cemetery

Dikkebus (in Flemish) lies three miles south-west of Ypres and the cemetery was on the front line during the first three months of 1915. It contains 40 British, three Canadian and one German burials of the 1914–1918 War. During 1940 the cemetery was again used by the British and a further 10 burials made. It is unusual for such a small site to have graves of both the wars.

Dickebusch New Military Cemetery and Extension

These two cemeteries are further along the track and each side of it, but are treated, so far as possible, as one site. The **New Cemetery** was begun in March 1915, in succession to the Old, and was used until May 1917 by nearby fighting and medical units. It contains 530 British, 85 Canadian and 10 Australian burials, including 100 artillerymen. The Extension was begun in May 1917 and used until the following January, even during the German attack which reached Dickebusch Lake on 8th May. It contains 520 British and 25 Australian burials, and small numbers from Canada, South Africa and Germany. These burials include 260 artillerymen.

As these two sites are treated as one the Stone of Remembrance is in the north-west corner of the New Cemetery and the Cross of Sacrifice at the western apex of its triangular extension.

Hautrage Military Cemetery

The village of Hautrage lies nine miles west of Mons ('Bergen' in Flemish) and the cemetery is to its south-east. The Germans were in occupation of the village for almost the whole of the 1914–1918 War and opened the cemetery in August 1914. The first burials were of German soldiers who died on 23rd August 1914 in the Battle of Mons. In the summer of 1918 they concentrated into it a large number of British soldiers who had also died in the battle and had been temporarily buried in the field by their comrades, the Belgian Red Cross, and the Germans. The cemetery now contains over 500 German burials and over 200 British, including a large proportion of unknowns. Among those buried here is Second Corporal Edwin Marsden RE, who died on 23rd August. He was the inventor of the improved trestle for bridge building accepted by the War Office and known as the Marsden Band Trestle.

Even though the cemetery has far more German than British burials, the Commission has, in agreement with the Volksbund, assumed responsibility for its maintenance, and all the graves are treated in exactly the same way. (St Symphorien Military Cemetery described below, also contains Commonwealth war graves from the early days of the Western Front.) A soldier who died on 8th November 1918, just before the end of the war, is buried in the single war grave in nearby Hautrage Communal Cemetery. He was Lance Sergeant C.T. Harris of the PPCLI (Canadian Infantry) of Regina, Saskatchewan, but born in Southampton, England.

Hedge Row Trench Cemetery, Zillebeke

This cemetery is about two miles from the village of Zillebeke, itself about that distance south-east of Ypres (Ieper). It was begun in March 1915 and used until August 1917, sometimes under the name of Ravine Wood Cemetery. It contains nearly 100 burials, nearly all British. The cemetery was very severely shelled over a long time and after the end of the war the exact positions of the individual graves could not be found. Therefore 44 of the headstones (all of which are 'special memorials') are unusually arranged in arcs of 11, themselves forming a circle around the Cross; the remaining markers are fairly equally distributed against the boundary of the square cemetery and opposite the gaps in the circle. All the markers face inwards. Typical of this area of intense fighting and many cemeteries, Woods Cemetery Zillebeke, and 1 DCLI Cemetery are within a few hundred yards of this site, easily spotted by their tell-tale Crosses of Sacrifice.

Hooge Crater Cemetery, Zillebeke

The cemetery is on the road from Menin to Ypres, the road along which the German Army made desperate attempts to advance in October and November 1914 to take Ypres. They were forestalled by the BEF, the 'Old Contemptibles'; and even though the Kaiser was present in person on 29th October 1914 to urge on his soldiers, Ypres was not taken. Hooge was taken by the Germans in May 1915 and the cemetery's title refers to a British mine exploded there, the crater of which can still be seen symbolically by the paved, sunken area surrounding the Stone of Remembrance. The area was the scene of the first use of liquid fire by the Germans on 30th July 1915 and pyrotechnic smoke or gas was seen issuing from the ground in the late 1970s.

The cemetery was begun in October 1917 but most of the burials were brought in from isolated sites on the battlefield after the Armistice. It contains over 5,000 British, 100 Canadian, 500 Australian and 120 New Zealand burials.

Lijssenthoek Military Cemetery

The cemetery is in the village of that name about two miles south-west of Poperinghe. The village lay close behind the extreme range of most enemy field artillery and was therefore a natural place for the establishment of casualty clearing stations, firstly by the French and later the British. The French opened the cemetery and the British began to use it in June 1915. Between that month and the Armistice, it became the second largest Commonwealth cemetery anywhere and is now the second largest in Belgium (Tyne Cot Cemetery is the largest). It contains nearly 10,000 Commonwealth burials of which 7,400 are British, over 1,000 Canadian, over 1,000 Australian, nearly 300 New Zealand, and 30 South African; the French burials number almost 700. As this cemetery served hospitals, the great majority of the dead were identified.

There are also about 30 graves of members of the Chinese Labour Corps, who were part of the British Army. The headstones were carved by the comrades and, in addition to the names and particulars in English and Chinese, a short motto chosen by the Chinese was inscribed, of which examples are 'A noble duty bravely done' and 'A good reputation endures for ever'; these two inscriptions are frequently seen in this and other cemeteries.

Nearby Poperinghe was the birthplace of the Toc H movement (Talbot House – Toc then being signaller's phonetic for the letter T), and the original club house is still in regular use. Its sign proclaims '1915–?'. Lieutenant G.W.L. Talbot, the Rifle Brigade, whose name was given to the movement, is buried in Sanctuary Wood Cemetery, Zillebeke.

Lone Tree Cemetery, Spanbroekmolen, Wytschaete

The cemetery is close to the originally named 'Lone Tree Crater', now known as Toc H's 'Pool of Peace', four miles south of Ypres. The crater was made by the detonation of one of the 19 (of 21 set up, two failed to explode) mines on the first day of the Battle of Messines, 7th June 1917. The cemetery's odd V shape is an indication that the burials were made during the battle when there was no opportunity for a careful layout. Eighty-eight soldiers of the United Kingdom are buried here, 60 of whom were from the Royal Irish Rifles of the 36th (Ulster) Division; nearly all died on that first day.

Passchendaele New British Cemetery

The village of Passchendaele is about seven miles north-east of Ypres and the cemetery is half a mile to the north-west of the village. The immediate area was, from October 1914 to the end of 1918, one of the most fought over in the war. The 5th Canadian Infantry Brigade captured the village on 6th November 1917 during the Second Battle of Passchendaele, itself part of the Third Battle of Ypres, 1917. However, the line was pulled back in the Battles of the Lys in April 1918 and the village not finally recaptured until Belgian forces took it on 29th September during the general Allied advance.

The cemetery was made after the Armistice by the concentration of burials from the battlefields of Passchendaele and Langemarck (at Langemarck there is a German Cemetery containing about 50,000 war dead). Almost all of those in Passchendaele Cemetery died in the autumn of 1917, a time of heavy and desperate fighting. The burials comprise 1,000 British, 650 Canadian, 300 Australian and 125 New Zealand, of whom more than three-quarters could not be identified by name.

Poelcapelle British Cemetery

Just over a mile from the village of Poelcapelle, which is itself seven miles north-east of Ypres, is the third largest Commonwealth war cemetery in

Belgium. Many of the dead were involved in the Third Battle of Ypres 1917 (often known as Passchendaele). Over 6,000 could not be identified by name, as they were not recovered until after the Armistice. The cemetery contains 6,500 British dead, nearly 550 Canadian, over 100 Australian and nearly 250 New Zealand. Private John Condon, age 14, is buried here.

Polygon Wood Cemetery, Zonnebeke

Zonnebeke is five miles north-east of Ypres, and Polygon Wood one mile south of the village. The wood was destroyed in the 1914–1918 War but was replanted with firs, which are now of substantial size. The wood was cleared by British troops in October 1914, given up on 3rd May 1915, taken in September 1917 by the Australians, again given up in the Battles of the Lys and finally retaken by the 9th (Scottish) Division on 28th September 1918. The cemetery is on the northern edge of the wood, opposite the entrance to Buttes New British Cemetery, which contains the Buttes New Zealand Memorial.

The Cross of Sacrifice stands on the path leading from the road to the cemetery proper which, oddly perhaps in view of its proximity to Polygon Wood, is hexagonal in shape. No attempt has been made to tidy the graves into plots and rows, and the dead still lie as they were buried during the fighting. The cemetery contains the graves of 30 British, 60 New Zealand, a score of unknowns and one German.

St Symphorien Military Cemetery

The village of St Symphorien is about three miles south-east of Mons. The cemetery is about half a mile south of the village and was constructed by the Germans for the burial of both their own and British soldiers who died in the Battle of Mons on 23rd August 1914. Most of the British dead were from the Middlesex Regiment (the Germans erected a still standing memorial to them and honoured them by referring to the 'Royal' Middlesex Regiment), the Royal Irish Regiment and the Royal Fusiliers. The cemetery contains the grave of probably the first Commonwealth man to die in battle on the Western Front, that of Private J. Parr, Middlesex Regiment, who died on 21st August 1914. There are also graves of probably the last battle deaths on that Front before the 1100 hours Armistice of 11th November 1918: Private G.E. Ellison, of the 5th Royal Irish Lancers and Private G.L. Price, 28th Battalion Saskatchewan Regiment (Canadian Infantry), both of whom died that day.

Also in this particularly interesting and unusually laid-out cemetery is the grave of Lieutenant M.J. Dease, Royal Fusiliers. After being wounded on several occasions he died on 23rd August and was awarded the first VC of the 1914–1918 War. Private S.F. Godley, Royal Fusiliers, who was fighting alongside Lieutenant Dease and survived the action was also awarded the VC. He is thought to have been the model for Captain Bruce Bairnsfather's famous cartoon soldier character 'Old Bill'.

The cemetery is laid out at different levels on a hillock caused by past mining of phosphates. It contains about 230 British burials (of whom 65 are not identified by name), about the same number of Germans, and two Canadians. There are certain similarities between this cemetery and Sage War Cemetery, Oldenburg, Germany, which is described below.

Burma

Thanbyuzayat War Cemetery

Both village (pronounced 'Tunboozyat') and cemetery lie about 40 miles south of Moulmein in southern Burma. In 1942 the Japanese, needing improved links to maintain their then victorious army in Burma, decided to complete the railway connecting Moulmein with Bangkok. It had been begun before the 1939–1945 War but abandoned with 250 miles remaining unfinished. The country is mountainous, covered with malarial jungle and experiencing high temperatures and humidity, and Thanbyuzayat was the Burmese terminal of the proposed line.

British, Australian, Dutch and American prisoners of war set up a base camp and hospital and started work in September 1942 and finished in December 1943. Unknown hundreds died of malnutrition, sickness, privation, ill-treatment and misery, and many were buried in the camp cemetery. Frequent Allied bombing raids also took their toll of the prisoners. Because of the severity of raids, the camp was evacuated in June 1943, and the prisoners sent to other camps on or near the railway. Nevertheless, Thanbyuzayat continued to be used as a reception camp for newly arrived prisoners. After the war the Army Graves Service brought in the remains of those who had been buried in the jungle or along the line and reburied them in the now expanding camp cemetery, laid out basically in its present form. It now contains 1,700 British, 1,350 Australian, and 15 Indian and 80 Malayan war dead, together with over 600 from the Netherlands. The American dead were sent home for burial.

The graves are marked by bronze plaques. The Cross of Sacrifice stands where the orignal wooden cross set up by the prisoners stood; that cross is carefully preserved in the entrance building and has an explanatory plaque below it.

Under the heading Thailand, below, Kanchanaburi – the cemetery at the Thai end of the railway – is described.

Egypt

Halfaya-Sollum War Cemetery

The cemetery is near the coast of the Mediterranean Sea, 11 miles from the Libyan border and over 300 miles west of Alexandria. It is near the village of

Sollum and adjacent to Halfaya Pass – the scene of heavy fighting in 1941 and 1942 and known to the soldiers as 'Hellfire Pass'. Few, if any, war cemeteries of the 1939–1945 War could be on a spot which witnessed so much advance and retreat in battle. The stages included Wavell's advance of the winter of 1940–1941; Rommel's advance to Sollum, where he was stopped in April 1941; an unsuccessful British attack on Sollum and Halfaya in June 1941; the cutting off and surrender of the German garrisons in Halfaya and Sollum, November 1941–January 1942; the re-entry of the Germans into Sollum in mid-1942; and the final expulsion of the Germans on 11th November 1942, following the Battle of Alamein.

The cemetery therefore contains the graves of all the stages of the Western Desert Campaigns. The dead include 1,100 British; 200 each from Australia and New Zealand; nearly 400 South Africans; and nearly 160 from India.

Each side of both the entrance buildings has a fine stone lioness guarding her cub; they were carved by Charles Wheeler. As this is a desert cemetery, with very little water, the layout displays few plants, and the surface is raked sand. Being so near the border with Libya, the area is sensitive and special local arrangements may have to be made before a visit.

France

AIF Burial Ground, Grass Lane, Flers

The village of Flers, almost in the middle of the battlefields of the Rivers Ancre and Somme, is about four miles south-west of Bapaume. Australian medical units stationed in caves in the vicinity (the local name is Aux Cavées) opened a cemetery known as the AIF (Australian Imperial Force) Burial Ground to receive those who were dying in the autumn of 1916. On 15th September 1916, the 41st and New Zealand Divisions entered the village during the battle of Flers-Courcelette in which the British-invented tanks were used for the first time – with great local success. The Germans retook the village in March 1918, and it finally fell to Commonwealth troops in August of that year.

This is a concentration cemetery and it was greatly enlarged after the war by bringing in burials from the battlefields and small burial sites. A large proportion of the burials are not identified by name. There are now 2,800 British, 70 Canadian, over 400 Australian, 90 New Zealand and 30 South African burials in the cemetery.

Anzac Cemetery, Sailly-sur-la-Lys

Sailly is in the Pas-de-Calais, between Merville and Armentières. Its church was burnt in the fluid fighting of October 1914 but from then until the spring of 1918 the village was comparatively unharmed. The Germans captured the village on 9th April 1918 and it remained in their hands until early September.

Anzac Cemetery is half a mile from Sailly on the road to Estaires, (where there was a Commission office in charge of the so-called Estaires Area of the Commission until the 1970s) and was begun by Australian units in July 1916, immediately before the attack on Fromelles. It contains many who died in that engagement, and continued to be used as a front line cemetery until April 1918 when it was used by the Germans for the burial of British soldiers. It was used again by the British when they re-occupied the village. It contains 110 Australian, 170 British and 10 New Zealand burials. It has a Cross of Sacrifice near the entrance but no Stone of Remembrance.

Sailly-sur-la-Lys Canadian Cemetery

The Canadian Cemetery is on the opposite side of the road from Anzac Cemetery – the two entrances are opposite each other. It was begun by Canadian units in March 1915 and used as a frontline cemetery until July 1916. It contains 10 Canadian, 285 British and 20 Australian burials. To complement Anzac Cemetery, it has a Stone of Remembrance at the rear but no Cross of Sacrifice.

The inclusion of 'Canadian' in the title is interesting as it shows clearly that the first unit to use a cemetery normally gave the site its name and this was kept and honoured by later users and by the Commission. What is not clear is why the Australians opened their cemetery on the other side of the road when this one was already in existence – perhaps there was a lack of suitable ground for expansion as there were many trenches and dugouts in the area. But it could also have been due to troops of these two countries not being too fond of one another; Haig was reported as ordering their units to be separated by British units.

Bazentin-le-Petit Communal Cemetery Extension

Bazentin is five miles to the north-east of Albert in the Somme and the Communal Cemetery is to the east of the village; the war graves Extension adjoins it. The village was held by the Germans until 14th July 1916, when the 3rd and 7th Divisions captured Bazentin-le-Petit and neighbouring Bazentin-le-Grand. The ground was lost in April 1918 but recaptured on 25th August by the 38th (Welsh) Division.

The Communal Cemetery Extension was begun immediately after the capture of the village and used until December 1916 as a front line cemetery. It was enlarged after the Armistice by the addition of 50 burials from the surrounding battlefield. The fact that it was indeed a front line cemetery is evident in its layout, which is perhaps as ragged as any in the Commission's care. There is only one recognizable row of any length – this is Row B, which contains nearly 30 burials, probably among those brought in after the war. Fifty-nine graves, mainly of the 1st Battalion, the Northampton

Regiment, were destroyed by shelling and the burials are now commemorated by special memorials, 36 along the wall near the entrance and the remainder along the wall at the rear. Over 50 of the burials are not identified by name.

The Extension (which in common with most extensions looks like, and is considered to be, one of the Commission's constructed sites) now contains 180 British burials, five Canadian and one Australian. One of the Canadians, Private Frederick Charles Daffin of the 4th Canadian Mounted Rifles (1st Central Ontario Regiment) was married to a lady with a Buffalo, New York, USA, address and was a native of London, England. It could be said that it took three nations to make this soldier!

Bény-sur-Mer Canadian War Cemetery

The village of Bény-sur-Mer lies about nine miles north-west of Caen and two miles from the beaches near Courseulles where the Canadian 3rd Division landed on D Day, 6th June 1944. On that day, over 300 soldiers of the division died. Most of them, and other Canadians who died in later stages of the Battle of Normandy, are buried in the war cemetery, which in fact is near the village of Reviers, a mile from Bény. The cemetery contains over 2,000 Canadian burials. This cemetery, and Bretteville-sur-Laize Canadian War Cemetery, contain most of the Canadian dead of the Normandy Campaign.

Béthune Town Cemetery

Béthune is about 20 miles north-west of Arras, and during the 1914–1918 War was an important military and hospital centre, No 33 Casualty Clearing Station being established here until the end of 1917. In the Battle of Béthune German forces advanced to within three miles of the town on 18th April 1918, and on 21st May it was heavily bombarded. Subsequently, there was almost constant shelling, ending only when the Germans withdrew in October. The Commonwealth graves are in the northern end of this civil cemetery. They include 26 soldiers of the Manchester Regiment who were killed by a bomb while marching to rest billets on 22nd December 1917. There are nearly 3,000 British, 55 Canadian, and 90 German burials from the 1914–1918 War. The cemetery also contains another 15 British and two Canadians of the 1939–1945 War, who died in the retreat of 1940 or the advance of 1944.

The grave of Lieutenant F.A. de Pass VC is in this cemetery. The personal inscription on his headstone is from a sonnet by his Rugby school-fellow, Sub Lieutenant Rupert Brooke, RNVR, who is buried on the Isle of Skyros, Greece. It reads: '. . . LOVED, GONE PROUDLY FRIENDED'.

The recording of a small group of British war graves here in 1914 was one of the first acts of the British Red Cross Society's Mobile Unit. From this there grew the Graves Registration and Enquiries Department of the Army and from it the Imperial (later Commonwealth) War Graves Commission. In one sense, therefore, this cemetery can be considered as holding the honour of being the Commission's first cemetery. However, as has been seen, the first three cemeteries to be constructed were Le Tréport, Forceville and Louvencourt, also in France.

Bourlon Wood Cemetery

Bourlon is a village in the Pas-de-Calais, between the roads from Cambrai to Arras and Bapaume, and about five miles from the former; the wood is on the village's south-east side. There was heavy fighting in the village and wood in the Battle of Cambrai in 1917, the 40th (Bantam), 62nd (West Riding) and the Guards Divisions bearing the brunt. The British troops were withdrawn at the end of the battle, but the wood and church were retaken, after more fierce fighting, by two Canadian Divisions, the 3rd and 4th on 27th September 1917.

Bourlon Wood Cemetery was opened by the Canadian Corps Burial Officer in October 1918 and contains many burials of this heavy and successful fighting. It now contains 230 Canadian burials, 15 British and three from the Chinese Labour Corps buried close to the right hand wall. Nearby is the Bourlon Battlefield Memorial erected by the Canadian Government in honour of the forcing of the Canal du Nord by the Canadian Corps on 27th September 1918 and the subsequent advance to Mons, Belgium, and ultimately to the River Rhine in Germany. Many of the trees in the memorial area still bear their battle scars in the late 1980s; the trees are carefully preserved.

Cabaret Rouge British Cemetery, Souchez

The village of Souchez and the war cemetery lie seven miles north of Arras, on the main road to Béthune. The village was completely destroyed in the 1914–1918 War. The Cabaret Rouge was a small café, so-called because of its distinctive red bricks and roof; it was destroyed in May 1915. Its name was taken for the sector of the front and a communication trench held here by the French and taken over by the British in March 1916. The cemetery is near the site of the café and was begun that month by the 47th (London) Division and the Canadian Corps. The original burials are in Plots I to V inclusive. After the war, more than 7,000 dead were brought in from small cemeteries and individual graves on the battlefields of Arras and other places in the Departments of Nord and Pas-de-Calais.

The cemetery has the third largest number of Commonwealth burials in France, containing 6,800 British, 750 Canadian, over 100 Australian , over 40 South African and 15 Indian burials. The majority are unidentified by name. Behind the Cross of Sacrifice, there is a hill crowned by (as it was known in the war) Gazoy Wood. It held the entrance to Cabaret Rouge trench and was used as an observation post.

The cemetery and the massive domed shelter building at the entrance were designed by Frank Higginson, then the architect for France, who, as Sir Frank Higginson, was later Secretary to the Commission (after Sir Fabian Ware). Higginson served in the Canadian Army on the Western Front in the 1914–1918 War. Exceptionally, a bronze plaque in his memory and explaining that he designed the cemetery was placed in the shelter building.

Dieppe Canadian War Cemetery

The cemetery is in the Commune of Hautot-sur-Mer, about two miles south of Dieppe. It will always be linked with Canada, for in the Dieppe Raid that took place on 19th August 1942 nearly 5,000 Canadians took part (of a total of just over 6,000). More than 3,600 Allied troops were killed, wounded, missing or captured, while the naval losses were 550. Many of those who died are buried in the cemetery which contains nearly 700 Canadian burials and over 200 British, with small numbers of Australian, New Zealand and Indian. Those 40 Canadians who died in landing craft or ships and were brought back to Britain are buried in two rows in Brookwood Military Cemetery, Surrey. Those who died and have no known graves are commemorated on the Brookwood Memorial in that cemetery.

A proportion of the British dead date from 1940; one of them was a woman Brigadier of the Salvation Army, M.J. Climpson, who died on 20th May of that year.

Etaples Military Cemetery

Etaples is a port in the Pas-de-Calais and this large cemetery is outside the town. The cemetery has been seen by generations of passengers travelling on the nearby main railway line from Calais to Paris, the usual route for land travellers from Britain to the Continent. It is the second largest war cemetery in France, with nearly 11,000 burials. Etaples Cemetery was used throughout the 1914–1918 War, as the area held a large number of reinforcement camps and 16 hospitals. The area was again in use by the British Army in 1939 and the cemetery from January to May 1940. The great majority of the burials of both the wars are of those who died of wounds or disease in the hospitals; it is therefore not surprising that the majority are identified by name.

The cemetery contains nearly 9,000 British burials, nearly 1,200 Canadian, 470 Australian, 260 New Zealand, 70 South African, 30 Indian and 30 from other Commonwealth countries. Included in these figures are 70 British and five Canadian burials from the 1939–1945 War.

London Cemetery and Extension, High Wood, Longueval

The cemetery is in the Department of the Somme and the nearby wood (known locally as the Bois des Fourcaux, but as High Wood to the soldiers) crowns a low but dominating hill which formed part of the main German defence line from the Flers Ridge to Thiepval during the First Battle of the Somme in 1916. The cemetery is a mile north-west of Longueval, itself about seven miles north-east of Albert. There was much loss of life on both sides for possession of the hill and its High Wood.

On 18th and 21st September 1916, in the middle of the Battle of the Somme, the 47th (London) Division buried 47 of their dead in a large shell crater opposite the wood. Fifty other bodies were later brought in, mainly of soldiers who had died on 15th September 1916, the day the London Division cleared the wood of the enemy. This small burial place was known as London Cemetery, and in 1934 it was extended to take nearly 4,000 burials from the surrounding battlefields. Understandably, most of these were now unidentifiable by name. The original cemetery is between the entrance gates and the shelter building; all the burials are to the left of the gates. An inscription on a stone states that 78 of the soldiers whose names are on the surrounding headstones are known to be buried close by, although the exact grave location is not known, as this spot, as mentioned earlier, had been a shell crater.

There are also the graves of soldiers of the 51st (Highland) Division who died in June 1940, fighting for the River Somme crossings, and others who died with British Second Army four years later. There are 3,350 British burials, 170 Canadian, 300 Australian, over 30 from both New Zealand and South Africa from the 1914–1918 War, and 160 British and three Canadian from the 1939–1945 War.

Ranville War Cemetery

Ranville, seven miles north-east of Caen and near the Normandy coast, was the first village to be liberated on 6th June 1944. The cemetery contains the graves of soldiers of the British 6th Airborne Division who landed by glider and parachute nearby to take the vital bridges over the River Orne and the Caen Canal. It lies next to the village churchyard, where there are 50 British burials. An old mill was on the site when the cemetery was begun; it has been reconstructed and is now used as the gardeners' toolshed. The cemetery contains over 2,000 British burials, 80 Canadian, small numbers of other countries and, in Plots VI and VII, over 100 Germans.

In the village churchyard is the grave of Lieutenant H.D. Brotheridge, Mentioned in Despatches, Oxfordshire and Buckinghamshire Light Infantry, who was probably the first Comonwealth soldier to be killed in the invasion.

St Pierre Cemetery, Amiens

Amiens is the main city of the Department of the Somme. The cathedral, one of the largest in the world, was the first in which tablets were erected to the memory of the million servicemen of the British Commonwealth and

Empire who died in the 1914–1918 War. At Amiens there are separate tablets commemorating the dead of Britain and Ireland, Canada, Australia, New Zealand, South Africa, India, and Newfoundland. In other cathedrals where such tablets have been erected, the design combines the arms of the various countries on a single memorial.

During the 1914–1918 War, Amiens was an important British base and hospital centre until January 1919, and one of the main objectives of the German offensive which started on 21st March 1918. That it did not fall was largely due to the stand made by the Australians at Villers-Bretonneux, some five miles to the east, and site of the Memorial of that name.

St Pierre Cemetery, which contains a large French National Plot, is on the north side of the road to Albert; the British Plot was first used in September 1915 and closed in October 1919. It contains 560 British burials, 10 Canadian, over 90 Australian, and small numbers of others. Amiens was heavily bombed by both the Germans and the Allies and was taken by German armoured forces on 20th May 1940 during the sweep to the Channel coast. It remained in German hands until 31st August 1944, when it was liberated by the British Second Army. The Commonwealth section of the cemetery was opened again for Commonwealth burials (mainly of airmen) in March 1941 and they number 60 British, 12 Canadian, and nine Australian.

Among those buried in the cemetery are Group Captain P.C. Pickard DSO and two Bars DFC RAF and Flight Lieutenant J.A. Broadley DSO DFC DFM RAF. They died in Operation Jericho, the brilliant low level attack of 18th February 1944 that breached the walls of Amiens prison and freed over 250 prisoners, many held for political reasons. The nine soldiers who are included in the 60 British burials were killed during the liberation of Amiens.

St Sever Cemetery and Extension, Rouen

Rouen is the old capital of Normandy and the place where William the Conqueror died. In the 1914–1918 War, the city was a British base and about 16 hospitals were established in the southern outskirts. Most of those who died here were buried in St Sever Cemetery or, from September 1916, in the Extension which lies south of it and was last used in April 1920.

There are also over 300 burials (260 British, 40 Canadian) from the 1939–1945 War. Some were killed during the German advance on Rouen, which they took on 9th June 1940; others were Canadians who died of wounds sustained at Dieppe on 19th August 1942; and others were British who died in the capture of Le Havre between 10th and 12th September 1944. The Cemetery and the Extension, which adjoin, together contain (including those of 1939–1945) over 9,600 British, 500 Canadian, 900 Australian, 200 New Zealand, 100 South African, 350 Indian and 90 British West Indian burials – a total of nearly 11,800. This cemetery and its extension have, therefore, the melancholy distinction of being the largest

Commonwealth war cemetery in France, surpassed only anywhere by Tyne Cot Cemetery, Belgium, which has 200 more. Being a hospital cemetery, the great majority of the burials are known, whereas two thirds of those at Tyne Cot, a battle and concentration cemetery, are unidentified by name. Unusually, but not uniquely, St Sever Cemetery has separate plots for officers.

Terlincthun British Cemetery, Wimille

Terlincthun is a village two miles from Boulogne. The cemetery contains the graves of men who died in hospital in Boulogne and Wimereux (the cemeteries there being full) the first being buried on 16th June 1918 and the last in July 1920. After the 1939–1945 War, however, the cemetery was re-opened for the burial of the bodies of Commonwealth soldiers who were still (and are still) being found accidentally on the 1914–1918 War battlefields in France. It is also used for the burial of soldiers and airmen of the 1940 Campaign who are found in northern France (those of the Normandy Campaign are buried in St Charles de Percy War Cemetery, Normandy). The largest number buried at one time in recent years were the 49 British and two Germans who were found at Ovillers-la-Boisselle, in the Department of the Somme, in November 1982. None could be identified by name, but the fact that the British were from five regiments was established. Terlincthun will continue as an 'open' cemetery, probably well into the twenty-first century.

In the late 1980s, the cemetery contained 3,900 British, 320 Canadian, 120 Australian, 30 New Zealand, 40 South African and eight Indian burials.

Thistle Dump Cemetery, High Wood, Longueval

Longueval is a village in the Somme, midway between Bapaume and Albert, but off the main road. High Wood (see London Cemetery and Extension, High Wood above) was taken by the 7th Division for a day, on 14th July 1916, and the southern part by the 33rd Division on the 20th. The struggle in the wood was continued by the 51st (Highland) Division until 7th August and on 15th September it was cleared by the 47th (London) Division. It was lost in April 1918 and retaken in August.

Thistle Dump Cemetery is in a field half a mile south of the southern apex of High Wood. It was begun in August 1916 and used as a frontline cemetery until the following February. The Germans buried some of their soldiers in it in the spring of 1918. Nearly 60 battlefield burials were added after the Armistice and the cemetery now contains over 100 British burials and just over 40 each from Australia and New Zealand; there are also the graves of seven German soldiers. Six of the soldiers buried here are not identified by name.

Toronto Cemetery, Démuin

The cemetery is a mile north of the village of Démuin. It is located deep in farming fields about a mile from the nearest main road, and is very isolated. It was begun by the 3rd Canadian Battalion (Toronto Regiment) in August 1918 and also used by other Canadian units for burials that month. It contains 75 Canadian burials, 20 British (some of whom died in the previous March), one Australian and four German.

Wimereux Communal Cemetery

Wimereux is a town in the Pas-de-Calais, on the coast about three miles north of Boulogne. From October 1914 until the end of the war, Wimereux and Boulogne formed an important hospital centre. Until June 1918 the medical units at Wimereux buried their dead in the Communal Cemetery north of the town; the south-eastern half of this cemetery was reserved for Commonwealth graves.

There are 2,300 British burials, over 200 each of Canadians and Australians, 80 New Zealand, 10 South African and 20 British West Indian. There is also a German plot with over 170 burials. About a dozen British burials were added in the 1939–1945 War. The nature of the ground – mainly its inherent instability – necessitated recumbent markers, an unusual feature. Boulogne Eastern Cemetery, which contains 6,000 Commonwealth burials, also has recumbent markers.

At Wimereux is buried the Canadian Lieutenant Colonel John McCrae, author of the poem *In Flanders Fields*. In his memory, a committee presented a seat, next to the road-side wall of the cemetery, and inscribed on it a verse from the poem.

Germany

Berlin 1939–1945 War Cemetery

The cemetery lies in West Berlin on the southern side of the Heerstrasse. The site was chosen by the British Occupation Authorities and Commission officials jointly in 1945, soon after the war's end, in one of the city's most attractive areas. The burials its contains were removed from the Berlin area and eastern Germany. Of those, about three-quarters were airmen who had died in Bomber Command raids, particularly during the winter of 1943–1944. The others were mainly soldiers who had died as prisoners of war in the region, or on forced marches from Poland, driven by their German captors away from the advancing Russians.

The cemetery contains nearly 2,700 British burials, 530 Canadian, 220 Australian, 60 New Zealand, 30 South African and 50 Indian. There is also a section for the burial of British troops now stationed in Berlin and their dependents, cared for by the Commission on an agency basis.

Reichswald Forest War Cemetery

The large Reichswald Forest (Forst Reichswald) lies in North Rhine Westphalia, between Cleves (Kleve) and Nijmegen in nearby Netherlands. After the end of the war in Europe in May 1945, thousands of soldiers' and airmen's remains were brought in from burial places in western Germany. Many of the soldiers died in the hard-fought battles of the Rhineland, others in fighting in the Reichswald itself, and yet others during the crossing of the Rhine in March 1945. Among the soldiers' graves is that of Major General Thomas Rennie, killed by a mortar bomb which exploded on his jeep. There are 4,000 airmen in the cemetery, most of whom died in the years of the bombing offensive and some in supporting the advance of the soldiers. They, like the soldiers, were concentrated after the war.

This, as mentioned elsewhere, is the largest Commonwealth war cemetery of the 1939–1945 War if only actual buried bodies, and not cremations, are included. (If they are included, then El Alamein War Cemetery, Egypt, with 7,950, is larger). The cemetery contains 6,400 British burials, 700 Canadians (all airmen, except for one soldier – Canadian soldiers who died in the area were interred in Groesbeek Canadian War Cemetery, Netherlands) over 300 Australian, 130 New Zealand and 70 Polish – a total of over 7,600.

Sage War Cemetery, Oldenburg

Sage, in north-west Germany, is about 15 miles south of Oldenburg. The cemetery is on the roadside a mile and a half to the south. Most of those buried here were airmen who died in raids on Germany and whose bodies were brought in from civil cemeteries in the north-west and the East Friesian Islands. A number of airmen died on 4th September 1939, making them (so far as is known) the first battle casualties of the 1939–1945 War. They were the crews of RAF Wellington bombers killed in the attack on ships of the German Navy in North Sea ports. Also in this cemetery are soldiers who died in the last days of the war in Europe – between 23rd April and 7th May 1945.

One of those buried is Squadron Leader I.G. McNaughton RCAF, who died on 23rd June 1942. He was the son of General A.G.L. McNaughton, Canadian commander in Britain. Another was Pilot Officer P.J.N. Robinson RAF, who died on 25th June 1941 and was the son of a VC, Rear-Admiral E.G. Robinson. Also in this cemetery are seven soldiers of the Royal Artillery killed in an ammunition explosion on 1st June 1945.

There are 650 British burials, 125 Canadian, 35 each of Australians and New Zealanders, and over 20 Polish. There are similarities between this cemetery and St Symphorien Military Cemetery, Belgium, described above.

Greece

Salonika (Lembet Road) Military Cemetery

This cemetery (then known as the Anglo-French Military Cemetery) was opened in November 1915 and had British, French, Serbian, Italian and Russian sections. The British section remained in use until October 1918, although from the beginning of 1917 burials were also made at Mikra (see below under Additional Cemeteries). The front line was 40 miles away and most of the burials are of soldiers who died in hospitals established locally. In February and March 1917 Salonika received two heavy air raids and many of the graves just north of the Cross of Sacrifice are of those killed in the bombing. The cemetery contains 1,650 British burials (of whom 15 were in the Malta Labour Corps) and three Canadian; 45 Bulgarians who died as prisoners of war are also buried here.

One of the more remarkable graves is that of Mrs Katharine Mary Harley, Croix de Guerre (France), age 62, who died on 7th March 1917. She was a sister of Field Marshal Sir John French, C-in-C of the BEF in France and Flanders in 1914–1915. Mrs Harley led a group of British nurses serving with the Serbian Army and she was killed in the bombing. Her grave bears a private memorial (as well as a recumbent Commission headstone) erected in 1917 by the Serbian Army and inscribed in two languages:

THE GENEROUS ENGLISH LADY AND

GREAT BENEFACTRESS OF THE SERBIAN PEOPLE

MADAME HARLEY

A GREAT LADY

ON YOUR TOMB INSTEAD OF FLOWERS

THE GRATITUDE OF THE SERBS

SHALL BLOSSOM THERE

FOR YOUR WONDERFUL ACTS YOUR NAME SHALL

BE KNOWN FROM GENERATION TO GENERATION

Though Mrs Harley, at an age when few men were serving, died nursing in the Serbian Army, she was typical of the many women who served with the nursing and similar forces of the Commonwealth forces and whose graves lie wherever those forces served.

Hong Kong

Stanley Military Cemetery

The Military Cemetery lies in the south of Hong Kong Island, and was used by the Hong Kong Garrison and their families as a burial place from 1841 to 1866. There were no further burials until the 1939–1945 War, when it was used for the burial of those who died while imprisoned by the Japanese in Stanley Jail or interned in the local camp. After the war, remains of men who had died in the Colony's defence in December 1941 or during the years of Japanese occupation were brought in from nearby burial places. The burials include nearly all of the casualties of the local defence forces, such as the Hong Kong Volunteer Defence Force, and also members of the British Army Aid Group. It is remarkable that in such a comparatively small cemetery, no fewer than five should have been awarded the George Cross. The cemetery contains 400 British, 20 Canadian, five Indian and 160 Hong Kong burials.

India

Imphal War Cemetery

Imphal is the capital of the State of Manipur in north-east India and borders on Upper Burma. The easiest route from Burma to India is through Imphal into Assam. After the invasion of Burma in the 1939–1945 War, Imphal became a focal point in the defence of India against the Japanese and the 900-mile retreat to India of the British Fourteenth Army ended there. In the spring of 1944 the Japanese, having taken Burma, tried to invade India but their advance was held round Imphal by the Indian IV Corps. Although completely surrounded by the Japanese and totally dependent on supply by air, the corps stood firm from the end of March until they were relieved late in June. During this period, the Japanese made repeated but unsuccessful attempts to break into the plain beyond but eventually were forced to withdraw through lack of supplies and loss of men, whereupon the initiative passed decisively to the Commonwealth forces.

There were originally over 900 burials in the war cemetery but, after hostilities had ceased, burials from isolated sites and two smaller cemeteries at Imphal were brought in. The cemetery contains 1,300 British burials, 10 Canadian, five Australian, 220 Indian, 40 East African, and 10 each from Burma and West Africa. The graves are marked by bronze plaques.

Kohima War Cemetery

Kohima is a town 4,500 feet above sea level in the Naga Hills of East Assam. It marks the farthest point reached by the Japanese in their attempted invasion of India in the spring of 1944 and was the scene of protracted, bitter and close fighting. On Garrison Hill a small force resisted repeated attacks by the Japanese, evenutally drove them off, and re-opened the road to Imphal. It was during this fighting that the heaviest casualties were sustained. Hand-to-hand fighting took place in the Deputy Commissioner's bungalow where, for a time, the tennis court was part of No-Man's-Land.

Kohima War Cemetery is on Garrison Hill. The graves are marked by bronze plaques, as they are at Imphal. The Cross of Sacrifice stands on a visitors' shelter to the side of the tennis court, which has been preserved, though the original white lines have been replaced by ones of concrete. The cemetery contains nearly 1,100 British burials, five Canadian and 330 Indian. There is also an Indian Cremation Memorial which commemorates by name over 900 other Indians (Gurkhas) who were cremated.

An eye-catching feature is a private memorial to the British 2nd Division. It is a large stone, such as the Nagas use to commemorate their dead, and stands in front of a semi-circle of bronze panels bearing the names of units of the division. When all mechanical means to move the memorial along the mountainous roads and tracks had failed, the stone was pulled and put into position by a hundred or more Naga tribesmen using nothing but human muscle-power and a sledge. Its inscription is at the head of Chapter 4.

Italy

Beach Head War Cemetery, Anzio

The cemetery is about two miles north of Anzio on the road to Rome. It was established in January 1944, following the sea-borne landings, near the site of a casualty clearing station. Burials were made both at the time and later, after the fighting had moved on. It contains 2,200 British, 70 Canadian, small numbers of Australian, New Zealand and 25 South African burials.

Castiglione South African Cemetery

Castiglione dei Pepoli is at a height of over 2,000 feet, about 30 miles north of Florence on the road to Bologna through Prato; the cemetery lies just to the north of the town. It was started in November 1944 by the 6th South African Armoured Division which had entered Castiglione at the end of September and remained holding positions in the area throughout the winter until the following April. Many of the burials were made direct from the Apennine Mountains battlefields. Four fifths of those buried here were South Africans, while the remainder were mostly from the British 24th Guards Brigade, then under the command of the South African Division.

There is a memorial building in the cemetery which the South Africans erected. It contains two tablets which were unveiled by Field Marshal Jan Christiaan Smuts, the South African statesman, which read:

TO SAVE MANKIND YOURSELVES YOU

SCORNED TO SAVE,

OM DIE MENSDOM TE DIEN HET JUL

VEILIGHEID VERSMAAD

The cemetery contains 400 South African and 100 British burials. It is the only war cemetery in the Commission's care with 'South African' in its title.

Forli Indian Army War Cemetery

The war cemetery lies in the Commune and Province of Forli in north-east Italy. The site of the cemetery, a mile and a half north of the town, was chosen in December 1944 by the 10th Indian Division, which had come into the Adriatic sector south of Cesena early in the previous October. The division buried not only their own dead but also some from 4th Indian Division which had preceded them in the area, and from the 8th Indian Division, which fought on this front in the spring of 1945.

The 10th Division had played an important part in the heavy fighting in appalling weather between their arrival and the end of the year, suffering considerable casualties. The cemetery contains 500 burials from India and another 750 names of Hindus and Sikhs on the Cremation Memorial. This is one of three cremation memorials in Italy, the others being at Rimini, and the Sangro River (the latter is described below).

Moro River Canadian War Cemetery, Ortona

The River Moro enters the Adriatic not far from Ortona in the Province of Chieti. On 6th December 1943 Canadian forces crossed the river near its mouth and at Rogatti, about four miles up-river, after overcoming stiff German resistance. They went on to take Ortona on the 28th, after a week of bitter street fighting. In that month alone the 1st Canadian Division suffered over 500 fatal casualties.

The site of the war cemetery, on high ground, was selected by the Canadian Corps in January 1944 and bodies were brought into it from the surrounding battlefields. The Canadians remained in this sector for a further three difficult months, undertaking offensive actions in January and patrolling throughout the period. The cemetery contains 1,400 Canadian burials, 170 British, 40 New Zealand, 15 South African and small numbers from Australia and India. This cemetery contains the largest number of Canadian burials in Italy.

Salerno War Cemetery

Salerno is the chief town of its province and the war cemetery is nearly 10 miles to its south on the coast road. It was near Salerno that British and American forces landed on 8th and 9th September 1943, in an attempt to cut off German units. There was fierce fighting for days in the beachhead, and not until the 16th did the Germans begin to withdraw and the Allied hold become secure. The site of the cemetery was chosen in November 1943 and contains those who died in the battles in and following the landings, some from the General Hospital near Salerno and others who were brought in from south-western Italy. The cemetery contains 1,750 British burials, 30 Canadian, 10 Australian, and 35 Indian, with small numbers of New Zealanders and South Africans.

Sangro River War Cemetery

One of the most difficult operations in the advance up the Adriatic coast in November and December 1943 was the crossing of the River Sangro. This, like the Moro and so many other rivers in Italy, runs off the central mountains to the sea, forming a formidable natural barrier to advances to the north or the south. The site of the cemetery lies two miles inland from the mouth of the River Sangro in the Province of Chieti. It was chosen by the British V Corps and into it were concentrated the bodies of men who had died in this sector during the fierce fighting and the subsequent static period. The 8th Indian Division was here during those months, 4th Indian arrived in January 1944, and 10th Indian in April; their participation is reflected in the number of their graves.

The New Zealanders, too, were engaged in this area against stiff German opposition and later beyond the Sangro. The Canadians, who have two graves in this cemetery, buried most of those who died near here in Moro River Canadian War Cemetery, about eight miles to the north-west.

Sangro River Cemetery contains 1,800 British burials, 360 New Zealand, 75 South African and nearly 400 Indian; there are also small numbers of Australian and former High Commission Territories' burials. The Cremation Memorial in the cemetery commemorates by name a further 520 Indians who were cremated in accordance with their faith. With a total of well over 3,000 burials and cremations this war cemetery ranks second in size (after Cassino War Cemetery) in Italy.

Japan

Yokohama War Cemetery

The war cemetery is about six miles south of Yokohama in Yuenchi Park in Hodogaya. The cemetery was constructed in 1945 by the Australian War Graves Group and is the only Commonwealth war cemetery in Japan. Unusually for a Commission war cemetery, it comprises four main separate sections, commemorating the dead from the United Kingdom; Australia; Canada and New Zealand; and India. A granite Cross of Sacrifice stands in each of the first three sections. A specially designed monument, in the form of a four-faced pylon, stands in the Indian section. On two faces is inscribed 'Indian Forces 1939–1945'; 'India' is on one face and 'Pakistan' on the other. In a niche on the north wall of this section are commemorated 20 Indians who died while serving with the occupation forces in Japan, for whom no burial or cremation information exists.

Commonwealth and Netherlands prisoners-of-war captured in the Pacific region disembarked near here to undergo captivity in Japan. Nearly all who died were cremated and after the war their remains were collected from camps and burial sites and buried in the war cemetery. The graves are marked by semi-recumbent bronze plaques. Deaths were from many causes, especially from pneumonia in the severe winters and, towards the end of the war, from Allied naval bombardment and air bombing of the dockyards and places where the prisoners worked.

The ashes recovered from two of the camps in the prisoner of war centre at Fukuoka were placed in two large urns. One of these is housed in a shrine in the United Kingdom section; the other, which contains the ashes of more Americans than of other countries, is in Jefferson Barracks National Cemetery, St Louis, USA. The names of those whose ashes are known to be in the Yokohama urn are inscribed on the walls of the shrine, known as the Yokohama Cremation Memorial; they include over 200 British, (more than half from the Royal Artillery), 50 Americans and 20 Netherlanders.

The numbers of burials in the cemetery are 1,000 (excluding the 200 mentioned above) British, 140 Canadian, 280 Australian, 15 each from New Zealand and India, and over 40 from Hong Kong.

Libya

Tobruk War Cemetery

Tobruk and its important deep-water harbour were first captured from the Italians (Libya was then an Italian colony) by General Sir Archibald Wavell in his successful advance in January 1941. Later, the Commonwealth forces in Tobruk were besieged by General Rommel, a siege which lasted from April to December 1941. Tobruk was relieved by General Sir Claude Auchinleck when he drove back the *Afrika Korps* to El Agheila – but that was not the end of the story, as Rommel's advance to El Alamein in the spring and summer of 1942 enabled him to take Tobruk on 21st June. It was not retaken until the war passed that way again after the Battle of El Alamein.

Hanging from the wall of the gate house is the bell from HMS *Liverpool*, to symbolize the critical part played by the Navy in bringing in essential supplies and ammunition during the seige. Without that help, Tobruk would have fallen. Inside the entrance, on the central path, is a stone obelisk commemorating the Australian dead, replacing the original concrete memorial erected by Australian soldiers. The cemetery, begun during the siege, stands five miles inland from the town, on the road to Alexandria, Egypt.

Bodies from outlying sites were brought in after the war and the cemetery now contains 1,200 British burials, three Canadian, 560

Australian, 40 New Zealand, 160 South African, over 20 each East and West African, 130 Poles, 15 Czech and smaller numbers of French and Greek.

Malaysia

Labuan War Cemetery, Sabah

The island of Labuan is off the west coast of the enormous island of Borneo and was invaded by the Japanese in December 1941. It is in that part of Borneo which was then known as British North Borneo, but is now part of Malaysia. There was heavy fighting during a rearguard action in Borneo by the British, Indians, and Dutch (most of Borneo was part of the Dutch East Indies) until the beginning of April 1942, when these isolated Allied troops were forced to surrender and the Japanese occupied the island.

Borneo was recaptured by the 7th and 9th Australian Divisions, supported by the RAAF, in the summer of 1945. By the middle of June, the Allies had established a base on the island of Labuan. Hostilities ceased in August and the spot where Major General G.F. Wootten, the Commander of the Australian Forces, received the Japanese surrender is marked on a plaque in the northern part of the island.

Labuan War Cemetery is two miles from the town of Victoria on the top of a hill. It was designed to receive burials from all over Borneo, not only from isolated sites but also from sites which had been regarded as being probably permanent but proved to have insuperable defects, such as flooding. Many of the burials were of Australians and British taken prisoner-of-war as a result of the fall of Singapore; their treatment by the Japanese was as bad as that inflicted on the prisoners working on the Burma–Siam railway. The Cross of Sacrifice was unveiled by the Governor of North Borneo, Major General Sir Ralph Hone, on 10th June 1953, eight years exactly after the 9th Division had landed on the beaches of Labuan.

The cemetery contains 1,200 Australian burials, 900 British, 120 Indian, 40 Malayans and 1,800 who could not be identified. The graves are marked by semi-recumbent bronze plaques. There is also in the cemetery a memorial commemorating 35 Indians whose remains were cremated; this figure is included in the number of burials. The Labuan Memorial to the missing is also in the cemetery.

Netherlands

Arnhem (Oosterbeek) War Cemetery

Arnhem is the capital of the Province of Gelderland; Oosterbeek is a village suburb about four miles from the city centre. It was in this area that the British 1st Airborne Division landed in September 1944 in their vain attempt to capture and hold the bridge over the Lower Rhine at Arnhem. The division made a stand within a gradually shrinking perimeter at Oosterbeek, holding out until all hope of relief by troops advancing from the south was abandoned and their supplies and ammunition were running out. Many of those who died were buried on the south side of Oosterbeek, in what was to become the cemetery when large numbers of others were brought in from temporary graves. The cemetery is the scene of an annual ceremony organized by the local people. It is also often visited by Poles, as a number of their countrymen are buried here.

The cemetery contains over 1,600 British burials, over 30 Canadian, four each from Australia and New Zealand and 80 Poles. There is an excellent museum nearby concerned with the fighting at Arnhem; it is owned and organized by the local authorities.

Bergen-op-Zoom War Cemetery

The war cemetery is about 100 yards east of Bergen-op-Zoom *Canadian* War Cemetery. Many of those buried here died, like their Canadian brothers-in-arms, in the operations on the northern shore of the Scheldt Estuary in the latter months in 1944 and in south-west Netherlands thereafter. The cemetery contains 1,200 British burials, 45 Canadian, 12 Australian and 23 New Zealand. There are also a few 1914–1918 War British burials which were brought in when their original graves became unmaintainable. It is not clear why these two concentration cemeteries, so close to each other, were not constructed as one.

Groesbeek Canadian War Cemetery

Most of those buried here are Canadians who died in the heavy fighting in the battle of the Rhineland in February and March 1945. The cemetery is unusual in that many of the dead were brought here from nearby Germany – one of the few cases where bodies were moved across international frontiers. So far as can be ascertained, all slain Canadian soldiers of the Rhineland battles, who were buried in German battlefields, were reinterred here (less one, who is buried in Reichswald Forest War Cemetery). General Crerar, who commanded Canadian land forces in Europe, ordered that Canadian dead were *not* to be buried in German soil.

The cemetery contains the largest number of Canadians, 2,350, interred in the Netherlands and there are also 265 British burials. As it is the 'open' cemetery from the Netherlands, these figures are rising slowly.

Canadian airmen who died in Germany and were buried there were not moved into Groesbeek, but into Commission cemeteries in that country.

New Caledonia

Bourail New Zealand War Cemetery

New Caledonia, discovered by Captain James Cook in 1774, lies about 1,000 miles east of Queensland, Australia, and is a French territory. In 1942 the Allies used the island as a training ground for jungle and island warfare and New Zealanders prepared here for the Solomon Islands Campaign. Noumea, the capital, was the headquarters of South Pacific Command and became the largest forward Allied military and supply base in the theatre. Bourail, on the west coast, was the headquarters of the 3rd New Zealand Division which opened a war cemetery four miles to the south-east for those who died on the island.

After the war, some of the New Zealanders who had died in the Solomons and other Pacific Islands were brought here for burial. The graves are marked by semi-recumbent bronze plaques. The Cross of Sacrifice was unveiled in 1955 by Major General Sir Harold Barraclough, Chief Justice of New Zealand, who had commanded the division from its arrival in New Caledonia until its disbandment in October 1944, when the Solomon Islands Campaign ended. The cemetery contains 240 New Zealand and five British burials.

The Bourail Memorial, which stands in the cemetery, commemorates by name 280 New Zealanders, the majority of whom were airmen who died in the southern Pacific and have no known graves. It also commemorates 170 soldiers of the Western Pacific Local Forces who died in the area and whose graves, too, are unknown.

Norway

Oslo Western Civil Cemetery

Olso was captured by the Germans in April 1940 and liberated on 10th May 1945, two days after VE Day. The Civil Cemetery is in the north-western outskirts of the capital and contains the Commonwealth War Graves Plot. There are also plots nearby of those of other nationalities.

Many of the airmen buried here were shot down while attacking Oslo Airport at Fornebu in November 1941. However, 43 soldiers and airmen were killed on the day of liberation (an unopposed landing) when two aeroplanes carrying airborne troops crashed accidentally – a particularly tragic way to die just after the end of the war in Europe. The Cross of Sacrifice was unveiled in November 1949 by General Otto Ruge, who commanded the Norwegian Army at the time of the German invasion. Facing the Cross, outside the plot, stands a memorial erected by the City of Oslo in honour of the men of the British forces who died in Norway in the 1939–1945 War; it represents the figure of a mourning woman and was unveiled by King Olaf in June 1960. The plot contains 90 British, eight Canadian and two Australian burials.

Papua New Guinea

Lae War Cemetery, New Guinea

Lae lies on the Huon Gulf on the north-east coast of Papua New Guinea, and it was Lae and its neighbouring airfields that were the objects of the Japanese air attacks in the early months of 1942. Lae was heavily bombed on 21st January, but Japanese land forces did not enter the area until 7th March, when 3,000 landed at Lae. There were landings, too, at Salamaua, 40 miles to the south of Lae which was also bombed on 21st January. Landings followed on 21st July at Buna and Gona, over 100 miles south-east of Salamaua, in preparation for an offensive over the Owen Stanley Mountains – the 'spine' of that part of New Guinea – to Port Moresby on the south coast. The vital stage of the New Guinea campaign dates from then and Lae became one of the bases from which the southward drive was launched and continued until it was stopped at Ioribaiwa Ridge, only 35 miles from Port Moresby. Lae was recaptured by the Australian 7th and 9th Divisions, with local help, on 16th September 1943. A base was established there and, with RAAF support, the Japanese were driven 500 miles westwards beyond the River Sepik. Few campaigns in the 1939–1945 War can have been as harrowing and as difficult as that facing the Australians in the steamy high jungle of the Owen Stanley Mountains and against a fanatically brave enemy.

The cemetery contains 2,400 Australian burials, 20 British and over 400 Indian. The Indians are almost all unidentified and had been taken prisoner in the fighting in Malaya and Hong Kong and put into working parties, largely on Japanese airfield construction.

In this cemetery stands the Lae Memorial which commemorates by name 350 Australian soldiers, sailors and airmen who died in these operations and have no known grave. The Cross of Sacrifice was unveiled by Field Marshal Viscount Slim.

A reminder of the 1914–1918 War is the single grave of a Australian who died in the occupation of this then German territory of North-East New Guinea on 12th September 1914. The original grave could not be properly maintained and his remains were therefore reburied here.

Thailand

Kanchanaburi War Cemetery

Kanachanaburi is a town on the River Me Khlong about 80 miles north-west of Bangkok and the war cemetery is on the outskirts of the town. It is a short distance from the former 'Kanburi' Prisoner of War Base Camp, through which prisoners passed on their way to other camps and is the largest of the three notorious (with Chungkai and Thanbyuzayat) camps set up for the completion of the Burma-Siam railway. Sufficient has already been said in the notes on Thanbyuzayat to show that Commonwealth and Allied prisoners of war were nowhere treated worse than in these three camps.

The war cemetery was established by the Army Graves Service who transferred to it all the burials, less Americans, from camp burial grounds and isolated sites along the southern half of the railway from Bangkok to Nieke. The graves are marked by semi-recumbent bronze plaques. The cemetery contains 3,600 British burials, 1,400 Australian, 12 Indian, 100 Malayan and 1,900 Netherlands.

Above the bronze door of the box containing the register of the names of those buried in the cemetery, is a bronze panel which reads in part:

IN HONOURED REMEMBRANCE OF THE FORTITUDE AND

SACRIFICE OF THAT VALIANT COMPANY WHO PERISHED

WHILE BUILDING THE RAILWAY FROM THAILAND TO BURMA

DURING THEIR LONG CAPTIVITY. THOSE WHO HAVE NO

KNOWN GRAVE ARE COMMEMORATED BY NAME AT RANGOON,

SINGAPORE AND HONG KONG AND THEIR COMRADES REST

IN THE THREE WAR CEMETERIES OF KANCHANABURI,

CHUNGKAI AND THANBYUZAYAT

Turkey

All but two of the cemeteries of the 1914–1918 War, Haidar Pasha and Chanak, are on the Gallipoli Peninsula, which stretches southwards for 60 miles from the Sea of Marmora in the north to Cape Helles in the south. The 31 war cemeteries are in three areas, all within 25 miles of Cape Helles. They consist of the Cape Helles group of cemeteries near the southern end of the peninsula where the British and Indians landed on 25th April 1915; the Anzac group of cemeteries in the so-called Anzac Area on the west of the peninsula about 15 miles north of Cape Helles, where the Australian and New Zealand Army Corps landed, also on 25th April; and the Suvla group of cemeteries near Suvla Bay, a few miles north of Anzac Area, where the British made new landings to support further Anzac attacks from 6th August 1915.

All troops, Commonwealth, French and Turkish, fought desperately and courageously in a bleak and difficult terrain, losses on both sides being high. But eventually the attempt to dislodge the Turks and gain control of the Dardanelles failed and, on 20th December, the last rear guards were taken off Suvla and Anzac. Early in January 1916, the last British troops were evacuated from Cape Helles. In all 25,000 British, 22 Newfoundlanders, 7,300 Australians, 2,400 New Zealanders, and 1,700 Indians (and perhaps 10,000 French) are buried or commemorated on this small strip of land. The Commonwealth graves are marked by semi-recumbent stone 'Gallipoli' plaques.

One great difference between the Gallipoli cemeteries and those elsewhere in the world is the abnormally high proportion of markers which bear a superscription making it clear that the exact place of burial in the cemetery is unknown. In many cases, the best that can be stated is 'Believed To Be Buried In This Cemetery'. Most of the cemeteries have an inscribed stone block near the entrance stating the number of unidentified burials.

The difficulty in locating the exact position of the graves and in identifying or otherwise is due to the nature of the close fighting during the nine months' campaign. No Army Graves Unit was able to visit the battlefields until after the Armistice, by which time many of the original wooden markers which had survived shelling and fighting had been displaced, lost, or destroyed by nature.

Azmak Cemetery, Suvla

Azmak is the most northerly of the cemeteries on the peninsula and was constructed at the end of the war. Its graves are of those who died on the Suvla plains in August 1915 or in later actions in the vicinity. It contains 560 British and 12 Newfoundland burials and 500 who are entirely unidentified.

Beach Cemetery, Anzac

The 3rd Australian Brigade landed at Anzac Cove on 25th April. The landing was to have taken place under Gaba Tepe, but an unknown sea current took the boats further north. The landing parties therefore had to scale steep, crumbling, thorny cliffs – as well as deal with the enemy. Beach Cemetery was made beneath the cliffs on what was known as Hell Spit, and was used throughout the campaign. It contains 300 Australian, 20 New Zealand and 50 British burials.

Lancashire Landing, Helles

The 29th British Division (later to serve with distinction on the Somme) landed at Cape Helles on 25th April in five small coves, codenamed S, V, W, X, and Y Beaches. The 1st Battalion Lancashire Fusiliers landed at W Beach under very severe fire and cut their way through wire and trenches to establish themselves on the hills inland. The beach became known as Lancashire Landing as a tribute to their endeavours.

The cemetery, the greater part of which was made between the landing in April 1915 and the evacuation in January 1916, contains 1,200 British burials, two Newfoundland, 30 Australian, 15 New Zealand and 20 unidentified.

Shrapnel Valley Cemetery, Anzac

Shrapnel Valley was so-named because of its heavy (even for this campaign) shelling by the Turks on 26th April, the day following the initial landings; it formed an essential roadway up from the beaches. Some water was obtained from wells sunk in the valley, and there were gun positions at its mouth.

The cemetery was started during the fighting, but was completed after the war by the concentration of burials elsewhere in the valley. It contains 530 Australian, 60 New Zealand, 30 British and 70 unidentified burials.

V Beach Cemetery, Helles

As mentioned above, V Beach was a codename for one of the coves in which landings took place on 25th April. The objective of those landing here was the old fort and village of Sedd-el-Bahr. Support was to be given by troops secreted in the collier *River Clyde* which was to be run aground, with the troops rushing out through sally ports and over lighters to the shore. The *River Clyde* positioned herself properly, but heavy fire from the Turks killed nearly half of the soldiers as they emerged; the remainder landed successfully that night. The French Corps' main body landed here on the evening of the 26th and the beach area was used as their base during the summer.

The cemetery was begun and ended, so far as 1915 was concerned in April and May, but after the end of the war a few more burials were brought in. It contains 700 British burials, of which only about 200 are named.

Walker's Ridge Cemetery, Anzac

The spur and the cemetery perpetuate the name of Brigadier General H.B. Walker. The ridge in question was the first objective of General Walker's New Zealand Infantry Brigade after the men had landed under heavy fire on 25th April; the New Zealanders occupied it that morning. The Turks launched a powerful attack on the ridge in May, but were repulsed by the New Zealand Mounted Rifles. Most of the soldiers buried here, in a cemetery which was created after the war, were killed during this attack. The Auckland Mounted Regiment suffered particularly heavy losses. Some Australians who died during an attack on the Turks in August are also buried here. The cemetery contains 50 New Zealanders, 30 Australians and 12 who are entirely unidentified.

United Kingdom

Cliveden War Cemetery, Taplow, Bucks

The cemetery is in an excavation in the high, steep hillside which forms the wooded left bank of the River Thames along the Cliveden House Estate formerly owned by the Astor Family. During the 1914–1918 War, Lady Astor opened this estate for the recuperation of wounded and the presence of a war cemetery in these surroundings is most unusual. It contains 42 burials of the 1914–1918 War, of which 28 were Canadian (two were nursing sisters), and two American; 19 Americans were repatriated after the Armistice. The other burials are British, Australian and New Zealand. The cemetery is laid out as a sunken Roman garden, with symbolic broken pillars, a large font, and an allegoric statue. The markers are the original, rather small plain stones still recumbent on the graves. The cemetery was used by the hospital at Taplow which, from December 1914 to September 1917, was known as the Duchess of Connaught Canadian Red Cross Hospital and then, until September 1919, became No 15 Canadian General Hospital. There are also one Canadian and one British burial of the 1939–1945 War. This cemetery and Cannock Chase War Cemetery are the only two in Britain to have 'War Cemetery' in their title.

Dover (St James's) Cemetery, Kent

Dover was heavily involved in the 1914–1918 and 1939–1945 Wars. In 1914–1918 it was the headquarters of the Royal Navy's Dover Patrol and scores of thousands of troops passed through the port on their way to the Western Front. In the 1939–1945 War the majority of the troops rescued from Dunkirk re-entered Britain through the port. The town was subject to air bombardment and shelling from long-range guns on the French coast throughout most of the war.

Most of the British burials of the 1914–1918 War are in the Zeebrugge Plot. The majority took part in the Zeebrugge raid, the attack on the Belgian port to deny its use to German submarines on 23rd April 1918 – St George's Day. The raid was led by Rear Admiral R.J.B. Keyes, who was recalled to service in the 1939–1945 War as Admiral of the Fleet Sir Roger Keyes. When he died in 1945 he was buried in the plot among his former sailors. (Admiral Keyes' son, Lieutenant Colonel Geoffrey Keyes, was posthumously awarded the VC for leading a raid on Rommel's headquarters in 1941, and is buried in Benghazi War Cemetery, Libya.)

There are 330 British burials of the 1939–1945 War in this cemetery, grouped in a plot at the south-east end.

Additional cemeteries

The following are other cemeteries which have some interesting or unusual details, and are well worth a visit.

Belgium

Essex Farm, Ypres   Lieutenant Colonel John McCrae, Canadian Army Medical Corps, wrote his poem *In Flanders Fields* near here. In the mid-1980s the Provincial Government of West Flanders erected a memorial by the roadside next to the cemetery in his memory. Colonel McCrae is buried in Wimereux Communal Cemetery, France (described above).

Gunners Farm   One of four cemeteries close together, and an example of burials by regimental groups. South-east of Ploegsteert.

Hotton   Marks the limit of the German advance in December 1944 and January 1945. Seventy miles south-east of Brussels.

Ridgewood Military   Chosen as a front line cemetery in May 1915. There was heavy fighting in this area from March to July 1918; 300 Canadian, 260 British, 45 Australian and smaller numbers of other nationalities are buried here. Two miles south of Ypres.

Schoonselhof   There are some very early 1914 burials here, and some caused by V2 rockets in the 1939–1945 War. Three miles south of Antwerp.

France

Adanac   The name is Canada spelled backwards. The cemetery contains Canadian burials from the 1914–1918 War. One of Canada's youngest VCs, James Richardson, is buried here. Near Courcelette, in the Somme.

Bapaume Australian   A front line cemetery, south-east of Bapaume, from the 1914–1918 War. It also contains 25 Germans; these burials were not removed when a German cemetery across the road had all its burials moved to the German cemetery at Villers-au-Flos.

Boiscarré British   An example of destruction in a cemetery by shelling during the 1914–1918 War. The irregular arrangement of rows is testimony to the difficult conditions under which burials were made. Fifteen miles north of Arras.

Bretteville   Of great Canadian interest; 3,000 soldiers are buried here as a result of the Normandy battles of 1944.

Cuckoo Passage   The fighting of early 1917 resulted in this front line cemetery (with this unusual name) receiving over 50 British burials, 40 from the Manchester Regiment. It has an unusual shape due to battle conditions. Some six miles south-east of Arras, near Heninel.

Ecouste   Two neighbouring but separate cemeteries attesting to the heavy fighting in this immediate area, 1917–1918. Ten miles south-east of Arras.

Guards   Near the line of Rommel's 1940 advance. It contains special memorial headstones to 'Buried Elsewhere' or 'Believed To Have Been

Buried In This Cemetery", and memorials to four cremated Indian soldiers. Four miles from Béthune.

Hangard Wood British   A cemetery resulted from frontline fighting in August 1918. It contains about 165 burials of which 20 are French; this area was the junction of British and French forces. Two miles south of Villers-Bretonneux.

Jerusalem (Chouain)   The smallest cemetery in Normandy with about 50 burials. It contains the youngest soldier (Private Jack Banks of the Durham Light Infantry age 16) to die in Normandy, a Baronet, Major Sir Robert Dalrymple, and two Padres (the latter side by side). Five miles south-east of Bayeux.

Le Paradis   The SS massacred nearly 100 Norfolk Regiment soldiers in May 1940, and they are buried here. Six miles north of Béthune.

Longuenesse   A cemetery containing many burials of Commission staff members. Contains graves from the 1914–1918 and 1939–1945 Wars. Near St Omer.

Mazargues   An example of cemetery in southern France, it contains burials of many nationalities of both wars, in Marseilles.

Meerut   Of Indian interest, this cemetery displays a type of headstone different from the Commission's standard marker. Near Boulogne.

Rookery British   A frontline cemetery near Heninel, south-east of Arras. It is unusual in that there is no Cross of Sacrifice (though it contains more than the 40 burials required) because trenches, dugouts and subterranean galleries made the ground too unstable. There is an odd arrangement of graves.

Germany

Cologne Southern   An example of 1914–1918 War cemetery in Germany. It contains the graves of prisoners of war. It also contains the burials of some who died as members of the occupying forces after the 1914–1918 War.

Greece

Suda Bay, Crete   There was heavy fighting on the island after the German parachute landings of May 1941. The cemetery contains 850 British burials, of whom 600 unidentified; 200 Australian, 60 unidentified; and 450 New Zealand, 100 unidentified.

Mikra, Salonika   A Macedonian Campaign cemetery including a memorial to those lost in troop ships during the 1914–1918 War.

Monastir, Salonika   Contains many Indian burials, of casualties sustained in the Macedonian Campaign of the 1914–1918 War.

Iceland

Reykjavik   The only sizeable cemetery in this country, for dead of the 1939–1945 War.

India

Imphal Indian   This cemetery contains nearly 1,700 burials or cremations, mainly of Indian servicemen of the 1939–1945 War.

Indonesia

Ambon and **Djakarta** are the two Commonwealth cemeteries in Indonesia. They commemorate dead of the 1939–1945 War.

Iraq

Kut   The cemetery of the infamous siege of Kut during the 1914–1918 War.

Israel

Jerusalem   A large cemetery resulting from General Sir Edmund Allenby's campaign against the Turks in 1917. Contains the Jerusalem Memorial.

Italy

Agira   Of great Canadian interest: burials here are of Canadians who died in Sicily fighting in 1943.

Anzio   A rare 'battlefield' cemetery in Italy, and close to Beach Head War Cemetery, Anzio.

Bari   A cemetery concentrating burials from other sites, and including victims of a vessel that exploded in the harbour in 1944. It also contains 100 1914–1918 burials from Brindisi, where the site was unmaintainable.

Bolsena   A tank battle was fought nearby, and Field Marshal Alexander's headquarters were on the site, after the liberation of Rome.

Cavalletto   A cemetery at 4000 feet, on the Asiago Plateau in northern Italy, containing burials of the 1914–1918 War. There are four other small British cemeteries nearby.

Ravenna   This cemetery includes the burials of Jews killed in British forces in 1939–1945. Their repatriation was requested by Israel, but the Commission refused on the principle of equality of treatment, that includes no repatriation. There are 400 Canadian, 300 British, 120 Indian and 100 New Zealand among the burials.

Rimini   Of great interest to Gurhkas and Indians. Includes two Gurkha VCs from the 1939–1945 War.

Libya

Knightsbridge (Acroma)   On the site of a key position in 1941–1942, this cemetery contains over 3,500 burials.

Madagascar

Diego Suarez   The cemetery of the Madagascar Campaign of 1942 against the Vichy French.

Namibia

Aus   A cemetery commemorating the campaign of the 1914–1918 War against the Germans in south-west Africa.

Netherlands

Bergen General   A communal cemetery containing over 250 Common-wealth airmen including graves of some of the 'Dambusters' who died in the attack on the Ruhr Dams of May 1943. Local people have erected a propeller blade as a memorial.

Bergen-op-Zoom   This Canadian cemetery ties in with 'British' War Cemetery 200 yards along the road, and both commemorate dead of the 1939–1945 War.

Brunssum   A cemetery resulting from the first operations on German soil by British soldiers, in 1944–1945.

Holten   Contains 1,400 Canadians died March–May 1945.

Hook   Burials include Irish and Welsh Guards, and Royal Marines who formed part of the guard of Queen Wilhelmina when she was evacuated in 1940.

Overloon   Near a good museum, this cemetery is on the site of a heavy battle in October 1944.

Schiermonnikoog   An unusual cemetery on an island in the west Friesian group; has special markers commemorating dead of the 1939–1945 War.

Valkenswaard   The first village liberated in the Netherlands, in September 1944.

Norway

Tromso   This is the most northerly cemetery – well north of the Arctic Circle. 36 British and one New Zealander from the 1939–1945 War are buried here; the latter is, perhaps, the serviceman buried furthest from home.

Papua – New Guinea

Port Moresby   The cemetery contains 3,350 Australian burials, and 440 unknowns from the Royal Artillery.

Poland

Poznan   This cemetery is one of only three Commission cemeteries in Poland, from both wars. The burials are mostly prisoners of war and airmen.

Sweden

Kviberg   A concentration cemetery of Sweden. The bodies of Canadian airmen found in 1970s are buried here, and it also contains dead from both the 1914–1918 and 1939–1945 Wars.

Switzerland

Vevey   The only Commission site in Switzerland, this cemetery is situated on the north-east shore of Lake Geneva. It contains burials from both the 1914–1918 and 1939–1945 Wars.

Syria

Damascus   The site of those who died fighting the Vichy French in the 1939–1945 War, this cemetery also includes 600 burials from the 1914–1918 War.

Thailand

Chungkai   Chungkai and Kanchanaburi are a pair of cemeteries at the Thai end of the Burma–Siam Railway. They will always be linked and remembered because of the prisoners of war who died there in Japanese captivity during the 1939–1945 War.

Tanzania

Morogoro   A cemetery from the East African Campaign of the 1914–1918 War. This campaign lasted for the whole of the 1914–1918 period, involving 20,000 German troops and locally recruited askaris.

Tunisia

Enfidaville   The last battle in the British Eighth Army's great advance across North Africa in the 1939–1945 War.

Turkey

Haidar Pasha   This cemetery contains 600 burials from the Crimean War and is near to the hospital where Florence Nightingale nursed. There are over 500 Commonwealth Army and Navy burials of the 1914–1918 War; and 40 British of the 1939–1945 War.

United Kingdom

Bath (Haycombe)   An example of a 1939–1945 cemetery in England.

Cambridge (City)   An air forces regional cemetery of the 1939–1945 War.

Dishforth   An example of an air base cemetery, this contains RAF and RCAF aircrew and some from New Zealand, South Africa and the United States.

Great Bircham   This cemetery contains the first Cross of Sacrifice erected after the 1939–1945 War, and was used in the 1914–1918 War also. It is located in the Royal Estate at Sandringham, Norfolk.

Harrogate (Stonefall)   Large number of Canadians from 1939–1945 War and a member of the Commission's staff murdered in Tunisia are buried here.

Lenham   All the graves here are the graves of servicemen who died of wounds or gas or were killed in action, such as the members of REME, killed by a V1 flying bomb in 1944; in Kent.

Ontario   Of Canadian interest, this cemetery contains mainly Canadian soldiers who died of wounds from the 1914–1918 War. Near Orpington, Kent.

Oxford   An air forces regional cemetery of the 1939–1945 War.

Torpoint. The resting place of 65 sailors and soldiers killed on 28th April 1941, during German air raid on their camp, HMS *Raleigh*, in Cornwall.

{ 15 }

The Memorials

To have reached thirty is to have
failed in life

'Saki' (Sergeant H.H. Munro,
who died on the Somme – 1870–1916).

T
O SOME VISITORS, THE COMMISSION'S MEMORIALS ARE
of even greater importance, and more moving than the cemeteries,
because the dead they commemorate are totally lost. In some
theatres there is just one memorial. In others, such as the Western Front,
several can be visited in a single day, representing well over 100,000
Commonweath war dead whose deaths were, perhaps, even harder to bear
for relatives than for those whose husbands and sons had known and marked
graves.

The Commission's memorials are not standard, except in one particular
– they all bear names. These may be of those with no known grave; lost or
buried at sea; cremated and whose ashes were scattered, as opposed to
buried; or whose grave cannot be maintained. The following brief
description and notes pertain almost completely to the first two categories –
that is, no known grave or lost or buried at sea. They will be taken in the
order of naval, land, and air.

There are about 200 memorials to the 750,000 missing of the
1914–1918 and 1939–1945 Wars, but it must be remembered that not all
memorials commemorate great numbers. For example, the Zeebrugge
Memorial in the churchyard of that name in Belgium bears just four names –
one the holder of the Victoria Cross. Each memorial has its own register of
names, containing an Introduction, as is the case of the war cemeteries. The
numbers of dead commemorated in the following descriptions are rounded as
appropriate. Following the section on Merchant Navy memorials are Notes
on Additional Memorials in very brief form (again in sections by countries)
on other sites well worth a visit. A list of the memorials described in this
chapter, less 'Additional Memorials', is provided in Appendix F.

Naval memorials

Canada

The Halifax Memorial is situated on a fine site in Point Pleasant Park, overlooking the harbour entrance. The original memorial which stood on Citadel Hill deteriorated badly and had to be demolished in the late 1960s. Its stonework was sunk in the Bedford Basin by the Royal Canadian Navy, who held a ceremony as the last blocks were lowered into the sea. The majority of the 3,000 men named were sailors and merchant seamen of Canada but the memorial also bears the names of soldiers of the Canadian Army stationed in Canada who died but have no known grave; just over 400 of those commemorated died in the 1914–1918 War. As mentioned elsewhere, the central feature of this memorial is the largest Cross of Sacrifice, standing about 40 feet high. The memorial was unveiled by the Honourable H.P. MacKeen, Lieutenant Governor of Nova Scotia, on 12th November 1967.

Even on this memorial a few names are still being added to the Addendum panel in the 1980s as details emerge of Canadian servicemen who died in Canada in the 1914–1918 War but whose place of burial is now unknown.

United Kingdom

The Chatham, Plymouth and Portsmouth Memorials In 1920 it was decided that a memorial at each of the manning ports would be the best way of commemorating the 25,000 sailors who had lost their lives in the Great War. The memorials would be similar and would take the form of a sea-mark near the shore, so combining the memorial with a beacon to guide ships. The memorials were designed by Robert Lorimer and stand on the Great Lines at Chatham, the Hoe at Plymouth (where Sir Francis Drake played his game of bowls while awaiting the Spanish Armada in 1588), and Southsea Common at Portsmouth. The globe which tops each column is supported by the figures of the four winds above the prow of ships.

The globe on the Plymouth Memorial bears an honourable scar which is unique in the Commission's memorials. It has a clearly visible dent on the seaward side where the trailing cable of a barrage balloon, which had broken free, struck it in the 1939–1945 War. Edward Maufe designed extensions to the three memorials to take panels bearing the even more numerous names of the 1939–1945 War.

The Chatham Memorial (1914–1918) was unveiled by the Prince of Wales on 26th April 1924, and the Extension by the Duke of Edinburgh (who had served in the Royal Navy) on 15th October 1952. The Plymouth Memorial bears the names of nearly 2,000 Australian and over 200 South African sailors, sailors from other Commonwealth navies, marines, and soldiers of the Maritime Regiments, Royal Artillery, in addition to sailors of the Royal Navy. The 1914–1918 memorial was unveiled by Prince George (later Duke of Kent, who had served in the Royal Navy and was killed on active service with the RAF in the 1939–1945 War) on 29th July 1924, and the Extension by Princess Margaret on 20th May 1954. Additional panels commemorating those sailors who died ashore but have no known grave were unveiled by Admiral Sir Mark Pizey on 11th November 1956.

The Portsmouth Memorial was unveiled by the Duke of York (who had served in the Royal Navy, was at the Battle of Jutland in 1916 and became King George VI in 1936) on 15th October 1924, and the Extension by his widow, Queen Elizabeth the Queen Mother, on 29th April 1953. Among many brave and dedicated sailors on this Memorial, none was more so than Captain F.J. Walker CB DSO and three Bars, of HMS *Starling*, whose group destroyed more German submarines than any other. He died on 9th July 1944. Chatham commemorates 19,000 war dead, Plymouth 23,000 and Portsmouth 26,000.

Land forces memorials

Belgium

The Messines Ridge New Zealand Memorial stands in the cemetery of that name, and commemorates 830 New Zealanders who died in or near Messines in 1917 and 1918 and have no known grave. The panels bearing their names form the base of the circular wall below the cemetery's Cross of Sacrifice. The Ridge dominates the low ground near Ploegsteert. The village itself was captured by the Germans in November 1914, recaptured by the New Zealand Division on 7th June 1917, retaken by the Germans in April 1918 from the South Africans and fell into British hands in September 1918.

The Ploegsteert Memorial (always 'Plug Street' to the soldiers), in Berks (the abbreviation for the Royal County of Berkshire in England) Cemetery Extension bears the names of the 22,500 British missing who died near the Franco-Belgian border, about a mile away. It takes the form of a large covered circular colonnade designed by H. Chalton Bradshaw; its entrance is guarded by two lions, one snarling, the other benign, carved by Gilbert Ledward.

The Extension in the title of the cemetery refers to the small cemetery on the opposite side of the road, Hyde Park Corner (Royal Berkshire Regiment) Cemetery, to which this is an extension. The Rifle Brigade, with 559 names, has the most numerous representatives. The memorial was unveiled by the Duke of Brabant (a Belgian Province) on 7th June 1931.

The Tyne Cot Memorial forms the seemingly unending rear wall of the largest war cemetery in the Commission's care, Tyne Cot Cemetery, Passchendaele. During consideration of the commemoration of the 100,000 missing of the Ypres Salient, it was found that a division of the names was desirable as well as inevitable. The Menin Gate was a natural site, as an enormous number of men had passed through it on the way to the front line and Ypres represented the obstinacy with which the British Empire had defended that area of Belgium for four years. There was also available space at Tyne Cot, close to the furthest point reached by the Commonwealth armies in Belgium until nearly the end of the war. It was therefore historically appropriate that Tyne Cot should be the site of a memorial and that a date in the summer of 1917, when the advance to Passchendaele was in progress, should be chosen to divide the names of British soldiers between Ypres and Passchendaele. The date chosen was the night of 15th–16th August 1917, when the Battle of Langemarck began. So, British soldiers' names are on the Menin Gate if they died before the 16th, and on Tyne Cot if they died later.

The memorial has no distinctive central feature, but the Stone of Remembrance and the Cross of Sacrifice on a German block house to its front are sufficient. No doubt, many of the thousands of the unknown soldiers buried in the cemetery are among the nearly 34,000 British and over 1,150 New Zealanders named on the memorial. The Lancashire Fusiliers, with 1,304 names, are the most heavily represented British regiment, for New Zealand it is the Otago Regiment with 287 names.

A service of dedication only was held on 19th June 1927.

The Ypres (Menin Gate) Memorial (its official name) spans one of the two main gateways into the town. It was through the Menin Gate, a roadway flanked by two stone lions where the medieval gate once stood, that hundreds of thousands of Commonwealth soldiers passed on their way to the battlefields of the Ypres Salient. The memorial was designed by Reginald Blomfield and joins the two ends of Vauban's defensive ramparts (which did exist even though the gate itself did not) by means of a great arch spanning the road to Menin. The panels inside the 120 foot-long arch, the stairways and upper loggias, bear the names of 40,000 British (who died before 16th August 1917), 7,000 Canadian, 6,000 Australian, nearly 600 South African, and 400 Indian soldiers who died in the Salient and have no known grave. New Zealand decided that the names of its missing should be commemorated on various New Zealand memorials nearer to the place where the missing were presumed to have died. The memorial was considerably damaged during the fighting of spring 1940, but it has been repaired, less a few honourable scars. The regiments most represented are King's Royal Rifle Corps with 1,444 names for the United Kingdom; the Canadian Mounted Rifles with 721; the Australian Machine Gun Corps with 244; 1st Regiment South African Infantry with 166; and 57th Wilde's Rifles (Frontier Force) with 79 names for India.

The memorial was unveiled by Field Marshal Lord Plumer of Messines in the presence of King Albert I of the Belgians on 24th July 1927. It is perhaps the best known war memorial anywhere. The main road which runs under the arch is closed by the police every day at 2000 hours, when members of the local fire service sound Last Post. This has happened daily since 1929, except during the German occupation of 1940–1944, and is a ceremony which is still well attended by local people, but particularly by visitors and pilgrims.

Burma

The Rangoon Memorial is situated in Taukkyan War Cemetery, about 20 miles north of Rangoon, and records the names of over 4,000 British, 50 South Africans, nearly 20,000 Indians, and well over 2,000 from East and West Africa who died in the Burma Campaign of 1941–1945 and have no known graves. The memorial, designed by Henry Brown, is composed of two long colonnades which form covered walks and bear the names. The two wings of the memorial are joined by an open rotunda which bears the dedicatory inscription. The memorial, the largest numerically of the 1939–1945 War, is testimony to the fierce fighting against the Japanese by the British Fourteenth Army.

The regiments and corps most represented are, for the United Kingdom, the Royal Artillery with 362 names; for South Africa the Native Military Corps with 40; for India the Royal Indian Army Service Corps with 2557; for East Africa the King's African Rifles with 484; and for West Africa the Nigeria Regiment with 611 names.

The memorial was unveiled by General Sir Francis Festing, Commander-in-Chief of the British Far East Land Forces, in the presence of the Honorable U Nu, Prime Minister of Burma, on 9th February 1958.

Egypt

The Alamein Memorial stands at the entrance to El Alamein War Cemetery and takes the form of a cloister 270 feet long. It commemorates nearly 9,000 soldiers of the Western Desert Forces and Eighth Army who died in the campaigns in Egypt and Libya, and in the operations in Tunisia up to 19th February 1943 – the date when the Eighth Army came under the overall command of General Dwight Eisenhower of the United States – and who have no known grave. It also commemorates those who died in Syria and Lebanon, Iraq and Persia (now Iran) and have no known grave. Nearly 5,000 of these were British, nearly 800 New Zealanders, over 300 Australian, 800 South African and 1800 from India.

For the British, the Royal Horse Artillery and Royal Artillery have the most names with 1020; for Australia, the 2nd/28th Battalion with 48; for New Zealand the Infantry with 551; for South Africa the Artillery and Cape Corps with 128 each; and for India, the Royal Indian Army Service Corps with 181.

The memorial also commemorates airmen who have no known grave and were based on the countries already mentioned and in addition on Greece, the Aegean, Ethiopia, Sudan, East Africa, Aden (now South Yemen) and Madagascar. Also commemorated are those who served in the Rhodesian and South African Air Training Scheme. Two thousand of these airmen were from Britain; 200 from Canada; 300 from Australia; 90 from New Zealand; and over 450 from South Africa.

The memorial was designed by Hubert Worthington and unveiled on

24th October 1954 by Field Marshal Viscount Montgomery of Alamein, the Commander of the Eighth Army at the Battle of Alamein.

France

The Arras Memorial stands in the Commission's cemetery at Faubourg d'Amiens, in south-west Arras near Vauban's Citadel. It is a cloister nearly 400 feet long, built up on Doric columns. At one part of the memorial the colonnade returns to form a recessed and open court, in which is the Flying Services Memorial. The names of the 35,000 British and 80 South African soldiers who died in the Battles of Arras from the spring of 1916 to 7th August 1918 (the eve of the advance to victory or the 'Hundred Days') and have no known grave are carved on the cloister walls. There is an exception in the case of those who died in the Battle of Cambrai (one of the Battles of Arras), who are commemorated on the Cambrai Memorial. The regiments with the largest number of names on the memorial are the Royal Fusiliers (City of London Regiment) with 1,422, and the Northumberland Fusiliers with 1,378.

The names of the 1,000 airmen in, or attached to, the Royal Naval Air Service, Royal Flying Corps (the Corps up to 31st March 1918) and Royal Air Force (from 1st April 1918, when the RAF was formed) who died on the whole Western Front, and have no known grave are on the Flying Services Memorial. They include those of 50 Canadians and 10 Australians, and that of Major Edward Mannock VC who, with 73 air victories, was the most successful airman on the Commonwealth side.

The memorial was designed by Edwin Lutyens; the Flying Services Memorial, of which the sculpture is by William Reid Dick, is a square pillar. On top of the pillar is a globe, oriented as Earth was poised in space at 1100 hours on 11th November 1918, Armistice Day. Five winged comets, representing the five years of the war, encircle the globe, symbolizing the forces of the air.

The Arras Memorial was unveiled by Marshal of the RAF Lord Trenchard ('Father of the RAF') on 31st July 1932.

The Bayeux Memorial stands on the opposite side of the road fronting Bayeux War Cemetery in Normandy. It was designed by Philip Hepworth (the principal architect of the war cemeteries in Normandy). It is an open colonnade and bears the names of over 1,500 British and nearly 300 Canadian soldiers who died in Normandy or in the advance to the River Seine between 6th June and 29th August 1944 and have no known grave. Bayeux is associated with William the Conqueror, whose invasion of England in 1066 is depicted in the Bayeux Tapestry. It was, perhaps appropriately, the first important French town to be liberated in 1944. The road alongside which the memorial and war cemetery stand was constructed during the campaign as a town by-pass and was named after Major General Sir Fabian Ware in recognition of his work for Anglo-French friendship while he was Vice-Chairman of the (then) Imperial War Graves Commission. The inscription in Latin (perhaps written tongue-in-cheek) may be translated as: 'We, once conquered by William, have now set free the Conqueror's native land.' The regiments with the largest numbers of names are, for the United Kingdom, the Gloucestershire Regiment with 171 and, for Canada, 1st Hussars with 35.

The memorial was unveiled by the Duke of Gloucester (then President of the Commission) on 5th June 1955.

The Beaumont-Hamel (Newfoundland) Memorial is, strictly, a battle-exploit memorial, and is maintained by the Commission on behalf of the Canadian authorities. The memorial proper is a large earth and stone cairn, surmounted by a defiant bronze caribou (the badge of the Newfoundland Regiment). The cairn has a spiral path on it for access to the caribou and heather and other plants grow on it. Set into the base of the cairn are bronze panels bearing the names of 800 soldiers of the Royal Newfoundland Regiment and sailors of the Newfoundland Royal Naval Reserve and Mercantile Marine who died in the 1914–1918 War and have no known grave or no grave but the sea.

The memorial park in which the memorial stands was opened by Field Marshal Earl Haig on 7th June 1925. It contains three Commission war cemeteries: Hawthorn Ridge Cemetery No 2, Hunter's Cemetery, and 'Y' Ravine Cemetery.

The Delville Wood Memorial stands in the Bois d'Elville, about seven miles north-east of Albert. It is South Africa's National Memorial, and it was decided that it should bear no names. The South Africans who died in France and have no known grave are commemorated on the memorials at Arras (80), Cambrai (5), Pozières (320), Thiepval (830) and Vis-en-Artois (16). The Delville Wood Memorial honours all South Africans who fell in the 1914–1918 War, not only in France, but in Flanders, Egypt, Palestine, East Africa and other theatres of war. Herbert Baker was the architect of the memorial and also of Delville Wood Cemetery, on the other side of its fronting road. A grass avenue, 750 feet long, leads from the entrance on the road to a semi-circular screen wall of knapped flint and dressed stone. In the centre is an arched building topped by a bronze charger between two men, symbolic of the comradeship between those of Dutch and English origin who, only about 15 years before, had been enemies in the Anglo-Boer War in South Africa. The memorial was unveiled on 10th October 1926 by Mrs Botha, widow of the South African statesman, General Louis Botha. He was Commander-in-Chief of the Boer forces in the Anglo-Boer War, later became Prime Minister, captured South-West Africa from the Germans in 1914–1915 and died in 1919. Present were France's Maréchal Joseph Joffre and Field Marshal Earl Haig.

On 5th June 1952, the memorial was re-dedicated and a new altar-stone, standing in front of the memorial, similar to the Stone of Remembrance was unveiled in memory of South Africans who had died in the 1939–1945 War. The unveiler was Mrs Swales, mother of Major Edwin Swales, a South African, who was awarded the VC posthumously in 1945 and is buried in Leopoldsburg War Cemetery, Belgium.

The Neuve-Chapelle Memorial is on the road from Estaires to La Bassée where it is crossed by the road from Armentières to Béthune. It was chosen as the site of the Indian Army's Memorial because the Indian Corps fought here with great gallantry in March 1915. It bears the names of the 5,000 Indians who died in France during the 1914–1918 War and have no known grave. (Most of their fighting troops were withdrawn in 1915 to fight on the Gallipoli Peninsula, and in the Middle East.)

The memorial was designed by Herbert Baker, who shared with Edwin Lutyens in the planning of New Delhi. It consists of a circular wall enclosing a sanctuary at the centre of which there is a Stone of Remembrance as focal point. Half of the circular wall is solid and bears the panels on which are the names of the missing. The other half of the wall is of pierced stonework after the Indian style. In the middle of the solid wall, and rising from it, is a 50-feet-high column, reminiscent of similar columns in India erected by Emperor Asoka, guarded by two flanking tigers carved by Charles Wheeler, looking out from the memorial.

The regiment and corps represented by the largest number of names are the 8th Gurkha Rifles with 306, and the Indian Labour Corps with 372. The memorial was unveiled by the Earl of Birkenhead, Secretary of State for India (whose home at 32 Grosvenor Gardens, London SW1, later became the Commission's Head Office), in the presence of Maréchal Ferdinand Foch, on 7th October 1927.

In 1964 a bronze panel was added to the memorial, bearing the names of 200 soldiers and seamen of undivided India whose graves at Zehrensdorf Indian Cemetery, East Germany, could not be maintained (the site was in a tank training ground).

The Thiepval Memorial stands near the rebuilt village of that name about four miles north of Albert in the Department of the Somme. It commemorates over 70,000 British and 830 South African soldiers who died during the period starting in July 1915, when the British Third Army took over from the French, through the Battles of the Somme in 1916 to 20th March 1918, the eve of the last great German offensive on the Somme.

The site was chosen partly because it was on high ground and partly for its historical associations. Of the positions attacked on 1st July 1916 (the day on which 20,000 British soldiers were *killed* on the Western Front – more than on any other day anywhere) Thiepval, garrisoned for nearly two years by the 180th Regiment of Württembergers, was perhaps the strongest and certainly the most obstinately defended of the Somme villages blotted out; it was even considered for permanent erasure from the list of French municipalities.

The memorial was designed by Edwin Lutyens and is the largest of the memorials built by the Commission. Its brick superstructure is carried on 16 masonry piers, which have four panelled faces (if internal piers) and three if they are external; the names are on the panels. In the decade ending in 1985, the brick facing was entirely replaced by new, even stronger, engineering bricks which are better able to resist the winter's freezing, rain-laden winds. It is about 150 feet high and its ground dimensions are 120 by 140 feet; its general aspect is that of a series of vast, brooding arches, supported by the piers. The focal point of the memorial is the Stone of Remembrance, which lies under the great arch and centrally between the piers. The regiments most represented are the Northumberland Fusiliers with 2931 names and the Royal Fusiliers (City of London Regiment) with 2502 names.

The memorial was designed to fly two flags at its summit, the Union Flag and the French flag, and was unveiled by the Prince of Wales on 1st August 1932 in the presence of M Albert Lebrun, President of the French Republic.

The virtually adjoining Thiepval Anglo-French Cemetery has a Cross of Sacrifice, and contains 300 Commonwealth and 300 French war dead, most of whom are unidentified. The Cross's podium bears a text, unusual on the Western Front, which reads in English and French:

THAT THE WORLD MAY REMEMBER THE COMMON SACRIFICE

OF TWO AND A HALF MILLION DEAD HERE HAVE BEEN LAID

SIDE BY SIDE SOLDIERS OF FRANCE AND OF THE BRITISH

EMPIRE IN ETERNAL COMRADESHIP.

The bodies of the Commonwealth soldiers buried here were found between December 1931 and March 1932, the majority being from the battlefields of the Somme of July to November 1916; they include four Canadians, ten Australians and a New Zealander.

The Villers-Bretonneux Memorial stands about ten miles to the east of Amiens, a little north of the road to St Quentin at the rear of Villers-Bretonneux Military Cemetery, Fouilloy. It is not only the National Memorial to the Australian feats of arms in France and Belgium during the 1914–1918 War, but also bears the names of nearly 11,000 Australians who died in the Battles of the Somme, Arras, and the 'Hundred Days' and who have no known grave. Other Australians who died in France and have no known grave are commemorated on the VC Corner Memorial, Fromelles.

The memorial was designed by Edwin Lutyens and its plan is in the form of an open quadrangle of high stone walls on which are inscribed the names of the missing. In the centre of the wall is a 100-feet-high tower which serves as an observation point for the vast area of the Somme battlefields. This, no doubt, explains why the memorial was severely damaged by shelling in the debacle of spring 1940 when the French made a stand for some days. Among its honourable scars is a bullet hole in the bronze door of the box containing the memorial's register of names. The greatest number of names is of soldiers from the 28th Battalion (Western Australia).

The memorial was unveiled by King George VI on 22nd July 1938 in the presence of Queen Elizabeth and M Albert Lebrun, President of the French Republic.

The Vimy Memorial stands on Hill 145, the highest point on the Ridge of that name about seven miles north of Arras. Its site was chosen in recognition of the Canadians' great feat of arms in April 1917 when, fighting as a corps, they took the heights which dominate the Plain of Douai.

It is, first and foremost, the National Memorial, erected on 250 acres of land given by France to Canada, in the country where most Canadian soldiers served and on the battlefield which made the Canadian Corps famous. Second, it is the memorial to the 11,000 Canadians who died in France and have no known grave and whose names are inscribed on the outer face of the enclosing wall. Despite the fact that this is not a Commission memorial, it was agreed between the Canadian government and the Commission that the inscription of the names of the Canadian missing in France would be fitting, and therefore further commemoration elsewhere by the Commission would be superfluous.

The memorial was designed by Walter S. Allward, a Toronto sculptor. Its essential parts are the retaining wall in front, the enclosing walls and the platform within them, and the two high pylons, visible from a score miles, rising from the platform. One of the pylons bears the crown and maple leaf, the other the fleur-de-lis and the laurel. Twenty sculptured figures, on or beside the pylons and the walls, symbolise Canada, her soldiers, and her ideals. The names of the Canadian provinces and Canadian units are carved on the inner side of the enclosing walls, and the Battle Honours and the dedicatory inscription are on the faces of the pylons.

The memorial was unveiled by King Edward VIII on 26th July 1936, in the presence of M Albert Lebrun, President of the French Republic.

Hong Kong

The Sai Wan Bay Memorial which is in the form of an 80-feet-long shelter building, stands at the entrance of the war cemetery of that name, seven miles from the capital, Victoria. There is a semi-circular forecourt leading to two entrances to the building and inside are inscribed the names of the 2000 Commonwealth soldiers and 100 Hong Kong Police who lost their lives in the Japanese attack on Hong Kong in December 1941, in subsequent captivity, or at sea, and have no known grave. There are 1300 soldiers from Britain; 230 from Canada; 300 from India; and 130 from the Hong Kong Local Forces. The regiments most represented are, for the United Kingdom, the Royal Artillery with 305; for Canada, the Winnipeg Grenadiers with 114; for India, the 7th Rajput Regiment with 187 and the Hong Kong Volunteer Defence Corps with 115.

The memorial and the war cemetery were designed by Colin St Clair Oakes. It now also commemorates the 72 British and Indians whose graves of the 1914–1918 and 1939–1945 Wars in China are now lost.

Italy

The Cassino Memorial stands in the war cemetery of that name (the largest in Italy), about a mile south-west of the town and about 85 miles south-east of Rome. Close behind it the hills rise rapidly to the dominating feature of Monte Cassino on which stands the famous monastery founded by St Benedict in 529 AD. Cassino was the most stubborn obstacle encountered by the Allies in the liberation of Italy which began in mid-1943 with the invasion of Sicily and steps to secure it included the destruction of the monastery by air bombing. After months of bitter fighting, the feature was taken in mid-May 1944. The memorial commemorates Commonwealth soldiers who died in the fighting in Italy (including Sicily) and have no known grave. It consists of a formal garden with an ornamental pool in the centre, on each side of which are marble pillars on which are inscribed the names of 2350 British, 200 Canadian, 55 New Zealand, 13 South African and 1450 Indian soldiers. The regiment most represented are, for the United Kingdom, the South Staffordshire Regiment with 144 names; for Canada, the Royal 22e Regiment with 19; for New Zealand, the Infantry with 49; and for India, the 5th Mahratta Light Infantry with 224.

The memorial was designed by Louis de Soissons, the Commission's principal architect for cemeteries of the 1939–1945 War in Italy. It was unveiled on 30th September 1956 by Field Marshal the Earl Alexander of Tunis, the former Commander-in-Chief in Italy and Governor-General of Canada from 1946 to 1952.

Singapore

The Singapore Memorial stands at the rear of Kranji War Cemetery, 14 miles north of the city and overlooking the Straits of Johore. The central avenue of the cemetery rises gently from the Stone of Remembrance near the entrance to the Cross of Sacrifice, beyond which flights of steps lead to the top of the hill on which the memorial stands. It consists of a building of a dozen piers carrying a flat roof, with a tall central tower surmounted by a star, the whole at first glance not unlike the tail unit of a giant aeroplane. The memorial commemorates 24,000 soldiers and airmen who died in the war against Japan from 1941 to 1945 and have no known grave. Six thousand eight hundred of these soldiers came from Britain; 1400 from Australia; 12,000 from India; and 1000 from Malaya (including the Malayan Police Forces). They died in the campaigns in Malaya and Indonesia or in subsequent captivity. The names also include many who died in the building of the Burma-Thailand railway, or lost their lives at sea while being shipped from Malaya to prison camps elsewhere. Two thousand five hundred of the airmen came from the United Kingdom; 200 each from Canada and Australia; 60 from New Zealand; five from South Africa; six from Malaya; and 50 from India. Their places of death were even more widely scattered than the soldiers' and were in the whole of southern and eastern Asia and the surrounding waters. The names of the dead, Land followed by Air Forces, are on panels fixed to the piers. The dedicatory inscription is on a curved panel at the foot of the central tower.

The regiments most represented are, for the United Kingdom, the Royal Artillery with 2235 names; for Australia, the 2nd/19th Battalion Australian Infantry with 246; for India, the 14th Punjab Regiment with 866; and for Malaya the Malay Regiment with 229.

The memorial and war cemetery were designed by Colin St Clair Oakes, and the memorial was unveiled on 2nd March 1957 by Sir Robert Black, who had been a prisoner of war of the Japanese and was then Governor and Commander-in-Chief, Singapore. He was later to become a Member of the Commission for many years.

Turkey

The Helles Memorial stands at Cape Helles at the south-west tip of the Gallipoli Peninsula. It is an obelisk 100 feet high and serves as a sea-mark for shipping. Few memorials can stand closer to the scene of the actual fighting where so many of those it commemorates died, for it was on the beaches below that the principal and most costly landings were made, starting on 25th April 1915. The obelisk stands on a raised platform and bears the dedicatory and other inscriptions. It is surrounded by a wall, on both sides of which are carved the names of the 19,000 British, 250 Australian, and 1500 Indians who died in the Gallipoli Peninsula Campaign from 25th April until the last British troops were withdrawn in January 1916 and have no known grave; or were buried at sea from hospital ships, or were on ships which were sunk while taking them to or from the Peninsula.

Of the regiments named on the memorial, the Lancashire Fusiliers, with 1246, sustained the heaviest losses. The memorial was designed by John Burnett.

United Kingdom

The Brookwood Memorial in the Military Cemetery of that name, commemorates 3500 men and women of the land forces who, in the 1939–1945 War, died at sea, in the campaign in Norway in 1940, as members of raiding parties that set out from the United Kingdom (including those against St Nazaire and Dieppe), or on service outside the main theatres of war and who have no known grave. The great majority are from Britain (3200) and Canada (200). The memorial, a rotunda of Portland stone with green slate panels bearing the names, was designed by Ralph Hobday, the Commission's own architect, and unveiled by Queen Elizabeth II on 25th October 1958.

The Brookwood (Russia) Memorial was completed in 1984. This commemorates all those from the Commonwealth (620 British, 26 Canadians and one Australian) who died in Russia or the Soviet Union in the 1914–1918 War and 1939–1945 Wars, whose graves are either unknown or, if known, unmaintainable or maintainable only with difficulty as access by Commission staff is infrequent. This is a rare (if not unique) case of the Commission accepting dual commemoration as the markers are being left standing, though many even of these are special memorial headstones bearing superscriptions to actual graves that are elsewhere. There was no formal unveiling.

The Hollybrook Memorial in the civil cemetery on the northern side of Southampton, is especially the memorial of those who, in the 1914–1918 War, went down in transports or other ships in home waters. It also includes the names of others who died in the United Kingdom or in distant areas and whose bodies could not be recovered. It is, so to speak, a clearing memorial to cover those who do not fall into such categories as to make them appropriate for any other memorial.

The memorial illustrates the Commission's principle of equality: the name of Field Marshal Lord Kitchener of Khartoum, Secretary of State for War, is carved in the same size and style of lettering as that of one Private Paraffin (he had no other name) of the South African Native Labour Corps, who died in a troop transport. The memorial bears nearly 2000 names, including those of 800 British, 60 Canadians, 160 Australians, and 700 South Africans.

The memorial was unveiled on 10th December 1930 by Field Marshal Sir William Robertson, Chief of the Imperial General Staff for most of the 1914–1918 War, and a soldier who was promoted through all ranks from private to field marshal.

The unit most heavily represented on the memorial is the South African Labour Corps, of which Private Paraffin was one of 596.

Air forces memorials

The principal air force memorials are those at Alamein and Singapore (combined with the Army's described earlier) and Runnymede and Malta (which follow), and Ottawa. There are others, with small numbers of names mainly in Australia and the south-west Pacific, some of which have been described. The great majority of those commemorated died while flying or in aircrashes, but there was a sizeable minority who died while not on flying duties – in troopships or in air attacks on their airfields. The essential point when deciding where an airman was to be commemorated was where he was based, not necessarily the area in which he was presumed lost.

Malta GC

The Malta Memorial stands in the Floriana District of Malta's capital, Valletta, and consists of a column, about 50 feet high, surmounted by a large gilded bronze eagle with outstretched wings. The column stands on a circular base, around which the names are commemorated on bronze panels; the memorial area takes the form of large garden, with approach paths. The 2300 Commonwealth airmen commemorated here died in the 1939–1945 War while based in and around the Mediterranean, and as far north as Austria and south to Tunisia, and have no known graves. The airmen were in the following Air Forces: 1550 in the RAF; 300 in the Royal Canadian; 200 in the Royal Australian; 85 in the Royal New Zealand; and 170 in the South African.

The memorial was designed by Hubert Worthington and unveiled by Queen Elizabeth II on 3rd May 1954. Her Majesty had previously been stationed in Malta as the wife of Prince Philip, while a serving officer in the Royal Navy.

United Kingdom

The Runnymede Memorial stands on Cooper's Hill, overlooking Runnymede, the Thames-side pastures three miles east of Windsor where King John signed Magna Carta in 1215. The large site was given to the Commission by Sir Eugen and Lady Effie Millington-Drake. (Sir Eugen was British Ambassador to Uruguay at the time of the Battle of the River Plate in December 1939.)

The design of the memorial consists of a square cloister. On the far side from the entrance is a tower, reminiscent of a war-time airfield control tower, available for access and giving fine views. The cloister on this side, which is on the edge of a wooded hill and overlooks the River Thames, has two curved wings, terminating in look-outs, one facing Windsor, the other Heathrow, London's main airport.

The tower has a central arched opening above which are three stone figures sculptured by Vernon Hill, representing Justice, Victory, and Courage. The focal point for ceremonies is the Stone of Remembrance on the lawn enclosed by the cloisters, and for contemplation, a chapel in the tower.

The memorial commemorates 20,000 airmen and airwomen of the Commonwealth Air Forces who, during the 1939–1945 War, died over north-western and central Europe, the British Isles, and the eastern Atlantic, while in any of the Air Forces Commands, and have no known grave. These airmen were in the following Air Forces: Royal Air Force 15,400 (including 25 from Newfoundland); Royal Canadian, 3050; Royal Australian 1400; Royal New Zealand 600; South African 17; Royal Indian seven, with others from the Women's Auxiliary Air Force, British Overseas Airways Corporation, etc.

The memorial was designed by Edward Maufe and was unveiled by Queen Elizabeth II on 17th October 1953.

Mercantile marine/merchant navy memorial

The Tower Hill Memorial in London is the only memorial which commemorates merchant seamen exclusively. Those from the other Commonwealth countries are on dual (or mixed) memorials.

The Tower Hill Memorial stands on a fine site near the Tower of London and commemorates (civilian) seamen of the Mercantile Marine (as it was known in the 1914–1918 War), and the Merchant Navy (1939–1945 War), and Fishing Fleets who died as a result of the two wars and have no grave but the sea. In one respect, the memorial is similar to the naval memorials at Chatham, Plymouth and Portsmouth, in that a 1914–1918 War memorial to those lost but who have no grave but the sea has been extended to take the more numerous names of the 1939–1945 War.

The 1914–1918 War Memorial was designed by Edwin Lutyens and takes the form of a portico or vaulted corridor. Bronze panels inside commemorate 12,000 British seamen, including two, Masters Parslow* and Smith, who won the Victoria Cross. It was unveiled by Queen Mary on 12th December 1928, in place of King George V, who was seriously ill.

The memorial is linked to the 1939–1945 War memorial, which was designed by Edward Maufe, by flights of stone steps leading into a sunken garden. The names of the 24,000 British and 50 Australian seamen are on bronze panels set against the retaining walls of the sunken garden. Between the 1914–1918 Memorial and Extension are two tall columns against which stand sculptured figures representing seamen of the Merchant Navy. These are the work of Charles Wheeler.

The memorial was unveiled by Queen Elizabeth II on 5th November 1955.

The following are other memorials which have some interesting or unusual details and are well worth a visit.

Additional memorials
Naval

Bangladesh

Chittagong 1939–1945 A memorial book in Bengali to sailors and seamen of the Indian Navy and Merchant Navy is displayed in Chittagong War Cemetery; the Hindi version is at Bombay, India.

---

* Now, 1988, known to be buried in Cobh Old Church Cemetery, Co. Cork, Republic of Ireland.

India

Bombay 1939–1945   The Hindi version of the Chittagong Memorial in the Indian Sailors' Home. The Home also contains the 1914–1918 Sailors' Memorial in the form of inscribed panels.

New Zealand

Auckland   The only New Zealand naval memorial for the 1939–1945 War; at Devonport Naval Base.

United Kingdom

Lee-on-Solent   The only memorial to the Fleet Air Arm of the Royal Navy.
Liverpool   The only memorial to those of the 'T124' Agreement, which covered seamen of the Merchant Navy who agreed to serve with the Royal Navy in the 1939–1945 War.
Lowestoft   The only memorial to the Royal Naval Patrol Service in the 1939–1945 War.

Land Forces

Belgium

Buttes New Zealand   Located in Polygon Wood Cemetery, Zonnebeke, commemorating the 1914–1918 War.
Nieuport   Commemorates some of the earliest British missing from action in 1914; freestanding.

Egypt

Chatby   A 1914–1918 memorial for land forces lost at sea; in Alexandria (Chatby) Cemetery.
Heliopolis (Aden)   A replacement memorial; the original bronze panels in Aden were stolen. In Heliopolis War Cemetery; most of the dead are from the Indian Army of the 1914–1918 War.
Heliopolis (Port Tewfik)   Also a replacement memorial, completed in 1980. The original, to 4000 soldiers of the Indian Army killed in the 1914–1918 War, was destroyed in Israeli-Egyptian fighting in the 1970s.

France

Cambrai   The memorial covering the 1917 battle where tanks were used in large numbers for the first time. It commemorates 7000 British soldiers.
Caterpillar Valley   This is the largest New Zealand memorial on the Western Front and bears 1200 names; Longueval, Somme.

Dunkirk The memorial to those who died in the first large-scale fighting in the west in the 1939–1945 War. Commemorates 4500 British soldiers.
Grévillers New Zealand Memorial to 450 soldiers who died March to August 1918.
Le Ferté-Sous-Jouarre The only memorial to British Regular Army *only*. Commemorates 3750 British soldiers lost August–October 1914.
Le Touret A large memorial to early 1914 and 1915 fighting. Commemorates 13,400 British soldiers lost from November 1914 to 24th September 1915. Located in Le Touret Military Cemetery, four miles north-east of Béthune in Pas-de-Calais.
Loos This memorial follows the period covered by Le Touret above. Located in Dud Corner Cemetery, six miles south-east of Béthune, it commemorates 20,500 British soldiers including Rudyard Kipling's son Lieutenant John, and Captain the Honourable Fergus Bowes-Lyon, the brother of Elizabeth Bowes-Lyon, who became Queen in December 1936, as Consort of King George VI.
Soissons This memorial commemorates 4000 British soldiers lost during May–July 1918. An unusual sculptured group of three soldiers in greatcoats is used as the main theme.
VC Corner Of much interest to Australians, this memorial commemorates their earliest fighting in France during July 1916; at Fromelles.
Vis-en-Artois One of the most handsome memorials, it commemorates nearly 20,000 British and 16 South Africans lost during the Advance to Victory 8th August 1918 to the Armistice. Located eight miles south-east of Arras in Vis-en-Artois British Cemetery, Haucourt.

Greece

Athens The only memorial to the Greek Campaigns of 1941 and 1944, and the last to be unveiled, on 10th May 1961. Nearly 3000 British, Australian and New Zealanders are commemorated here.
Doiran The only memorial to the Macedonian Campaign of 1914–1918; it bears 2000 names.

India

Delhi Of great interest to Indians, this memorial commemorates 1200 British and 12,300 Indian soldiers lost in or beyond the North-west Frontier Province in the 1914–1918 War.
Delhi 1939–1945 In Delhi War Cemetery is a book in Hindi that commemorates 25,000 names and corresponds to the Karachi Memorial, Pakistan.

Iran

Tehran   Of great interest to Indians of whom 3400 are commemorated, plus 200 British.

Iraq

Basra   The only memorial to the Mesopotamian Campaign ('Mespot' to the soldiers), and one of the Commission's largest, commemorating 7000 British and 33,000 Indian soldiers lost in the campaign against the Turks 1914–1918. Until the 1960s this memorial was in full view from the Shatt-al-Arab, the river formed by the confluence of the Rivers Tigris and Euphrates, but is now obscured by a wall-like memorial, erected by the Iraqis. The Commission has not yet, in the late 1980s, been able to have the wall removed and in view of the current Iraq–Iran situation, no early resolution is in sight.

Israel

Jerusalem   The only memorial to the missing of Allenby's victorious campaign against the Turks in the 1914–1918 War. Located in Jerusalem War Cemetery.

Kenya

East Africa   The only memorial to the East African Campaign of the 1939–1945 War. Located in Nairobi War Cemetery.

Malaysia

Labuan   Of great significance to Australia, this memorial commemorates 2300 of her soldiers, including 50 airmen, plus 65 local forces who died as prisoners-of-war at the hands of the Japanese in Borneo and in the Philippines from 1941–1945. Located in Labuan War Cemetery, Sabah.

Netherlands

Groesbeek   The only memorial to the period from 30th August 1944 (crossing of the River Seine, France) to VE Day. Located in Groesbeek Canadian War Cemetery. It commemorates 950 British (including 180 airborne troops, most lost at Arnhem in 1944) and 100 Canadians. Its architectural merit may be apparent after contemplation.

Pakistan

Karachi   This memorial commemorates 25,000 dead from the 1939–1945 War and is located in Karachi War Cemetery. It corresponds to the Delhi 1939–1945 Memorial and is a book in Urdu.

Papua New Guinea

Rabaul   The memorial commemorates 1300 Australians lost in fighting against the Japanese 1942–1945.

Sudan

Khartoum   The only memorial in Sudan – 25 of those named were discovered in 1981. It commemorates dead of the 1939–1945 War. Located in Khartoum War Cemetery.

Tunisia

Medjez-el-Bab   Located in the war cemetery of that name, this memorial commemorates 1800 British, 40 New Zealanders and 140 Indians from the British First and Eighth Armies.

Turkey

Chunuk   Of great interest to New Zealand as 850 of her soldiers who died in 1915 are commemorated; this memorial is at Anzac, Gallipoli Peninsula.
Lone Pine   Over 4200 Australian soldiers are commemorated on this memorial located at Anzac, Gallipoli Peninsula.

Air Forces

Canada

Ottawa   This memorial commemorates 800 airmen and women of the Commonwealth air forces lost while serving from bases in Canada, USA and the Caribbean during the 1939–1945 War.

{ 16 }

Victoria Cross and George Cross recipients who died in the war periods

Cowards die many times before their deaths,
The Valiant never taste of death but once

William Shakespeare (1564–1616).
Julius Caesar

I
N GENERAL, ALL THE MEN AND WOMEN WHO DIED IN THE two world wars have graves with uniform markers, or if there is no known grave, or remains were cremated, or the grave is unmaintainable, their names are inscribed on a Commission memorial. An exception to the principle of equality of treatment was made for those who had been awarded the Victoria Cross, and for the George Cross after its institution in 1940. A visitor usually feels a particular interest in the grave or the place of commemoration of the serviceman who received one of the decorations which take precedence over all others and are, perhaps, the most highly-prized decorations for bravery in the world. A facsimile of the decoration on a grave marker, instead of the religious emblem, was instituted. When a name appears on a memorial, the letters VC have usually been placed in front of the surname, to catch the eye of the viewer. None of this applies, of course, to those graves of VCs and GCs buried by the next of kin in their own home countries, and subsequently marked by permanent private memorials.

The Victoria Cross was instituted in 1856 under Queen Victoria, but made retroactive to the autumn of 1854, to cover the period of the Crimean War. It is awarded for acts of valour or self-sacrifice of the highest order – virtually always in the face of the enemy. Women in the services are eligible, but no award has been made to date.

The George Cross was instituted in September 1940 and was intended primarily for civilian men and women who, as with the Victoria Cross recipients, performed acts of great valour, but not necessarily in the face of the enemy. Members of the armed services were also eligible. Several women have been awarded this cross. Appendix D lists the recipients of the VC and GC entitled to 'war graves treatment' in alphabetical order of the

172

countries and sites in which they are buried, or the memorials on which they are commemorated.

According to available information, there are 259 holders of the VC from the 1914–1918 War and 111 from the 1939–1945 War (a total of 370) who are commemorated by headstones or, if they have no known grave, or no grave but the sea, were cremated, or the grave is unmaintainable, by the inscription of the name on a Commission memorial. Sixty-six recipients of the GC are similarly commemorated. At least another eight were awarded the Albert Medal (AM) which, had they lived, would have been exchanged for the GC.

The cemeteries with the largest numbers of VCs and GCs are: Taukkyan War Cemetery, Burma (7 VCs, 1 GC); Stanley Military Cemetery, Hong Kong (5 GCs); El Alamein War Cemetery, Egypt (4 VCs); and Sfax War Cemetery, Tunisia (4 VCs). The memorials with the largest number of VCs and GCs are: the Arras Memorial, France (13 VCs); the Portsmouth Naval Memorial, England (8 VCs, 4 GCs); the Rangoon Memorial, Burma (6 VCs, 3 GCs); the Menin Gate Memorial, Belgium (8 VCs); the Cambrai Memorial, France (7 VCs); the Thiepval Memorial, France (7 VCs); the Runnymede Memorial, England (1 VC, 5 GCs); the Basra Memorial, Iraq (5 VCs); and the Helles Memorial, Turkey (5 VCs).

To give an insight of the character of, or facts about, the recipients of the Victoria Cross or the George Cross, brief notes follow on 25 recipients of the VC of the 1914–1918 War and 14 of the 1939–1945 War. Similar notes on the actions of eight recipients of the GC are included. In each cemetery or memorial the register contains the citation for the award after the casualty's personal entry.

VCs 1914–1918 War

Captain A. Ball VC DSO and Two Bars, MC

The Sherwood Foresters, attached to the Royal Flying Corps
Died: 7.5.1917
Buried: Annoeullin Communal Cemetery, German Extension, France.

Captain Ball was credited with shooting down 44 enemy aircraft before crashing behind the German lines, where he was buried. His father, Sir Albert Ball, then Lord Mayor of Nottingham, England, wanted his son's remains to be repatriated but, by then, repatriation had been forbidden. Hearing this, Sir Albert insisted that his son's grave be undisturbed and, when the remains of the other 23 Britons were moved to Cabaret Rouge British Cemetery, Souchez, his wishes were respected. The grave is the only one of a Commonwealth casualty in this German war cemetery and is marked by a private memorial paid for and erected by Sir Albert Ball.

Captain A. F. W. Beauchamp-Proctor VC DSO MC and Bar, DFC

RAF
Died: 21.6.1921
Buried: Mafeking Cemetery, South Africa

Captain Beauchamp-Proctor was credited with shooting down 54 enemy aircraft before the Armistice of 1918, and subsequently left the RAF to return to his native South Africa. Later, however, he rejoined the RAF and, following aerobatics in his aircraft near Upavon, on Salisbury Plain, crashed and was killed on 21st June 1921, within the war period which ended on 31st August of that year. He was buried in the Church Cemetery at Upavon on 24th June 1921, as the church records clearly show.

According to some authorities, however – but not the Church in Upavon nor any ecclesiastical authority in England – his body was exhumed and reburied in Mafeking, contrary to the policy of non-repatriation. Some years later, a non World War service-pattern headstone was erected by the service authorities over his 'empty' grave in Upavon and it still stands. The South Africans had held an impressive funeral at Mafeking for their 'air hero' and are convinced that he is buried there. It seems odd that Church records which so meticulously state the date of death and burial, and grave location, should not state that the body was exhumed shortly afterwards – surely an important event, and obviously very much more unusual than burial. The service authorities probably erected the headstone in the belief that, as Captain Beauchamp-Proctor had died in 'peace time', it was their responsibility to do so, having overlooked the fact that all service burials were the responsibility of the Commission until 31st August 1921, no matter what the manner of death.

The Commission recognises Captain Beauchamp-Proctor's burial place as Mafeking, but others may wish to draw their own conclusions.

Second Lieutenant F. Birks VC MM

Australian Infantry Force
Died: 21.9.1917
Buried: Perth Cemetery (China Wall), Zillebeke, Belgium

Lieutenant Birks had already been awarded the MM for bravery in the ranks when he was awarded the VC 'for most conspicuous bravery' in attacking strong points and machine guns, killing some of the enemy and taking many prisoners. It was typical of this fine soldier that he should be killed by a shell while trying to extricate some of his men who had been buried by another shellburst.

Lieutenant Commander G. N. Bradford VC

RN
Died: 24.4.1918
Buried: Blankenberghe Communal Cemetery, Belgium

Brigadier General R. B. Bradford VC MC

Commands and Staff (formerly Durham Light Infantry)
Died: 30.11.1917
Buried: Hermies British Cemetery, France

These remarkable men were brothers (there are three other instances of brothers who were both awarded the VC). Lieutenant Commander Bradford was killed during the attack on Zeebrugge on St George's Day 1918, when attempts were being made by the Royal Navy to block the port to enemy submarines. Brigadier General Bradford was awarded the VC as a battalion commander, but it is not without interest that he died commanding the 186th Brigade at the age of 25.

Lieutenant J. Brillant VC MC

Canadian Infantry
Died: 10.8.1918
Buried: Villers-Bretonneux Military Cemetery, Fouilloy, France

The Canadian Corps was much to the fore in the 'Hundred Days' advance which led to the Armistice. Lieutenant Brillant, though wounded, led his party against the enemy capturing 150 troops and 15 machine guns. He died leading a charge on an enemy field gun. Brillant came from the small Canadian town of Mont Joli, Quebec. On this town's memorial to their World War I fallen, listing 10 men, is also recorded the name of another VC recipient, Corporal Joseph Kaeble whose VC action took place two months before Brillant's. He lies a scant 15 miles from his Mont Joli comrade in Wanquentin Communal Cemetery Extension.

Captain N. G. Chavasse VC and Bar, MC

RAMC
Died: 4.8.1917
Buried: Brandhoek New Military Cemetery, Belgium

This medical officer was attached to the 10th (Scottish) Battalion of the King's Liverpool Regiment – and he normally wore their Scottish headgear. He won his first VC for saving the lives of men, while under fire by day (in view of the enemy) and night, personally carrying an urgent case 500 yards to safety, and being wounded in the process. He went out again that night into no-man's land to rescue more and to bury others, saving in all about twenty badly wounded soldiers, over and above his work in the forward aid station.

A year later he virtually copied the action for which he had won the VC, though he had earlier been wounded in the scalp and, in this episode, was severely wounded in the arm and abdomen. He kept up his searches and succour to wounded men until he collapsed. He died about two days later, much loved and missed by the battalion. Chavasse was the second man to win a VC and Bar; he had earlier also been awarded the MC – not the DSO as stated in some accounts. (The first man to win two VCs was Lieutenant Colonel A. Martin-Leake, also of the RAMC, who won awards in the Boer War in 1901 and in Belgium in 1914. He died in 1953.)

In 1982 the Chief Records Officer of the Commission suggested that Chavasse's headstone should show two VCs in facsimile; this was agreed and the new headstone is unique. There are three Brandhoek cemeteries, all within a few hundred yards of each other. Chavasse's fiancée went to visit the grave in the 1920s (when travel was difficult) but, because of confusion in the names, never actually saw it.

Sergeant L. Clarke VC

Canadian Infantry
Died: 19.10.1916
Buried: Etretat Churchyard, France

Company Sergeant Major F. W. Hall VC

Canadian Infantry
Died: 20.4.1915
Commemorated: The Menin Gate Memorial, Ypres, Belgium

Lieutenant R. Shankland VC DCM

Canadian Infantry
Date of award action: 26.10.1917
Died: 20.1.1968 (Not entitled to war graves treatement)

All three of these recipients lived within one block of one another in Winnipeg, Manitoba, Canada, before joining up. The street is now called Valour Road.

Major W. La T. Congreve VC DSO MC

Rifle Brigade
Died: 20.7.1916
Buried: Corbie Communal Cemetery Extension, France

The son of a VC – Captain (later Lieutenant General Sir) William Congreve – Major Congreve was also awarded the French Légion d'Honneur. Beloved by his soldiers, he was buried in a grave at the end of a row: they set him askew to it, as a mark of respect. His fascinating diary *Armageddon Road* was published in 1982.

Boy J. T. Cornwell VC

Royal Navy
Died: 2.6.1916
Buried: Manor Park Cemetery, East Ham, Essex, England

Boy Cornwell died of wounds after the Battle of Jutland. At 16 years and 4 months, he is the youngest VC entitled to war graves treatment and the third youngest to win the award. (The two youngest, Hospital Apprentice A. Fitzgibbon, and Drummer T. Flinn, were both aged 15 years and 3 months. Fitzgibbon was awarded his VC for action at the Taku Forts, China, 21st August, 1860; Flinn's action took place on 29th November 1857, during the Indian Mutiny. Both survived their VC battle.)

Lance Corporal F. Fisher VC

Canadian Infantry
Died: 24.4.1915
Commemorated: The Menin Gate Memorial, Ypres, Belgium

Corporal Fisher was the first Canadian-born man to win the VC while serving with the Canadian Army. The place of the action where he won his award, St Julien, near Ypres was that of the first gas attack by the Germans. Coming forward from St Julien, Fisher discovered that some Canadian guns were being fired with the German infantry close on top of them. Capture of these guns seemed imminent, but Fisher set up his machine gun in advance of the battery, and held off the enemy until the guns got away. During this encounter Fisher's small section was under concentrated fire and four of his six men were killed. Returning to St Julien, he got four men and endeavoured once more to push up the front line alone. Here he continued to render valuable service up to the moment of his death.

Brigadier General C. Fitzclarence VC

Commanding 1st Guards Brigade (formerly Royal Fusiliers)
Died: 12.11.1914
Commemorated: The Menin Gate Memorial, Ypres, Belgium

It is perhaps odd that the Brigade Commander, a VC at that, should have
no known grave, but it is indicative of the intensity of the fighting in the
First Battle of Ypres between the original BEF and the Germans and,
secondly, that not all generals were château-bound as certain authors
would have people believe.

Brigadier General Sir John E. Gough VC KCB CMG

Chief of Staff, First Army (formerly Rifle Brigade)
Died: 22.2.1915
Buried: Estaires Communal Cemetery, France

Brigadier General Gough was the son and nephew of VCs – these three
are the largest number of VCs in a family group.

The Reverend (Chaplain 4th Class) T.B. Hardy VC DSO MC

Royal Army Chaplains' Department
Died: 18.10.1918
Buried: St Sever Communal Cemetery Extension, Rouen, France

The Reverend Hardy believed that the right place for a chaplain was at
the 'sharp end' with the soldiers. As he was in his mid-fifties, he could
properly have opted for a less-demanding posting in England or at the
base.

Captain G.S. Henderson VC DSO and Bar, MC

Manchester
Died: 24.7.1920
Commemorated: The Basra Memorial, Iraq

Captain Henderson, who had been awarded two DSOs and an MC during
the 1914–1918 War, was involved in the rebellion of over 100,000 armed
tribesmen which broke out at Tel Afar, Iraq on 4th June 1920. During
subsequent actions to put down the uprising, nearly 400 British and
Indian soldiers became casualties at Hillah, 70 miles south of Baghdad
and Captain Henderson, fighting gallantly, was one of these.

Captain C. S. Jeffries VC

Australian Infantry Force
Died: 12.10.1917
Buried: Tyne Cot Cemetery, Passchendaele, Belgium

This gallant officer attacked concrete bunkers and took prisoners and enemy machine guns. He repeated the performance shortly afterwards, by which time he and his soldiers had captured over 60 of the enemy. He was killed during this attack and is buried near one of the bunkers (which are still in the cemetery), very probably one of those he captured.

Brigadier General F. W. Lumsden VC CB DSO and Three Bars

RMA
Died: 4.6.1918
Buried: Berles New Military Cemetery, Berles-au-Bois, France

The decorations themselves speak for this general. (He also held the French Croix-de-Guerre.)

Major J. T. B. McCudden VC DSO and Bar, MC and Bar, MM

Royal Flying Corps and Royal Air Force
Died: 9.7.1918
Buried: Wavans British Cemetery, France

Major McCudden is one of the most highly decorated servicemen to have been commemorated by the Commission. His six decorations cover his score of 57 enemy aircraft. Very close to him in this little war cemetery is the grave of an illustrious Australian airman who won the DSO and Bar and DSC and Bar for destroying 47 enemy aircraft, Flight Commander R. A. Little, RAF and formerly RNAS.

Lieutenant A. A. McLeod VC

Royal Air Force
Died: 6.11.1918
Buried: Kildonan Cemetery, Winnipeg, Canada

This gallant Canadian airman, aged 19, who was wounded five times during an attack on his aircraft, nevertheless managed to rescue his also badly wounded observer when on the ground and with the aircraft on fire. He was then again wounded by a bomb. It is particularly sad that he should have succumbed to influenza some months later. McLeod was probably the youngest recipient of the VC for air operations in the

1914–1918 War. (The youngest VC (also 19) for air operations in the 1939–1945 War was Sergeant John Hannah, RAF, who is buried in Birstall Churchyard, Leicestershire, England.)

Major E. Mannock VC DSO and Two Bars, MC and Bar

Royal Engineers and Royal Air Force
Died: 26.7.1918
Commemorated: The Arras Memorial, France.

The top scoring ace on the Commonwealth side with 73 enemy aircraft to his credit, Major Mannock is also one of the most highly decorated men commemorated by the Commission. His burial place has not been established beyond doubt, but it seems highly likely that he is the unknown airman in Laventie Military Cemetery, La Gorgue, France. As a boy he lost most of his sight in his left eye. To overcome this and become the top ace indicates 'fearless courage, remarkable skill, devotion to duty, and self-sacrifice' – as stated in his citation.

Lieutenant W.B. Rhodes-Moorhouse VC

Royal Flying Corps
Died: 27.4.1915
Buried: Parnham Private Cemetery, Beaminster, Dorset, England

Lieutenant Rhodes-Moorhouse's VC was the first awarded for air action. The action took place in Belgium and he died there of his wounds the next day. His death occurred before the prohibition of the repatriation of remains and his next of kin had them returned for burial in their private burial ground, where they still lie, marked by a private memorial. Lieutenant Rhodes-Moorhouse's son, born posthumously, was killed in action while flying as an RAF officer in the Battle of Britain in 1940 and his ashes were buried next to his father's grave.

Private J.P. Robertson VC

Canadian Infantry
Died: 6.11.1917
Buried: Tyne Cot Cemetery, Passchendaele, Belgium

Private Robertson captured a machine gun from the enemy and then used it on them, enabling his platoon to advance. He then led the platoon onto the objective, still using the captured machine gun, but was killed on a second trip rescuing wounded soldiers from no-man's land. His actions are thought to have taken place very near the spot in which he is buried.

Company Sergeant Major J. Skinner VC DCM

King's Own Scottish Borderers
Died: 17.3.1918
Buried: Vlamertinghe New Military Cemetery, Belgium

This remarkable warrant officer had been wounded on *eight* occasions before being killed by a sniper while trying to rescue a wounded soldier. His coffin was brought to the cemetery on a gun carriage drawn by horses and carried to the grave by six VC winners of the British 29th Division (which had served, among other places, on the Gallipoli Peninsula and the Somme). This unique event illustrates the high esteem in which he was held by his fellow soldiers. After his investure for his VC at Buckingham Palace he was directed to a post in Scotland. Somehow he evaded this order to return to his men in Belgium. He also held the French Croix de Guerre.

Major F. H. Tubb VC

Australian Infantry Force
Died: 20.9.1917
Buried: Lijssenthoek Military Cemetery, Poperinghe, Belgium

Major (then Captain) Tubb won the VC for great gallantry at Lone Pine Trenches, Gallipoli Peninsula, Turkey on 9th August 1915 – the Gallipoli Campaign being, for its area and duration, one of the most bitterly fought of the war.

VCs 1939–1945 War

Jemadar Abdul Hafiz VC

9th Jat Regiment
Died: 6.4.1944
Buried: Imphal Indian Army War Cemetery, India

Jemadar Abdul Hafiz is but one of many Indians who won the VC in the 1939–1945 War; he is buried in the Indian Cemetery, about a mile from Imphal War Cemetery. He showed astonishing bravery in attacking the Japanese enemy over a bare, steep slope, being wounded and capturing a machine-gun. He was again wounded, even more severely, but succeeded in inspiring his men to capture the position; he died shortly after.

Corporal S. Bates VC

Norfolk Regiment
Died: 8.8.1944
Buried: Bayeux War Cemetery, France

Corporal Bates is the only VC buried in Normandy and, even though he was a Londoner, he was in the Norfolk Regiment which won more VCs (five) than any other regiment in the 1939–1945 War.

Gunner W. E. Brown VC DCM and Bar

Royal Australian Artillery
Died: 28.2.1942
Commemorated: The Singapore Memorial

This very brave Gunner had been awarded the VC at Villers-Bretonneux France on 6th July 1918. He was also awarded a double DCM during the 1914–1918 War. As if he had not done enough for his King and Country, he rejoined the Australian Army in 1939, aged 54. He died in the conquest of Malaya by the Japanese, but has no known grave.

Major General J. C. Campbell VC DSO and Bar MC

Commands and Staff (formerly RHA and RA)
Died: 26.2.1942
Buried: Cairo War Memorial Cemetery, Egypt

General Campbell was awarded the VC as a brigadier – possibly the most senior officer to receive the decoration in that rank in the World Wars. He was killed shortly afterwards in a traffic accident.

Sergeant A. Cosens VC

Queen's Own Rifles of Canada
Died: 26.2.1945
Buried: Groesbeek Canadian War Cemetery, Netherlands

Sergeant Cosens is a gallant example of the Canadians who liberated a large portion of the Netherlands and were involved in the heavy fighting on the Rivers Maas and Rhine. During the engagement for which he was awarded the VC his platoon commander was dead, casualties were heavy, and his platoon had been beaten back twice. He alone made yet another attempt and killed or captured the enemy in strongly-defended buildings, but was shot by a sniper on walking back to his headquarters after this action. In the words of the official citation he had engaged in 'the capture of a position which was vital to the success of the future operations of the brigade'.

Corporal J. H. Edmondson VC

Australian Infantry Force
Died: 14.4.1941
Buried: Tobruk War Cemetery, Libya

The Australians will always be associated with Tobruk and its sieges. During an attack by the Germans, Edmondson's officer was directly attacked and in danger of death. Despite the fact that he was already fatally wounded in the neck, Edmondson went to the officer's assistance and saved his life, but himself died later.

Flying Officer D. E. Garland VC; Sergeant T. Gray VC

Royal Air Force
Died: 12.5.1940
Buried: Heverlee War Cemetery, Louvain, Belgium

In an aircraft action over the Albert Canal in Belgium, on 12th May 1940, this pilot and his navigator attacked a crucial bridge to delay the German advance. Their zeal in the face of fierce anti-aircraft fire by the enemy resulted in their death. This is the only instance of two recipients of the VC being buried next to each other.

Wing Commander G. P. Gibson VC DSO and Bar, DFC and Bar

Royal Air Force
Died: 19.9.1944
Buried: Steenbergen-en-Kruisland Roman Catholic Cemetery, Nether-
   lands

Wing Commander Gibson was the leader of the successful air attack on the Mohne and Eder Dams in Germany on 16th May 1943, personally making the initial attack on the former and then circling for half-an-hour to draw anti-aircraft fire away from those aircraft still attacking. In addition, he made a single-handed attack on highly-defended objectives such as the German battleship *Tirpitz*. He flew some 175 sorties, many as a Pathfinder. He was killed over the Netherlands. Apparently Steen-bergen was asked for permission to rebury Gibson's remains in nearby (British) Bergen-op-Zoom War Cemetery but the town demurred, wanting this gallant airman to remain in their cemetery. He is buried with his navigator, Squadron Leader J. B. Warwick DFC, RAFVR.

Lieutenant R. H. Gray VC DSC

Royal Canadian Navy Volunteer Reserve
Died: 9.8.1945
Commemorated: The Halifax Memorial, Canada

Lieutenant Gray, a Canadian serving with a squadron of the Royal Navy's Fleet Air Arm in HMS *Formidable* off the coast of Japan, pressed home his attack and sank a Japanese destroyer, with a direct bomb hit, despite the fact that his aircraft was hit and ablaze. His was the last VC awarded in the 1939–1945 War, earned just before VJ Day.

Major A. F. E. V. S. Lassen VC MC and Two Bars

Special Boat Service, Special Air Service Regiment
Died: 9.4.1945
Buried: Argenta Gap War Cemetery, Italy

Major Lassen, born a Dane, was serving in the British Army. A most gallant officer, he had already been awarded the MC on three occasions before his particular valour won him the VC and cost him his life, just a month before VE Day.

Pilot Officer R. H. Middleton VC

Royal Australian Air Force
Died: 29.11.1942
Buried: Beck Row Churchyard, Suffolk, England

Pilot Officer Middleton was an Australian, one of the many who came to serve in Bomber Command. He died in the sea off Kent, when returning from a bombing mission on Turin, Italy, after guiding his aircraft back despite severe facial wounds and the windshield knocked out. Facing cold winds of 150 mph, he battled for hours to get his badly damaged aircraft to the English Coast, only to crash a few miles short of land. He was a Flight Sergeant at the time, but posthumously promoted to Pilot Officer.

Lieutenant Colonel D. A. Seagrim VC

Green Howards
Died: 6.4.1943
Buried: Sfax War Cemetery, Tunisia

Colonel Seagrim is one of a pair of unique brothers. He won the VC and his brother, Major H.P. Seagrim, DSO, MBE, won the GC for gallantry in Burma, also posthumously.

Major E. Swales VC DFC

South African Air Force
Died: 23.2.1945
Buried: Leopoldsburg War Cemetery, Belgium

Major Swales was one of the elite master bombers guiding a force of aircraft that attacked Pforzheim, Germany. Two of his aircraft's engines were destroyed by fighters, but Swales issued the aiming instructions to the force to ensure a successful attack. He then skilfully flew to friendly territory with an aeroplane which was ever more difficult to control, to enable his crew to bale out while he remained, and died at the controls. His mother, Mrs O.M. Swales, unveiled the Altar Stone, which lies in front of the South African Memorial at Delville Wood, Somme, France in 1952.

George Cross

Captain M. A. Ansari GC

7th Rajput Regiment
Died: 29.10.1943
Buried: Stanley Military Cemetery, Hong Kong

This gallant Indian prisoner-of-war's citation is brief, leaves much to the imagination and is standard for many GC winners – 'Awarded the George Cross for most conspicuous gallantry in carrying out hazardous work in a very brave manner'. In fact, as Captain Ansari was related to the ruler of an Indian State, the Japanese tried to persuade him to renounce his allegiance to the British and spread subversion among the other Indian prisoners. When he refused, he was jailed, starved, tortured and finally executed, together with 30 other Indian, Chinese and British prisoners. His name is on a Special Memorial indicating that the exact location of his grave in the cemetery is not known.

Mr J. A. Fraser GC MC and Bar

British Army Aid Group
Died: 29.10.1943
Buried: Stanley Military Cemetery, Hong Kong

Mr Fraser was a civilian who had won two MCs during the 1914–1918 War. He was a member of the British Army Aid Group of Hong Kong, a military establishment and war-time creation which came into being early in 1942 to encourage and facilitate escapes, to assist escapers and to get information and medical supplies into the camps. The group gradually developed into an organization for the collection of intelligence of military value and later into an escape and evasion organization for the American Air Force. Many of the Group's members were caught and executed by the Japanese. Fraser was caught but gave nothing away despite torture. His fortitude was commented upon by the prison guards.

Private B.G. Hardy GC; Private R. Jones GC

Australian Infantry
Died: 5.8.1944
Buried: Cowra War Cemetery, New South Wales, Australia

During the 1939–1945 War there was a prisoner-of-war camp of over 1000 Japanese at Cowra, which was the scene of a mass outbreak. Privates Hardy and Jones of the Australian Military Forces who lost their lives while on duty during this incident were posthumously awarded the GC. The citation for these Australians ends by stating 'Private Hardy (Jones) met his death in the true British (sic) spirit of sacrifice for his country'. These two soldiers are buried next to one another – the only other example of GC recipients being so buried is in Coventry (London Road) Cemetery, England, where Second Lieutenant A.F. Campbell and Sergeant M. Gibson are buried, both Royal Engineers.

Corporal J. Hendry GC

Royal Canadian Engineers
Died: 13.6.1941
Buried: Brookwood Military Cemetery, Surrey, England

Brookwood Military Cemetery contains the largest number of war burials (nearly 6000) of any cemetery in the United Kingdom, of which only two are of holders of the GC, both of whom were Canadians (the other is Sergeant J. Rennie). Corporal Hendry could easily have saved his own life when he found an explosives store on fire. Instead, he warned others to escape (and all but one were able to do so) and tackled the dangerous blaze; he was killed in the subsequent explosion.

Section Officer N. Inayat-Khan GC

Women's Auxiliary Air Force
Died: 13.9.1944
Commemorated: The Runnymede Memorial, Surrey, England

Section Officer Noor Inayat-Khan is the only woman holder of the GC on this memorial. She did excellent work in France with Special Operations Executive clandestine forces (which also earned her a

Mention-in-Despatches), but was later betrayed to the Gestapo. Following imprisonment and torture over a period of twelve months, she was taken to Dachau Concentration Camp where she was shot.

Ensign V. R. E. Szabo GC

Women's Transport Service, First Aid Nursing Yeomanry
Died: 25.1.45/5.2.45
Commemorated: The Brookwood Memorial, Surrey, England

Ensign Violette Szabo (who was married to a French officer who was killed in action in North Africa) originally served with a heavy anti-aircraft artillery regiment in England. She volunteered, partly because she spoke perfect French, to serve with the SOE forces in France. She was eventually captured and tortured by the Gestapo, but gave away no secrets. Later, she was sent to a concentration camp and murdered. Her story was so heroic and moving that a popular film, entitled *Carve Her Name With Pride*, was made in the 1950s, based on her life.

Captain J. R. O. Thompson GC

Royal Army Medical Corps
Died: 24.1.1944
Commemorated: The Brookwood Memorial, Surrey, England

Any act of bravery takes guts, but several acts over days takes perhaps even more courage. Captain Thompson's GC was awarded for his medical services and continual bravery over four years, from 1940 to 1944. His award was for gallantry and devotion to duty, including actions in May 1940 aboard HM Hospital Carrier *Paris* at Dunkirk; 10th–14th July 1943 aboard Hospital Carrier *St David* at Sicily; 10th–15th September 1943 at Salerno; and 23rd–24th January 1944 at Anzio. At Anzio, under enemy attack and shell fire, Thompson remained with his last patient as his ship was sinking, having managed to remove all the rest of his patients from the burning vessel. He went down with the ship: a man, officer and doctor in the mould of Chavasse and Martin-Leake described previously in this chapter.

{17}

Miscellany

*The Universe is so vast and so ageless
that the life of one man can only be
justified by the measure of his sacrifice*

Pilot Officer Vivian Rosewarne (1916–1940)
Last letter to his mother, published
in The Times, 18th June 1940.
(See complete letter at the end of this
chapter.)

THERE IS MUCH INFORMATION ABOUT THE
Commission and the subject of war graves in general which does not
fit easily into any particular chapter, but which is nevertheless
important, curious or simply of interest. The following is a small selection of
such facts and figures:

VC and Bar

The only man to be awarded the VC and Bar and to be recorded by the
Commission is Captain Noel Godfrey Chavasse MC RAMC, who is buried
in Brandhoek New Military Cemetery, west of Ieper, Belgium, Grave
III.B.15.

Youngest general officer to die

Brigadier General Roland Boys Bradford VC MC, late Durham Light
Infantry, was 25 and commanding 186th Brigade when he was killed on 30th
November 1917. He is buried in Hermies British Cemetery, France, Grave
F.10.

Youngest known battle deaths 1914–1918

Private John Condon, 2nd Battalion, Royal Irish Regiment, who died on
24th May 1915, age 14, and is buried in Poelcapelle British Cemetery,
Belgium, Grave LVI.F.8.

Rifleman Valentine Joe Strudwick, 8th Battalion, The Rifle Brigade, who died on 14th January 1916, age 15, and is buried in Essex Farm Cemetery, Boesinghe, near Ieper, Belgium, Grave I.U.8.

Youngest known battle death 1939–1945

Galley Boy R.V. Steed MN, SS *Empire Morn*, who died on 26th April 1943, age 14, when his ship was mined and is buried in Ben M'Sik Cemetery, Casablanca, Morocco, Grave 1. (Next to his grave in this civil cemetery is the non-world-war grave of Field Marshal Sir Claude Auchinleck, who died in 1981, age 96. As field marshals never officially retire, he was the 'oldest serving soldier' when he died.)

Oldest known battle deaths 1914–1918

Lieutenant Henry Webber, 7th Battalion, South Lancashire Regiment, Mentioned in Despatches, who died of wounds on 21st July 1916, age 68, and is buried in Dartmoor Cemetery, Bécordel-Bécourt, Somme, France, Grave I.E.54.

Private W.W. Speight, 13th Battalion, Royal Welch Fusiliers, who died on 1st August 1917, age 62, and is buried in New Irish Farm Cemetery, St Jean-les-Ypres, Belgium, Grave IV.B.16.

Oldest known deaths 1914–1918

Captain and Quartermaster G.W.V. Clements, Royal Dragoons, who died on 3rd March 1916, age 85, and is buried in Norwich Cemetery, England.

Colonel Ross Thompson, late Royal Engineers, who died on 5th December 1919, age 81, and is commemorated on the Madras Memorial, India. His grave, in Bangalore (Hosur Road) Cemetery was deemed unmaintainable.

Earliest battle deaths 1914–1918

Royal Navy

Many sailors are buried in Shotley Cemetery, Suffolk, England. They include Stokers 1st Class J. Foster and A. Martin and Leading Stoker H. Copland, who died in HMS *Amphion* when she was sunk by a mine at 0630 hours on 6th August 1914. HMS *Amphion* had sunk SMS *Königin Luise*, the German layer of this mine, on the 5th, and some of the latter's crew are also buried in this cemetery. Both ships sank off Great Yarmouth, Norfolk.

Army

(In West Africa) – Private Bai (his only name), Gold Coast Regiment, who died on 15th August 1914, probably at the Affair at Agbeluvoe, 50 miles north of Lomé, Togo (the German protectorate of Togoland from 1894–1914). He is commemorated by name on the Kumasi Memorial, Ghana.

Lieutenant George Masterman Thompson, Croix-de-Guerre with Palms (France), 1st Battalion Royal Scots and Gold Coast Regiment, who died on 22nd August 1914, age 24, and is buried in Chra Village Cemetery, Togo.

Lieutenant Thompson was the first British Army officer to be killed in action in the war. A special French Army order was published on 20th October, commending his gallantry and the fine example he set to the French soldiers temporarily under his command.

(On the Western Front) – Private J. Parr, 4th Battalion, Middlesex Regiment, who died on 21st August 1914 and is buried in St Symphorien Military Cemetery, Belgium, Grave I.A.10.

Last battle deaths 1914–1918

Private G.E. Ellison, 5th Lancers (Grave I.B.23) and Private G.L. Price, 28th Battalion, Canadian Infantry (Saskatchewan Regiment), age 25, (Grave V.C.4), both of whom died on 11th November 1918 and are buried in St Symphorien Military Cemetery, Belgium. (The first VC of the war, Lieutenant M.J. Dease RF is also buried here.)

Earliest battle death 1939–1945

Royal Air Force

Several airmen who died on 4th September 1939 are buried in Sage War Cemetery, Oldenburg, West Germany. The include Flight Lieutenant W.F. Barton, Flying Officer H.L. Emden and Sergeant O.L.D. Howells, who were killed while attacking German naval units in their North Sea ports.

Oldest Knight/Air Gunner to die

Pilot Officer (Air Gunner) Sir Arnold Talbot Wilson KCIE CSI CMG DSO was killed in action on 31st May 1940, age 56. As a Gentleman Cadet he had been awarded the King's Medal and Sword of Honour at the Royal Military College, Sandhurst. Before joining the RAF very early in the 1939–1945 War he had been a Lieutenant Colonel in the Indian Army, and later Member of Parliament for Hitchin, Hertfordshire, England. He is buried in Grave 2 of Eringhem Churchyard, 10 miles south-west of Dunkirk, France.

Baronet who died while serving as a rating

Ordinary Seaman Sir Robert Peel Bt RN died on 5th April 1942 when HMS *Tenedos* was struck by Japanese bombers in Colombo Harbour, Ceylon (now Sri Lanka). He is buried in Colombo (Kanatte) General Cemetery, Joint Grave 4A. Peel was the sixth and final Baronet and the son of Lady Peel, perhaps better known as Beatrice Lillie, the Toronto-born actress.

Father and Son buried together

Sergeant George Lee RFA, age 46 (father), and Corporal Robert Frederick Lee RFA, age 19 (son) of 'A' Battery, 156th Brigade, Royal Field Artillery, were killed in action on 5th September 1916 and are buried in adjoining graves in Dartmoor Cemetery, Bécordel-Bécourt, Somme, France, Graves I.A.35 and 36.

Brothers buried in Commission cemeteries

126682 Gunner Geoffrey Nutter RHA, age 25, and 126683 Gunner Harry Nutter RHA, age 27, died on 6th February 1917 and are buried in adjoining graves in Eclusier Communal Cemetery, Eclusier-Vaux, Somme, Graves A.10 and 11.

5511523 Private Thomas Gronert AAC and 5511524 Private Claude Gronert AAC (twins) died on 17th September 1944 and are buried in adjoining graves in Arnhem (Oosterbeek) War Cemetery, Netherlands, Graves 18.A.17 and 18.

14620854 Private John Cairncross, Gordon Highlanders, and 14620855 Private Thomas Cairncross, Gordon Highlanders (twins), died on 4th February 1944, age 19, and are in Anzio War Cemetery, Italy, but, for unknown reasons, are unfortunately buried apart: John in Grave II.T.8 and Thomas in Grave I.B.4.

Sergeant (Wireless Operator/Air Gunner) Joseph Gerald Fitzgerald RAF (VR) died on 25th September 1941, age 19, and is buried in Brookwood Military Cemetery, Surrey, England, Grave 21.A.3. His brother Leslie, also a Sergeant (WO/AG), died on 31st March 1943, age 29, and is buried in the same grave.

In Theale Churchyard, Berkshire, England, is the grave of Flying Officer Wynne Herbert RAF, who died on 26th January 1942, age 26; and his brother Flying Officer Gerald Herbert RAF, who died on 14th February 1943, age 20. On the headstone there is also a reference to the third brother, Flying Officer Richard Herbert RAF, who died over Greece on 13th April 1941, age 21; he is buried in Phaleron War Cemetery, Athens, Grave

IV.C.19. These three were the only children of Air Commodore and Mrs P.L.W. Herbert.

In the Dieppe Canadian War Cemetery lie Private K.J. Ingram, killed 19th August 1942, age 20; and his brother, Sergeant R.D. Ingram, killed 13th August 1944, age 23, of The Royal Regiment of Canada. They were the only sons of George and Mary Ingram of Toronto, Canada.

In Calais Canadian War Cemetery are the graves of Major P.K. Kennedy, age 29, and Major D.P. Kennedy, age 26, both of the Highland Light Infantry, who were killed within two days of each other, on 17th and 19th September 1944. They came from Guelph, Ontario, Canada.

Next to each other in Flatiron Copse Cemetery, Mametz, Somme, France, lie Lieutenant Arthur Tregaskis, age 32, and Lieutenant Leonard Tregaskis, age 33, both of the 16th Battalion, Welch Regiment, and who were both killed on the same day – 7th July 1916– in action at Mametz Wood. They were sons of Mr and Mrs George Henry Tregaskis, Millbrook, Jersey (Channel Islands).

The smallest Commission cemetery

Probably the smallest Commission cemetery is Ocracoke Island (Cunningham) Cemetery, off the coast of North Carolina, USA. It contains the graves of four British sailors from the armed trawler HMS *Bedfordshire*, a ship well known to the people of North Carolina's Outer Banks, which was torpedoed by a German submarine on 11th May 1942. There were no survivors, but the bodies of Ordinary Telegraphist S.R. Craig and Sub Lieutenant T. Cunningham and two unidentified sailors were washed ashore later.

The graves were maintained for years by the US Coastguard on behalf of the Commission and in a ceremony during Bicentennial Year, 1976, a perpetual lease of this tiny site (only a few yards square) was granted to a representative of the Commission by the North Carolina State Property Office.

The smallest Commission Memorial

Other than sites where special memorial headstones have, for reasons which are not clear, been classed as 'memorials', the smallest Commission memorial is the Zeebrugge Memorial in Zeebrugge Churchyard, Belgium. It commemorates four sailors, including a VC, who were killed in the Zeebrugge Raid of 23rd April 1918.

Most isolated graves and memorials

Perhaps the most isolated (and certainly the southernmost) grave is that of Stoker 2nd Class A. Phipps RN, of HMS *Bristol*, who died on 26th March 1915 and is buried in Magallanes (now Punta Arenas) Fiscal Cemetery, Tierra del Fuego, Chile.

In Timbuktu Cemetery, Republic of Mali, are buried two British Merchant Navy seamen, Able Seaman J.B. Graham and Chief Engineering Officer W. Soutter, who died on different dates in May 1944. That they died in the desert, 1,000 miles from the ocean, seems strange indeed and even, perhaps, romantic.

Probably the most isolated memorial is the Gan Memorial, situated near the old airfield Officers' Mess on Addu Atoll in the Republic of Maldives in the Indian Ocean, 400 miles south-west of Sri Lanka. It commemorates by name 70 men of the Indian Forces, who died while serving on the island in the 1939–1945 War and who have no known grave, were cremated, or whose graves were unmaintainable (having been, so far as is known, engulfed by the airfield runway).

Graves in tiny European States

Two of the smallest European states, Monaco and San Marino, each accommodate two war dead that are the responsibility of the Commission. The burial place of the two RAF dead in San Marino had been very carefully marked and was tended by the local people, but the personal details inscribed on the single headstone were inaccurate enough to have the Commission add a plaque giving the correct facts about the two buried there.

An unknown soldier identified by the next of kin

Like any other honest organization, the Commission does not claim always to 'get it right' and the following is one such example.

There is a Commission plot of 80 soldiers and seven airmen in Warhem Communal Cemetery in the Pas-de-Calais, France. Nearly 40 of the soldiers were unidentified by name and virtually all, known and unknown, died in late May and early June 1940, during the Dunkirk Campaign. Colin McCorquodale's father, Major Angus McCorquodale, Coldstream Guards, was missing and therefore commemorated only by name on a panel of the Dunkirk Memorial. Mr McCorquodale knew from his own research that his father had died near Warhem on 1st June 1940 and it seemed to him highly probable that the missing major would be among the unknown soldiers in the plot, who included some from his father's regiment.

On a visit to the cemetery, the son spotted the inscription on the headstone of a serviceman unidentified by name which, in accordance with Commission practice, gave all the information which was known about the burial in the grave. The inscription read that it was the grave of an unknown major of the Coldstream Guards. Major McCorquodale was the only major of that regiment listed as missing on the memorial, so the son got in touch with the Commission, and said that it followed that the remains could only be those of his father. The Commission could only agree that this was obviously the case.

As it happened, the Commission still had the reburial report (the casualty had first been buried in a temporary grave) and the details tallied with those given by the son. The Chief Records Officer accepted at once that a mistake had been made, and promptly had all records and the memorial and cemetery registers amended. A new headstone was quickly made, inscribed with the name of Major Angus McCorquodale and full details, and erected on the grave. Colin McCorquodale has since visited the marked grave several times. Had it not been for his intervention, the mistake would probably never have been spotted.

Either . . . or

La Clytte Military Cemetery, Reninghelst, Belgium, contains a grave (VI.C.15) with an unusually worded marker. It commemorates two soldiers by name – Privates W. Lumber and H.G. Noyce, both of the Hampshire Regiment and both of whom died on 30th June 1918 – but states that only one of them is buried in the grave. One can only speculate on the events which made such wording necessary, but most probably the two soldiers had been seen together being blown up by a shell. Presumably after the explosion only one, unidentifiable, body could be found for burial and so the occupant of the grave is either Private Lumber or Private Noyce – but both are commemorated.

Black Mountain, Province of Quebec, Canada

An RCAF aeroplane with over 20 on board crashed on Black Mountain during the 1939–1945 War and their collective grave was marked by a cairn. As the place is exceedingly difficult to reach, the Canadian Agency of the Commission suggested that the grave should be declared unmaintainable and that the names should, exceptionally, be added to those on the Ottawa Memorial commemorating those with no known graves. This was agreed, and the aeroplane's complement are commemorated by a special bronze panel on the memorial.

Bamfield Isolated Grave, Vancouver, British Columbia, Canada

From time to time, sites which have previously been unknown or unmaintainable become accessible through new roadways or exploitation.

One such site is a forest-covered hilltop near Bamfield, British Columbia, where an RCAF aeroplane crashed in 1945, killing all 12 RCAF airmen and airwomen on board. A cairn with a bronze plaque bearing all the names was erected on the two collective graves and unveiled, in 1983, by the Canadian Minister of Veterans' Affairs. The dead were previously commemorated on the Ottawa Memorial; all records and registers have been amended.

Australian Flying Corps

The Royal Flying Corps consisted of airmen seconded from many of the Commonwealth countries but mainly from Britain, Canada, and Australia. In 1917 the Australians decided to form their own flying units, and the Australian Flying Corps served in many parts of the world.

There is a cemetery at the village of Leighterton in Gloucestershire, England, in which are buried about 30 members of the Corps who died in accidents while training at the local aerodrome in the 1914–1918 War. One of them was not in fact entitled to war graves treatment, as he died about 10 years after the Armistice. However, as he had spent all the time between discharge from the AFC and his death in hospital, it was probably thought right at the time to bury him with, and in the same style as, his comrades.

One of the training unit's former Australian commanding officers revisited the cemetery in 1983.

Re-use of a War Grave

There was one grave of the 1914–1918 War in Volo (now Volos) Municipal Cemetery, on mainland Greece's eastern coast (the port from which Jason and his Argonauts sailed in antiquity). It was privately owned and marked and contained the remains of Lieutenant Commander F.G. Burns of the RNVR, who had married a lady who was very probably local. The grave was inspected from time to time by Commission staff and for years it seemed in good order. However, the local regulations were such that after a certain number of years the (civil) graves in the cemetery reverted to the local authority and could be re-used.

During a routine Commission inspection it was discovered that, despite the existence of the still standing privately owned headstone, a fresh interment had been made in the grave of a person unrelated to Lieutenant Commander Burns. The Commission, presented with this *fait accompli* and unable to trace the next of kin, could do little but complain formally and watch. Some years later, during another inspection, it was found that the grave had been opened again and the skeletal remains of the second (civil) burial removed and placed in an ossuary.

As the grave was still open, it was noted that this burial had been made at a shallow depth and the Commission decided to ascertain if the remains of the Lieutenant Commander were undisturbed. It turned out that they were buried much more deeply than the civil burial had been and were indeed undisturbed. The Commission followed its procedure for exhumation and, to ensure that no further interments were made over this war burial, decided on reburial in its 'open' cemetery for 1914–1918 War dead, at Kirechköi-Hortaköi Cemetery in Macedonia.

Lieutenant Commander Burns is now buried in this cemetery and his new grave, safeguarded and maintained in perpetuity, is marked by a standard Commission headstone. This is a good example of the dangers of privately owned graves in isolated sites. It did not show any intentional disrespect on the part of the authorities, only that they genuinely did not realize that the the grave they had opened was a war grave, protected (as they are in many countries) by a War Graves Agreement between the host government and the participating governments.

Lieutenant Prince Maurice of Battenberg

In Ypres Town Cemetery there is a standard Commission headstone to Lieutenant His Highness Prince Maurice of Battenberg, age 23, who was killed in action at Zonnebeke on 27th October 1914. The register entry adds that he was 'Son of Prince and Princess Henry of Battenberg and Grandson of Victoria, Queen of Great Britain and Ireland, Empress of India. Grave I.B.' There was a strong suggestion at one time that his remains should be repatriated for permanent burial. Correctly, he was left undisturbed in the cemetery in which he was originally buried and the Commission's principles of no repatriation and equality of treatment were not violated.

A Captain who re-enlisted as a Private

Arthur Arnold Crow was educated at Harrow School and Haileybury College and enlisted in the Artists' Rifles in August 1914. He was commissioned but had to resign his captaincy in the Loyal North Lancashire Regiment because of ill health in July 1916. He found on recovery that he could not regain his former rank without abandoning the chance of foreign service (he was probably too valuable at home as an instructor who had experience of service at the front) and he re-enlisted as a private soldier. He was killed in action as Private A.A. Crow, Essex Regiment, on 10th October 1917 and is buried in Cement House Cemetery, Langemarck, Belgium, Grave IX.C.9.

From Sub Lieutenant, Royal Navy, to Gunner, Royal Artillery

Sub Lieutenant William St John Wilson RN was born in Nagasaki, Japan, and lived in Yokohama. While serving in HMS *Tiger*, he decided that he wished to transfer to the Army; he resigned his commission and enlisted as a private soldier. While serving with 124th Brigade, Royal Field Artillery, as Gunner Wilson, he died of wounds on 19th September 1917. He is buried in Locre (now Loker) Hospice Cemetery, Belgium, Grave II.B.9.

The Lady from Worthing, Sussex, England

A lady music teacher telephoned the Chief Records Officer in the early 1980s and asked if a headstone could 'now be erected' over the grave in the 1939–1945 Minturno War Cemetery, Italy, which, she had been told, contained the body of her husband, an infantryman. She was kindly informed that a headstone had been in position for very many years. This surprised her, she said, as she had told the Commission in the late 1940s that she believed that her husband had not died in the true sense, but that he would, by God's grace, reappear, and for that reason no headstone was necessary and that was to be the end of the matter. However, she had become reluctantly convinced that her husband would not reappear, and it seemed wrong to her that the grave should remain unmarked.

It was a very sad story, but the offer immediately made to her by the Commission of adding a personal inscription to the standing headstone relieved and comforted her. The inscription of her choice was added and a photograph of the headstone sent to her. She said that, next to her husband's reappearance, this was the best thing that could happen and added, philosophically, that it would not be so very many years before she would in any case meet him again. A lady of true faith and strength.

General Wladyslaw Sikorski

General Sikorski, Commander-in-Chief of the Free Polish Forces and Premier of the Polish Government in exile from June 1940 in London, was killed in an air crash in the sea off Gibraltar on 4th July 1943. All on board died, except the pilot. (Scurrilous stories were later spread that he had been killed to order, but these were disproved.) General Sikorski's body was recovered, brought to England and buried in the large Polish Plot in Newark Cemetery, Nottinghamshire.

In the early 1980s there were requests from Poland that the General's body should be repatriated for burial there, but these came to naught. Had he been a Commonwealth serviceman, he would have been buried in Gibraltar or, ironically, buried at sea, as were many of those killed on the 'Rock', the names of whom are inscribed on the Gibraltar Memorial.

The man who never was

In Heulva Roman Catholic Cemetery, on the coast of south-west Spain, is the single war grave of a casualty who had been dubbed 'The man who never was'. The story of that man has been made famous by a book and film of that name, and the briefest of accounts will suffice here.

A body was cast adrift in the sea from a Royal Navy submarine by a British intelligence team under Lieutenant Commander Ewan Montagu RNVR. The body was accompanied by bogus documents and information to persuade enemy agents in Spain that seaborne landings would take place in

Greece and other places in the Mediterranean, rather than at the selected locations in Sicily. It seems likely that this information did in fact lead to the wrong disposition of the enemy's defensive forces.

The relatives of 'The man who never was' expressed a wish that his identity be kept secret; this has been respected and his grave accepted as a war grave. The original recumbent stone is still on the grave and records him a 'Major William Martin', who died on 24th April 1943. When that stone eventually needs replacement, a Commission marker with the badge of the Royal Marines ('Major Martin's' supposed service) will be erected. 'Major Martin's' supposed details are recorded in the Commission's cemetery register.

Private John Simpson and Donkey Duffy

Private John 'Simpson' (his real name was Kirkpatrick from South Shields, County Durham) served as a member of the Australian Army Medical Corps in the Gallipoli Peninsula Campaign in Turkey. He achieved fame by making journey after journey from the front to the medical facilities a mile to the rear, transporting wounded men on the back of a donkey which he had named 'Duffy'. This went on for a period of three weeks until both he, age 22, and Duffy were killed on 19th May 1915. Private Simpson (he chose the name for himself) is buried in Beach Cemetery, Anzac, Gallipoli Peninsula, Grave I.F.1.

Artists, Poets and Writers

The following are the details of some of those of the world of the arts who died during the 1914–1918 and 1939–1945 Wars. Some have been mentioned elsewhere, but for ease of reference, they are listed again here, each with the title of one of his best known works.

BROOKE, Sub Lieutenant Rupert Chawner RNVR, Hood Battalion, Royal Naval Division, died 23rd April 1915, age 27. He died en route to the landings on the Gallipoli Peninsula and was buried in a privately marked, isolated, grave on the Greek island of Skyros in the Aegean Sea. On the south coast of the island is Trebuki Bay, and the grave is situated in an olive grove about half a mile north-north-east of the head of the bay. (One of the burial party was his friend Bernard Freyberg, who won the VC DSO and Two Bars in the 1914–1918 War and a third Bar to his DSO in the 1939–1945 War.) Poet: *The Soldier*.

CRISP, Second Lieutenant Francis Edward Fitzjohn, 1st Battalion Grenadier Guards, died 5th January 1915, aged 33. He is buried in Le Trou Aid Post Cemetery (near Armentières/Fleurbaix), France, Grave D6. Artist: Gold Medalist of the Royal Academy, 1907.

GRENFELL, Captain the Honourable Julian H.E. DSO, 1st Royal Dragoons, was wounded on 13th May 1915, near Ypres and died 26th May, age 27. He is buried in Boulogne Eastern Cemetery, France, Grave II.A.18. He was the son of Lord and Lady Desborough, whose then home at Taplow Court is within easy view from the Commission's office at Maidenhead. Poet: *Into Battle*.

McCRAE, Lieutenant Colonel John, Canadian Army Medical Corps, died 28th January 1918, age 45, and is buried in Wimereux Communal Cemetery (three miles north of Boulogne), Pas-de-Calais, France, Grave IV.H.3. Poet: *In Flanders Fields*.

MUNRO, Lance Sergeant Hector Hugh (pseudonym Saki), 22nd Battalion, Royal Fusiliers, died 14th November 1916 in the Battle of the Somme, age 46. He has no known grave and is commemorated on the Thiepval Memmorial, France. Royal Fusiliers' names are on Piers and Faces 8C, 9A and 16A of the memorial. Writer of short stories.

OWEN, Lieutenant Wilfred Edward Salter MC, 5th Battalion Manchester Regiment, died 4th November 1918, age 25, and is buried in Ors Communal Cemetery, France, Grave A3. Ors is a village on the Canal de la Sambre between Le Câteau and Landrecies. The *Communal* Cemetery is near the railway, and is not to be confused with Ors *British* Cemetery, about a mile away. Poet: *Anthem for Doomed Youth*.

ROSENBERG, Private Isaac, 1st Battalion, King's Own Royal Lancaster Regiment (formerly of the Suffolk Regiment), died 1st April 1918, age 27, and is buried in Bailleul Road East Cemetery, St Laurent-Blagny (north-east of Arras) France, Grave V.C.12. Poet: *Dead Man's Dump*.

THOMAS, Second Lieutenant Philip Edward, 244th Siege Battery, Royal Garrison Artillery, died 9th April 1917 and is buried in Agny Military Cemetery, Pas-de-Calais, France, Grave C.43. Poet: *Early One Morning*.

WHISTLER, Lieutenant Rex John, Welsh Guards, died 18th July 1944, age 39, and is buried in Banneville-la-Campagne War Cemetery, Normandy, France, Grave III.F.2. Artist: Murals in the Tate Gallery, London, England.

Of course, other well-known poets, writers and artists survived the two wars. Remarkable among these was Robert Graves, who was so severely wounded while serving with the Royal Welch Fusiliers in the 1914–1918 War that his obituary notice was mistakenly published in *The Times*. After the war he wrote, among many other poems and books, *Good-bye to All That*, one of the best autobiographical accounts of life and action on the Western Front. He lived until 1985, but his son, Lieutenant John David Nicholson Graves, also of the Welch Fusiliers, died in Burma on 18th March 1943, age 23. He had no known grave and is, therefore commemorated by name on Face 9 of the Rangoon Memorial.

Vernon and Irene Castle

In their day, before the 1914–1918 War, dancers Vernon and Irene Castle were as world famous as Fred Astaire and Ginger Rogers were to become in theirs. Captain Vernon Blythe Castle, Royal Flying Corps, died on 15th February 1918 as a result of an aeroplane accident. He is buried in New York (Wood Lawn) Cemetery, but the register does not give the exact grave location. A well-known Astaire-Rogers films of the later 1930s was called *The Story of Vernon and Irene Castle*.

Husband and wife buried in adjoining graves

The only known case of a husband and wife who were both in the Commonwealth forces being buried in adjoining graves is that of Craftsman Edward John Brewster, Royal Canadian Electrical and Mechanical Engineers, of Lakeview, Peel County, Ontario and Private Winifred Lilian Brewster, Canadian Women's Army Corps, of Lower Edmonton, Middlesex, England. They were both killed in the Netherlands on 15th April 1946 and are buried in Holten Canadian War Cemetery, Plot X, Row H, Graves 8 and 7. There is at least one other case of a husband and wife being buried together, but the wife was not in the forces: this couple were in an aeroplane which crashed. They were Air Chief Marshal Sir Trafford and Lady Leigh-Mallory, who died on 24th November 1944 and are buried in Allemont (le Rivier) Communal Cemetery, Isère, France, 21A Centre Plot, Graves 1 and 2.

Military Cross and Three Bars

The only known war fatality to have been awarded the Military Cross four times was Lieutenant Colonel Humphrey Arthur Gilkes of the British Army General List (i.e. he did not belong to a regiment or corps). He died on 11th July 1945, age 49, and is buried in Jibuti New European Cemetery, Djibouti, East Africa, Collective Grave 184–190. Brigadier General F.W. Lumsden VC, buried in Berles New Military Cemetery, France, and Captain F.J. Walker RN, commemorated on the Portsmouth Naval Memorial, were both awarded the DSO four times.

Cabinet Ministers' sons

Lieutenant Raymond Asquith, Grenadier Guards, the British Prime Minister's son and a brilliant student at Oxford, died on 15th September 1916 and is buried in Guillemont Cemetery, France, Grave IB3.

In the 1939–1945 War Anthony Eden was the British Foreign Secretary. He had served in the Rifle Brigade in 1914–1918 War and had been awarded the MC. His son, Pilot Officer Simon Gascoigne Eden RAF, died on 23rd June 1945, age 20, and is buried in Taukkyan War Cemetery, Burma, Collective Grave 25 J 9–12.

Amy Johnson CBE – Airwoman

Born at Hull, Yorkshire (now Humberside), Miss Johnson was an English airwoman. She flew solo from England to Australia in 1930, England to Japan via Siberia in 1931 and England to Cape Town in 1932, making new records in each case. These flights were in a biplane with an open cockpit. She became a pilot in the Air Transport Auxiliary (ATA) in the 1939–1945 War and was drowned after baling out of an aeroplane over the Thames Estuary in 1941. She was 38.

As a pilot with the ATA, Amy Johnson was a civilian but as she had been flying on duty when she died, she was accepted for war graves treatment. Her body was never found and therefore she was commemorated by name on the Runnymede Memorial, England. She was at one time married to James Mollison, an airman who also was a maker of records.

Service Numbers

Soldiers were frequently proud of their service numbers as they appeared to reflect their seniority and length of service. Two who must have been particularly well satisfied with theirs were:

No. 1 Barber (this was his rank and trade category) Shankar (his only name), 14th Punjab Regiment, Indian Army, who died on 19th January 1941 and is buried in Khartoum War Cemetery, Sudan. He was one of the 25 soldiers discovered in the early 1980s in the three graves at Derudeb to which reference is made elsewhere in this book.

No. 1 Private James Smith, 1st Battalion, Black Watch, who died on 31st October 1914, age 19, and is commemorated by name on the Menin Gate Memorial, Ypres.

A soldier who may well have pondered on his service number was No. 3565½ Havildar Mansur Khan, 58th Vaughan's Rifles (Frontier Force), who died on 30th August 1917 and is buried in Slobozia Military Cemetery, Romania. (In addition one cannot help but wonder what quirk of fate led this Indian soldier to die in such an obscure place.)

Alteration of commemoration according to changing circumstances

On 21st March 1945 an RAF aeroplane, carrying probably three British and one New Zealand airmen and three Belgian soldiers, crashed in the Grand Duchy of Luxembourg in mountainous, forested country which was difficult to reach. Two of the British airmen, the New Zealander and the Belgians were killed, and buried next to the aeroplane wreck by the local people, who also provided and erected permanent stone markers.

The site was very rarely visited, and in 1964 the Commission decided that the graves were unmaintainable and that the three Commonwealth airmen should be alternatively commemorated by the erection of special memorial headstones in the nearest Commission site, Hotton War Cemetery in the Province of Luxembourg, Belgium. The Belgians were not included in this decision as alternative commemoration almost always concerns only Commonwealth war dead. ('Almost' as there has, for example, been alternative commemoration of 13 Belgians buried in Birtley Cemetery in the north of England.) The alteration of the Commission's statistics and records meant that the total of Commonwealth war dead in Luxembourg decreased by three from 26 to 23, and increased by that number in Belgium.

The matter remained unchanged until the early 1980s, when it was ascertained that the graves in Luxembourg were still identifiable by their private markers; that the site was being visited not infrequently; and that the virtually complete aeroplane was also still there, a most stark memorial of its own. The Commission decided to revoke its 1964 decision, to accept the three burials as Asselborn (Maulesmuhle) Isolated Grave, Luxembourg, and to cancel the alternative commemoration in Hotton. And so, the figure of Commonwealth war dead for the small country of Luxembourg is again 26, and the enormous number for Belgium has, for once, decreased. Circumstances and flexibility brought about this satisfactory re-adjustment.

Cemetery names

The Commission's cemeteries often have odd, romantic, historical or humorous names, given by the soldiers and perpetuated by the Commission's adopting them as the sites' official titles. The following is a small selection of these. Some are mentioned elsewhere but, for ease of reference, have also been included here. The names listed are of cemeteries in Belgium and France and on the Gallipoli Peninsula and all relate to the 1914–1918 War.

Belgium

Bedford House Cemetery, Zillebeke   Bedford House was the name given by the Army to Château Rosendal, a country house.

Belgian Battery Corner Cemetery, Ypres   This was the name given to the point where the Rue Brielen joined a spur of the Ypres-Dickebusch road. The origin of the name is evident, but details of the battery are not known.

Buttes New British Cemetery, Polygon Wood, Zonnebeke   The Buttes (properly Butte) is a long 20 feet high artificial mound formerly used as a small-arms butt in target training; it forms the north-east side of the cemetery.

Divisional Collecting Post Cemetery, Boesinghe   This is a reference to a post to which casualties were brought from the front line.

Dozinghem Military Cemetery, Westvleteren In July 1917, at the beginning of the British offensive, groups of casualty clearing stations were established in readiness at three positions called by the soldiers Bandaghem, Dozinghem and Mendinghem – a good example of their sardonic humour.

Haringhe (Bandaghem) Cemetery (see Dozingham).

Hop Store Cemetery, Vlamertinghe The cemetery was opened next to the village hop store.

Maple Leaf Cemetery, Romarin, Neuve-Eglise The village of Romarin was occupied by the Advanced Dressing Station of the 3rd Canadian Field Ambulance from July 1915 to April 1916, and the cemetery thus acquired its name.

Mendinghem British Cemetery, Proven (see Dozinghem).

Mud Corner Cemetery, Warneton Mud Corner was the name given to a road junction on the northern edge of Ploegsteert Wood; it was entirely descriptive.

No Man's Cot Cemetery, Boesinghe The name was coined by the soldiers from a nearby building; it probably has some connection with No Man's Land. 'Cot' is the abbreviation of 'Cottage'.

Packhorse Farm Shrine Cemetery, Wulverghem The name was given to the farm by the soldiers who established the cemetery at a nearby shrine.

Perth (China Wall) Cemetery, Zillebeke The reason why 'Perth' is in the title is unknown, but it is perhaps because the cemetery was adopted by the 2nd Scottish Rifles in June 1917. 'China Wall' comes from the name of a nearby communication trench known to the soldiers as the 'Great Wall of China'.

Railway Dugouts Burial Ground (Transport Farm), Zillebeke As the railway runs next to the cemetery, its soldiers' name is obvious; the dugouts were long used by medical units. The cemetery was also called 'Transport Farm', the name they gave to local farm buildings, perhaps used by the then common horse-drawn transport.

France

Blighty Valley Cemetery, Authuile Wood, Aveluy The name Blighty Valley was given by the soldiers to the lower part of the deep valley running through Authuile Wood; the upper part was called Nab Valley. 'Blighty' was a slang word for England and the name therefore arose from the number of soldiers shipped home from the valley – after being severely wounded.

Brewery Orchard Cemetery, Bois Grenier   The cellar of the brewery was used as a dressing station and the cemetery was started in the orchard next to it.

2nd Canadian Cemetery, Sunken Road, Contalmaison   The Sunken Road was part of the Contalmaison-Pozières road. As a sunken road, it was much sought for shelter and therefore equally by the enemy artillery for destruction. The prefix 2nd was given to differentiate the cemetery from Sunken Road Cemetery.

Caterpillar Valley Cemetery, Longueval   'Caterpillar' was the name given by the soldiers to a narrow ribbon of woodland shaped like that creature; the valley ran below it.

Dud Corner Cemetery, Loos   This name alludes to the large number of unexploded shells found there after the war.

Hunter's Cemetery, Beaumont-Hamel   The origin of the name is not known, but may have been that of the company commander who, at the time, ordered this former shell hole to be used as a burial place for 46 soldiers of the 51st (Highland) Division.

L'Homme Mort Cemetery, Ecoust-St Mier   The name is the unhappy one of a hamlet nearly two miles away. As both St Leger and Vraucourt were only one and a quarter miles away, one might be justified in thinking that lugubrious soldier humour brought about the adoption of the more distant place name.

Post Office Rifles Cemetery, Festubert   The cemetery originally contained the graves of men of the Post Office Rifles, part of the 8th Battalion, London Regiment.

Quebec Cemetery, Cherisy   The title refers to the many Canadian soldiers – mainly from the 22nd and 24th Battalions, both from Quebec – who are buried here.

Redan Ridge Cemeteries, Nos 1, 2 and 3, Beaumont-Hamel   Redan Ridge lies north of the village. The cold numbering is a reflection of how close to each other some cemeteries on the Somme are situated.

Regina Trench Cemetery, Grandcourt   Regina Trench was the name given to a German earthwork. It was captured for a time by the 5th Canadian Brigade on 1st October 1916, attacked again by the 1st and 3rd

Canadian Divisions on 21st October and finally cleared by the 4th Canadian Division on 11th November 1916.

Unicorn Cemetery, Vend'huile   The name is taken from the divisional badge of the 50th Division, who buried members of the 18th Division after a battle. (The 50th's badge in the 1939–1945 War was two superimposed capital letter 'T's, representing the two English rivers flowing in their recruiting area – the Tyne and the Tees.)

'X' Farm Cemetery, La Chapelle d'Armentières   'X' Farm and 'Y' Farm were Army codenames for the farms to differentiate what were probably, in the end, piles of rubble. There is also a cemetery at 'Y' Farm.

'Y' Ravine Cemetry, Beaumont-Hamel   The cemetery is in Newfoundland Park, near 'Y' Ravine; not in this case a codename, but a description of its length with two short arms forking at its end.

Turkey (Gallipoli Peninsula)

Courtney's and Steel's Post Cemetery, Anzac   Courtney's Post was named after Lieutenant Colonel R.E. Courtney of the 14th Australian Infantry Battalion and the adjacent Steel's Post (officially Steele's Post), named after Major T.H. Steel of the same battalion. The posts, which were held from 25th April 1915 until the evacuation, gave their names to the cemetery.

Green Hill Cemetery, Suvla   The names Green Hill and Chocolate Hill (together forming Yilghin Burnu) refer to the respective colours of these features; only the first has a cemetery named after it.

Johnston's Jolly Cemetery, Anzac   From an observation point nearby, Brigadier General G.J. Johnston, Commander of the 2nd Australian Division Artillery, was said frequently to have directed the fire of the guns so that their shells would 'jolly up' the enemy.

New Zealand No 2 Outpost Cemetery, Anzac   During the fighting nearby, there had been two outposts – No 1 and No 2. No 2 Outpost Cemetery had already been established, so the Nelson Company of the New Zealand Forces named the cemetery they opened New Zealand No 2 Outpost Cemetery.

Circular memorial plaques

Very rarely a four-and-three-quarter-inch-diameter circular bronze plaque is to be seen fixed to a Commission headstone on a grave which is not in a Commission cemetery or plot. About a tenth of an inch thick, the plaques bear the casualty's first given name and surname, a large background figure of

Britannia and, in the foreground, a small lion. They also carry the inscription: 'He Died For Freedom And Honour.'

These plates were sent to the next of kin, together with a letter from Buckingham Palace, which read in full: 'I join with my grateful people in sending you this memorial of a brave life given for others in the Great War. George RI.'

The plaques were manufactured in Britain by the Memorial Plaque Factory at 54/56 Church Road, Acton, London W3. They were not the Commission's concern but some next of kin felt that the best place to display them was against a headstone, particularly as the reverse of the plate was blank.

Old wooden cross markers

Some next of kin asked if they could be given the graves' original wooden cross markers after they were replaced with the stone headstones. The Commission consented and a number of these originals – complete with names, regiments and other details – were eventually installed in large houses, cloisters and churches. The latter setting was most usual, with the cross fixed to the wall of the church in the town or village in which the man had lived.

The next of kin of those who had no known grave could, if they wished, have a cross which had originally marked the grave of an unidentified soldier. In such cases, the marker had a black brass label, with yellow brass lettering, which read:

1914–1918
This Cross
temporarily
marked the grave
of an unknown
British soldier
on the
Western Front
and is entrusted
to your care
by the
Imperial
War Grave
Commission

Private memorial plaques in a church

In the little church of Eye, near Leominster, Herefordshire, England, is a plaque which was privately erected by Sir Frederick Cawley Bt MP (later

Lord Cawley) and his wife, Lady Cawley; they lived at Berrington Hall, three miles away. The plaque commemorates their sons:

Major J.S. Cawley, Mentioned in Despatches, 20th Hussars, who died on 1st September 1914 at the Affair at Néry, France, and is buried in a privately marked grave in Néry Communal Cemetery in the Department of the Oise.

Captain the Honourable Oswald Cawley, 10th Battalion, King's Shropshire Light Infantry, who died on 22nd August 1918 on the Western Front, and whose body was interred at Néry in his brother's grave.

Captain H.T. Cawley MP, 6th Battalion, Manchester Regiment, who died on 23rd September 1915 and is buried in Lancashire Landing Cemetery, Helles, Gallipoli Peninsula, Turkey.

The two officers at Néry share their grave with Lieutenant J.D. Campbell, 'L' Battery, Royal Horse Artillery and Captain E.K. Bradbury VC, 'L' Battery, Royal Horse Artillery, both of whom were also killed in the Affair at Néry (along with many of their soldiers). The private memorial there is a stone pylon bearing the four names (but not very easy to read), set up over the grave and close to the cemetery wall.

In the early 1980s it was felt that Commission headstones should be added to the private memorial as one of those buried there was one of the first VCs of the 1914–1918 War. (It was one of three awarded to artillerymen of 'L' Battery, Royal Horse Artillery that day and indeed the present day 'L' Battery is designated 'L' (Néry) Battery, Royal Artillery.) It transpired that the best way to do this was by fixing two headstones to the wall, one on each side of the private memorial. The headstones are now in place, one commemorating Bradbury only (to give sufficient space for the large facsimile VC and a short inscription), the other to the brothers Cawley, and Campbell.

So three brothers of an old family died, but that was not to be all. There is now a more recent plaque next to the original in Eye Church. It is to Captain the Honourable H.K.J. Cawley, 1st Battalion, King's Shropshire Light Infantry, who died on 5th May 1943 and is buried in Massicault War Cemetery, Tunisia. He was the son of the second Lord Cawley.

Hadrian's Wall and the Aurelian Wall

Hadrian's Wall is the ancient Roman wall which stretched the 70 miles from Carlisle to Newcastle in northern England; the Aurelian Wall is part of the city of Rome's ancient defences – both were named after the Roman emperors who instigated them. The people of Carlisle thought that a stone from 'their' wall would be appropriate in Rome War Cemetery, a boundary of which is the Aurelian Wall. Therefore in the 1960s a commemorative stone, with an explanatory panel, was let into the brick platform on which

Rome's Stone of Remembrance lies. The following is the inscription on the panel:

> This Stone From Hadrian's Wall The Northernmost Boundary Of The Ancient Roman Empire Was Placed Here At The Wish Of The Citizens Of Carlisle England In Commemoration Of The Cumbrian Servicemen Who Died During The Second World War.

The memorial to Ahmed Mohammed Kinawi

So far as is known, Gardener Kinawi, an Egyptian, is the only member of the Commission's staff to be killed by enemy action in war while on duty in his cemetery. A plaque in Arabic and English was erected in his memory in Suez War Memorial Cemetery in June 1980, 10 years after his death there in an Israeli air-bombing raid.

Long service: Moustafa Aly Hassan

There are many cases of long service by members of the Commission's staff, but few, if any, can surpass the 50 years' service of Egyptian Head Gardener Hassan, much of it in Alexandria (Hadra) War Memorial Cemetery, Egypt. He retired in 1981.

Cross of Sacrifice in the USA

On 11th November 1927 a Cross of Sacrifice, erected by Canada in Arlington National Cemetery, Virginia, USA, was unveiled in honour of the Americans who served in the Canadian Army and died in the 1914–1918 War.

'MacRobert's Reply'

Lady MacRobert, widow of Sir Alexander MacRobert Bt (first baronet), had three sons. The first, Sir Alasdair (second baronet), was accidentally killed flying his own aeroplane in 1938. His successor, his brother, Flight Lieutenant Sir Roderick MacRobert RAF (third baronet), died over Mosul, Iraq, in May 1941. Sir Roderick's younger brother Pilot Officer Sir Iain MacRobert RAF (fourth and final baronet), died over the North Sea on 30th June 1941. The two younger baronets are commemorated in Mosul War Cemetery, Grave I.B.6., and on the Runnymede Memorial, Panel 33, respectively.

On 10th October 1941 Lady MacRobert made a gift of a Short Stirling four-engined bomber to the RAF. Named 'MacRobert's Reply', it flew on 12 operational missions and was subsequently used on training. The plaque and name on the bomber were then transferred to another Stirling which was later lost over Denmark during a mine-laying sortie.

An estimate of the number of Commonwealth war dead of the 1914–1918 and 1939–1945 Wars by religions

The table below gives an estimate of the number of Commonwealth war dead by religious faiths. As a large proportion of the final verification forms could not be sent to next of kin or were not returned to the Commission, accurate figures cannot be given, but the following provide a fairly good guide.

Buddhists/Confucians	10,000
Jews	10,000
Pagans	15,000
Muslims	65,000
Hindus/Sikhs	100,000
Christians	1,500,000
TOTAL	1,700,000

Civilian war dead

Over 65,000 British civilians were killed by enemy action during the 1939–1945 War. The worst single incident in Britain in the war was at New Cross in south London on 25th November 1944 when a V2 rocket fell on a Woolworth store and killed 149 and wounded many others, of whom 14 died later. The names of the dead are on the Civilian Roll of Honour. The last air attack on London which caused heavy loss of life was at Stepney on 27th March 1945 when a V1 flying bomb killed 134 people.

Ammunition

It is not uncommon to see piles of recovered shells, grenades, and other ammunition of the 1914–1918 War heaped by the roadside in Belgium and France. Usually such items are placed there by farmers after they have surfaced after ploughing or prolonged rains; sometimes visitors to battlefield sites may still discover ammunition. Such ammunition should never be touched, prodded, or in any way interfered with, as it almost certainly contains very unstable high explosive or gas. Any shock or damage to the rusty metal casing could well make the device explode, and shells should never be taken away as souvenirs. No action is required by the visitor if an item has obviously been dumped and is awaiting collection, but should the visitor find, say, a grenade close to a track, he could helpfully report the matter to the local police, or to a member of the Commission's staff.

Private memorials set up by the Commission

As has been seen, the Commission does not normally erect memorials except those designed to bear the names of the missing, but there are exceptions, of which the following are examples.

At one time the Commission held exhibitions in various cities and towns in the United Kingdom and abroad (in Arras and Ieper) to make its work better known and at which models, photographs, examples of stonework, copies of documents, records and registers, and such like were displayed. Often held in cathedrals, these exhibitions were usually well attended by the public.

One such exhibition was held at Chester Cathedral in Cheshire, England, in the summer of 1978. During discussions with the cathedral authorities following a successful exhibition, the Commission offered a tree to mark the 60th anniversary of the end of the 1914–1918 War and, indirectly, as a memento of the exhibition.

The first choice of tree seemed to be a lime, as a 'traditional precinct tree', but the final choice was an oak because of its traditional place in English history and its longevity. Just as important was the fact that the badge of the local county regiment, The Cheshire Regiment, is an oak-leaf spray with acorns.

It was agreed that, to give the presentation greater significance, the young tree should have started its life in a Commission site on the Western Front. A sapling oak, which had until then been growing in Tyne Cot* Cemetery, Passchendaele, was brought over from Belgium and planted during a small ceremony. A stone plaque, inscribed in the Commission's workshops at Arras, France, reads:

> This oak tree from Tyne Cot Cemetery, Passchendaele in which 12,000 Commonwealth soldiers of the First World War lie buried, was presented by the Commonwealth War Graves Commission to mark the 60th anniversary of the 1918 Armistice.

For a totally different reason – the Queen's Silver Jubilee of 1977 – the Commission donated a tree to the town of Maidenhead. It was planted in Kidwell's Park, which adjoins the Commission's Head Office, but there is no plaque to distinguish it.

---

* The cemetery still contains several German bunkers which, to the soldiers, looked like 'Tyneside Cottages'.

Overleaf is a copy of 'An Airman's letter' copied from *The Times* dated 18 June 1985.

Copied from The Times
dated 18 June 1985

ON THIS DAY

JUNE 18 1940

*Among the personal belongings of a
young RAF bomber pilot who had been
reported missing was found a letter to
his widowed mother with his wish that
it be sent to her if he was killed. It had
been left open – in compliance with
security – and was read by the station
commander. The spirit and wording of
the letter prompted him to ask the
mother if it could be published
anonymously. Following publication in
The Times thousands of requests came
in asking for a copy and within a
month about 500,000 copies were sold.
On February 18, 1981 a correspondent
contributed an obituary notice to* The
Times *of Mrs Lillian Rosewarne the
mother of the airman (her only child),
Vivian Alan William Noall Rosewarne
who was killed with his crew of 36(B)
Squadron during the evacuation at
Dunkirk.*

◆

[AN AIRMAN'S LETTER]

Dearest Mother, Though I feel no
premonition at all, events are moving
rapidly, and I have instructed that
this letter be forwarded to you should
I fail to return from one of the raids
which we shall shortly be called upon
to undertake. You must hope on for a
month, but at end of that time you
must accept the fact that I have
handed my task over to the extremely
capable hands of my comrades of the
Royal Air Forces, as so many splendid
fellows have already done.

First, it will comfort you to know
that my role in this war has been of
the greatest importance. Our patrols
far out over the North Sea have
helped to keep the trade routes clear
for our convoys and supply ships, and
on one occasion our information was
instrumental in saving the lives of the
men in a crippled lighthouse relief
ship. Though it will be difficult for
you, you will disappoint me if you do
not at least try to accept the facts
dispassionately, for I shall have done
my duty to the utmost of my ability.
No man can do more, and no one
calling himself a man could do less.

I have always admired your amazing
courage in the face of continual
setbacks; in a way you have given me
as good an education and background
as anyone in the country; and always

Note: Buried in Veurne Communal Cemetery Extension, Belgium. Grave B1

kept up appearances without ever losing faith in the future. My death would not mean that your struggle has been in vain. Far from it. It means that your sacrifice is as great as mine. Those who serve England must expect nothing from her; we debase ourselves if we regard our country as merely a place in which to eat and sleep.

History resounds with illustrious names who have given all, yet their sacrifice has resulted in the British Empire, where there is a measure of peace, justice, and freedom for all, and where a higher standard of civilization has evolved, and is still evolving, than anywhere else. But this is not only concerning our own land. Today we are faced with the greatest organized challenge to Christianity and civilization that the world has ever seen, and I count myself lucky and honoured to be the right age and fully trained to throw my weight into the scale. For this I have to thank you. Yet there is more work for you to do. The home front will still have to stand united for years after the war is won. For all that can be said against it, I still maintain that this war is a very good thing; every individual is having the chance to live and dare all for his principle like the martyrs of old. However long the time may be, one thing can never be altered – I shall have lived and died an Englishman. Nothing else matters one jot nor can anything ever change it.

You must not grieve for me, for if you really believe in religion and all that it entails that would be hypocrisy. I have no fear of death; only a queer elation . . . I would have it no other way. The universe is so vast and so ageless that the life of one man can only be justified by the measure of his sacrifice. We are sent to this world to acquire a personality and a character to take with us that can never be taken from us. Those who just eat and sleep, prosper and procreate, are no better than animals if all their lives they are at peace.

I firmly and absolutely believe that evil things are sent into the world to try us; they are sent deliberately by our Creator to test our metal because He knows what is good for us. The Bible is full of cases where the easy way out has been discarded for moral principles.

I count myself fortunate in that I have seen the whole country and known men of every calling. But with the final test of war I consider my character fully developed. Thus at my early age my earthly mission is already fulfilled and I am prepared to die with just one regret, and one only – that I could not devote myself to making your declining years more happy by being with you; but you will live in peace and freedom and I shall have directly contributed to that, so here again my life will not have been in vain.

Your loving Son,

Glossary
of Commission and military terms

In general military terms are given the meanings which were current during the 1914–1918 and 1939–1945 Wars. The present-day definitions may be very different.

A

Adjutant-General The senior staff officer at Army Headquarters dealing with administrative business (e.g. personnel, medical, welfare and pay matters).

Admiralty The British Department of State responsible for all aspects of the Navy's operations, supplies, ordnance, pay, manning etc. (now incorporated in the tri-service Ministry of Defence).

Advance to Victory The title sometimes given to the period starting on 8th August 1918 and finishing on Armistice Day, 11th November 1918.

Agency Service A task undertaken by the Commission on repayment by the contracting authority which is extra to its official duties (e.g. the maintenance of certain battle-exploit memorials).

Airman/Airwoman For Commission purposes, anyone of any rank who was serving in any capacity in the air forces.

Alternative Commemoration The commemoration by name in a place other than where the known grave is of one who died in war. There are a variety of reasons for such a commemoration, the most common being that the grave is unmaintainable.

American Battle Monuments Commission The United States 'War Graves Commission'; Head Office is at Washington DC.

Anzac
(a) This is an acronym and stands for the Australian and New Zealand Army Corps, which was formed in the 1914–1918 War. It can also refer to a member of the Anzac.
(b) The area of about two and a half square miles on the west coast of the Gallipoli Peninsula which was the landing place of the Anzacs on 25th April 1915 and whose full name was Anzac Area. The name was used in the Treaty of Lausanne (which assures the permanence of the war cemeteries on the Gallipoli Peninsula) because the cemeteries in the area are too closely clustered for individual reference. The

214

cemeteries at Cape Helles, which are fewer in number but contain more dead, are mentioned individually.

Area   In Commission parlance, one of its administrative units, usually covering a geographical area (e.g. Western Mediterranean Area). The Area Office reports direct to the Commission's Head Office.

Armed Merchant Cruiser   A merchant ship which was armed with guns and used as a cruiser. Being unarmoured and large, they were very vulnerable. They were generally manned by merchant seamen serving under the 'T124' Agreement, by which they agreed to serve with the RN.

Army   Two or more corps under the command of a general; generally between 120,000 and 200,000 all ranks.

Army Group   Two or more armies under the command of a field marshal; generally between 400,000 and one million all ranks. The largest land force formation.

Axis
(a)   Rome-Berlin. A term denoting the political collaboration between Fascist Italy and Nazi Germany. The metaphor was invented by Mussolini in a speech on 1st November 1936, in which he said, 'This Berlin-Rome line is not a diaphragm but rather an axis'. It was widened into an alliance in 1939 and led to Italy's entry into the war in 1940. Germany and Italy were usually referred to as the 'Axis' or the 'Axis Powers'. Later, it came to include Japan.
(b)   The general and main line of movement of a body of troops.

B

Balloon   See Barrage Balloon

Bar   The second, and any further, award of the same decoration for gallantry (eg DSO and bar, or DSO*, means two DSOs; MM and two Bars, or MM**, means three MMs). The 'Bar' itself is of metal and is fastened across the ribbon on which the decoration hangs. If only the ribbon is worn, the Bar is indicated by a metal rosette on the ribbon.

Barrage   A concentration of artillery shells arranged to fall in 'lines' ahead of the infantry to destroy the enemy or make him keep his head down. The lines are 'lifted' to positions further on as the infantry advance.

Barrage Balloon   Sausage-shaped, hydrogen-filled, non-dirigible balloons, moored by a cable by which they could be raised or lowered. Their purpose was to force enemy aircraft to fly higher out of fear of entanglement in the cables, where they would be at greater risk from heavy anti-aircraft guns or fighters.

Battalion   The basic fighting unit of infantry, commanded by a lieutenant colonel and comprising about 35 officers and about 750 soldiers; this varies widely from army to army and from period to period.

Battery A body of between 150 and 180 soldiers of the Royal Horse Artillery or Royal Artillery, commanded by a major and armed with (c.) eight guns. Roughly the equivalent of an infantry company, but far more independent. Each of the three batteries in an RA regiment was normally allocated to one of the three battalions in the brigade.

Battle-Exploit Memorial Commission parlance for memorials set up by governments or regiments to commemorate feats of arms etc., and which are maintained by the Commission on an agency or repayment basis; ownership remains with the government or regiment. The function of these memorials is totally different from those of the Commission, which mainly exist to record the names of men with no known graves.

Battle cruiser A warship, nearly as large as a battleship (or, in rare cases, larger), but faster and with smaller armament and thinner armour.

Battleship Generally speaking the largest warships used in the 1914–1918 and 1939–1945 Wars, with the heaviest gun armaments and armour.

Beachhead The landing site on enemy territory after having crossed a large expanse of water. One cemetery (Anzio Beach Head) includes the term in its title.

Blighty British Army slang for England and home. A 'Blighty one' was a wound of such severity as to ensure the casualty's return to the United Kingdom. From Anglo-Indian corruption of Hindi 'bilayati' – European or English.

Blitzkrieg (and Blitz) German for 'lightning war'; the concept was to keep the enemy off balance by using shock-tactics. Most evident in Poland in September 1939, in France and Belgium in May and June 1940, and in the early months of the invasion of Russia which started in June 1941. The term 'Blitz' was coined by the British as a noun and verb for the air attacks on Britain; *the* 'Blitz' was on London in the last few months of 1940.

Botticino (limestone) The stone was initially used in Italy, where it is quarried at Brescia in the north; it is now being used for replacement of weathered Portland headstones.

Brigade The smallest fighting formation, commanded by a brigadier, comprising three battalions with artillery, engineers, signals, etc. Some brigades had four battalions. A brigade had between 4,000 and 5,000 men. Also (1914–1918 only) the parent unit of several artillery batteries (called a 'regiment' in the 1939–1945 War).

Brigade Group A brigade reinforced by certain administrative troops (and sometimes by combatant troops) to enable it to take part in operations independently, as opposed to within a division.

British Expeditionary Force (BEF) The name given to the original four infantry and one cavalry divisions of the Regular British Army which went to France in August 1914. Later the name was to cover all Commonwealth forces.

Burial Ground   See Site

Burning Ghat   A place where Hindus cremate their dead.

Bushido   The code of honour and morals evolved by Japanese warriors (the Samurai). The word translates as 'military knight way'.

Butt   A mound behind a target on a range to bring the bullet to a safe stop. 'Butts' is normally used to denote the rifle range as well as the mound.

C

Casualty   In military terms, anyone who is killed, wounded or missing. It is even stretched in barracks to include sickness, courses, and other events, including – yes – marriage!

Cemetery Extension   The title the Commission gives to an extension to a (usually) civil cemetery for the burial of Commonwealth war dead. This in effect forms a new war cemetery, but one which is linked with the original.

Cenotaph   Sepulchral monument (literally 'empty tomb') to person whose body is elsewhere. Perhaps the best known is the Cenotaph in Whitehall, London, England, which commemorates the dead of the 1914–1918 and 1939–1945 Wars. (This, and village and town cenotaphs, are not the Commission's responsibility.)

Chairman of the Commission   Is ex officio the Secretary of State for Defence of the United Kingdom (formerly Secretary of State for War).

Chemin d'Accès   Translates as 'access path' and is the usual Commission term for a footpath across fields etc. providing the recognized approach to a particular war graves site. The Commission is usually responsible for the maintenance (eg keeping the grass-way mown).

Chindit   The name of a mythical beast, and given to the forces raised by Major General Orde Wingate DSO** (formerly of the Royal Artillery). The role of the Chindits was to fight independently, while being supplied by air, behind the Japanese lines in Burma. Two forays took place, in February 1943 and March 1944; the second was larger and more costly in lives. Their military value has always been a matter of debate. Wingate was killed in an air crash in Burma in 1944.

Collective Grave   A war grave containing three or more Commonwealth war dead.

Command   In the Army, a non-operational, geographical district (eg South-Eastern Command, England); in air forces, an operational branch which performs a specific function (eg Coastal Command, Bomber Command).

Commandos   Assault troops employed in special roles. Originally a Boer term used in the Boer War.

Commemoration Book   In some cases those with no known grave are commemorated by the Commission by name in special books rather than by name on memorials; the Book is accepted as the memorial.

Commissioned Officer   See Officer

Commissioner   A member of the policy-making body of the Commission, not of its permanent, professional staff. Often referred to as a 'Member of the Commission'.

Common Grave   A grave not owned by the Commission, which contains more than one set of remains, at least one of which is of a war fatality. Common graves are not marked by the Commission, as they are often public property.

Communal Cemetery   A cemetery belonging to the *commune*. Many on the old Western Front contain Commonwealth war graves, either individually or in plots; many of the plots of war graves are in effect war cemeteries.

Company   A body of about 100 soldiers, commanded by a major or captain. There are four companies to a battalion. Although basically a unit of infantry, certain other branches do use the term.

Concentration   In Commission parlance, the gathering in of war dead from outlying battlefield graves and their reburial within a war cemetery.

Conspicuous Gallantry Medal (CGM)   The naval and air equivalent of the Distinguished Conduct Medal (DCM).

Contemptible   See Old Contemptible.

Convoy   A group of merchant ships sailing together under the protection of naval forces; sometimes slow-moving, as its speed is that of the slowest vessel. The word is also used for columns of motor vehicles.

Corps
(a)   Two or more divisions (it is flexible) under the command of a lieutenant general; generally between 30,000 and 60,000 all ranks.
(b)   See Departmental Corps.

Crater   The hole in the ground caused by a shell, bomb, mine, etc. Can be any size from one or two feet across to hundreds of feet in diameter. Some craters were used for burials, and became Commission war graves or cemeteries. As individual marking in the latter was impossible, the names were engraved on a specially erected screen-wall.

Cremation memorial   A memorial which lists by name those whose remains were cremated in that area and whose ashes were scattered (as opposed to buried) there or elsewhere.

Cross of Sacrifice   A stone cross, which usually comes in one of four sizes, erected in Commission sites containing 40 or more war dead. However, there are cases where a Cross has been erected over the graves of a smaller number. The Cross bears a sword.

Cruiser A fast, medium-sized warship with medium armament and armour. Often used as the mainstay of the defence of a convoy or of a patrol to safeguard shipping lanes from enemy surface ships.

D

D-Day D stands for 'Day' in military parlance and is the day on which any operation is due to start. Hence D + 1 is one day after the operation has started, and D − 10 is 10 days before. By using this system, the date of an operation remains more secure and can easily be altered (as the best known D-Day, in Normandy, was altered from 5th to 6th June) without having to amend all documents. There were any number of D-Days, but to the laymen the term means Normandy, 1944. The French use Jour J.

Dedicatory Inscription The fine words or thoughts on a memorial: literally inscribed on stone, but raised on bronze (on the latter therefore it is, to be strict, not an 'inscription').

Departmental Corps One of the supporting corps of the Army (eg Royal Army Medical Corps, Royal Army Ordnance Corps).

Depot
(a) The base of the regiment or departmental corps, where servicemen are trained and kitted out before joining units (eg battalions, batteries) or held, for example, after being in hospital.
(b) A place for stores, ammunition or fuel.

Destroyer A warship armed mainly with torpedoes and anti-submarine devices. The small, fast, manoeuvrable maid-of-all-work of the navies; originally a 'torpedo-boat destroyer'.

Director-General, Secretary to the Commission The Commission's senior permanent member of staff.

Distinguished Conduct Medal (DCM) For bravery in the field; awarded to non-officer army ranks. The DCM is equivalent to the DSO.

Distinguished Flying Cross (DFC) The air equivalent of the Military Cross (MC).

Distinguished Flying Medal (DFM) The equivalent for non-officer air force ranks of the Distinguished Flying Cross (DFC).

Distinguished Service Cross (DSC) The naval equivalent of the Military Cross (MC).

Distinguished Service Medal (DSM)   The equivalent for non-officer naval ranks of the Distinguished Service Cross (DSC).

Distinguished Service Order (DSO)   For bravery or as a recognition of good service in the field; normally awarded to majors (and other service equivalents) and above. In especially deserving cases it may be awarded to junior officers (ie captain and below). Equivalent to the DCM and, as an immediate decoration, often second only to the VC.

Division   The formation by which the strength of an army is usually calculated; it is commanded by a major general. It comprises three brigades, and is self-sufficient in that it has its own artillery, engineers, workshops, medical services etc. The infantry division is usually about 15,000 strong; the cavalry or armoured division has two or three thousand fewer men.

Duce (Il)   The leader of Fascist Italy, Benito Mussolini; Il Duce translates as the Chief. Shot by Italian Communist partisans in 1945.

Dud (shell)   A shell which fails to explode after having been fired from a gun; it is usually referred to merely as a 'dud'. It remains dangerous until expertly defused and emptied of high explosive.

E

Endowment Fund   See Imperial War Graves Endowment Fund.

Extension   See Cemetery Extension.

F

Fascism (Fascismo)   Principles and organization of the right-wing movement in Italy, which culminated in the dictatorship of Benito Mussolini; the Italians were imitated by Fascist organizations in other countries. The name was taken from the organization's symbol, a fascine (a bundle of sticks) with an axe. The Italians' leader was known as the Duce.

Field Marshal   The highest rank in the British Army. The other services' equivalent ranks are Admiral of the Fleet and Marshal of the Royal Air Force. Officially they are never retired.

Final Verification Form   The form sent by the Commission to the next of kin, giving the war dead's known personal details (eg given names and religion). Next of kin were asked to check and amend if necessary and, for those dead with known graves, to add a personal text for inscription on the marker, if desired. Many forms were either not sent or not received because next of kin's addresses were frequently not known, wrongly given, or had changed by the time the form arrived after the war; some were simply not returned to the Commission.

Fleur The French word for 'flower'. A repair to a piece of stone done by removing an irregularly shaped ('flower-like') piece and replacing it with stone or stone substitute. The irregular shape is less noticeable than a repair with straight edges.

Foreign Headstone The marker peculiar to a particular country and used by the Commission to mark graves of dead of that country which are in the Commission's sites. They were designed in agreement with the countries concerned.

Foreign War Grave The grave of any foreigner (ex-Allied or ex-enemy) which is in a Commission site and maintained with the site's Commonwealth war graves. Foreigners who served in the Commonwealth forces are considered 'Commonwealth' by the Commission and their graves are marked by standard Commission markers.

Formation The army term for a body of troops larger than a battalion (eg brigade, division).

Free French Those forces of France which rallied under Général de Brigade Charles de Gaulle from 18th June 1940 to continue the fight against Nazi Germany.

Front Line(s) See Line(s).

Führer (Der) Adolph Hitler (1889–1945), an Austrian by birth, was Führer (Leader) of Germany from 1933 to 1945, when he committed suicide in Berlin.

G

Gallipoli Often, inaccurately, used by people when they mean the Gallipoli Peninsula, Turkey. There was much fighting on the Peninsula; none at or near the town of Gallipoli (Gelibolu in Turkish), which was nearly 20 miles from the battlefield.

Gas Poison gas delivered to the enemy by release from a container or by shell; used by both sides, but only in the 1914–1918 War. With the prevailing westerly wind over the Western Front, it was of greater use to the Allies. Normally mustard, phosgene or chlorine.

Gentleman Cadet A cadet at the Royal Military College, Sandhurst, (now Royal Military Academy Sandhurst) or at the Royal Military Academy, Woolwich, London, (now no longer in existence) was so known before the 1939–1945 War.

George Cross (GC) Awarded for acts of gallantry not necessarily in the face of the enemy, the George Cross is equal in merit to the Victoria Cross, though the latter is the senior decoration in the order of precedence. It may be awarded during peacetime to the military or civilians. Holders of the Empire Gallantry Medal at the time of the George Cross's inception (24th September 1940) had the medal exchanged for the GC. Living holders of the Albert Medal have also had their medals exchanged for the GC. The obverse is inscribed simply, 'For Gallantry'.

George Medal (GM)   For deeds of the type for which the George Cross is awarded, but not involving the same extreme element of danger and/or courage.

Ghat   See Burning Ghat

Gift of Land Tablet   A tablet in stone frequently seen at the entrances to war cemeteries with a text in English and the local language(s) explaining how the site came to be held as a war cemetery – usually as a 'Gift of Land' from the host country.

Grave   The excavation which has received the remains (ie body or buried, as opposed to scattered, ashes) of one who is entitled to war graves treatment. A grave may contain almost any number of sets of remains, but most often contains only one.

Great War   The title by which the 1914–1918 War was generally known before the 1939–1945 War. It will be noticed that the inscription on the headstone of an unknown burial of the 1914–1918 War refers to the 'Great War'. The term 'World War' was not used.

Group   An RAF formation, roughly equivalent to an Army division, in Bomber Command (eg No. 6 (Canadian) Group).

Gurkha   A native of Nepal. For Commission purposes, a soldier of a Gurkha regiment.

H

Headstone   The definitive upright grave marker. It can be one of several types of stone, but Portland is by far the most common in temperate latitudes; granite is, for example, used in Canada, South Africa and Scandinavia. Replacements for Portland headstones are now usually made of Italian Botticino limestone.

Headstone beam   The concrete beam which is laid under the surface of the headstone border at the head of lines of graves and into which the headstones are slotted and fixed. This ensures a neat and tidy appearance of the lines and upright and stable headstones.

Headstone border   The carefully cultivated border, usually about two feet wide, in which the markers are fixed. It usually contains flowers, bushes or other plants.

H-Hour   Performs a similar function to D-Day: it is the time the operation starts on D-Day. Time is expressed in the same way as days, hence H − 2 mins is two minutes before the time of the start of the operation and H + 7 mins, is seven minutes after. (In the 1914–1918 War and earlier part of the 1939–1945 War the term 'Zero Hour' was used.)

Historical Notice   The Commission's name for the stainless steel notices in war cemeteries and at memorials which explain how these came to be situated there. The notice normally also has a map and is in English and the local language. In the case of predominantly Canadian or South African cemeteries, French or Afrikaans is used in addition to English and the local language. It is hoped that about 1,000 cemeteries and memorials will have notices by the 1990s.

Holland   North Holland and South Holland are provinces of **The Netherlands**.

Home Guard   A body of volunteer British civilian men recruited under a scheme announced by Anthony Eden (then British Secretary of State for War) after the disaster of Dunkirk in June 1940; they were armed scantily, but as well as possible. Organized on local defence infantry lines, they existed until 1944, by which time they were a useful adjunct to the Army in Britain; they helped to man anti-aircraft batteries, for example. At the time they were stood down, they were around a million strong. Their title on formation (for a few weeks) was the awkward-sounding Local Defence Volunteers (LDV).

Honourable Scars   Those marks on memorials which bear witness to shell bursts, bullet strikes etc. and have been left by the Commission for historical reasons and interest. Any scars which might have affected the safety or structure of the memorial or which obscured an inscription or name were repaired. There are, for example, minor honourable scars on the Villers-Brettoneux Memorial and extensive scars on the Memorial at Neuve Chapelle.

Hundred Days (The Battle of the)   The Commonwealth and Allied offensive which lasted the 96 days from the morning of 8th August to 1100 hours on 11th November 1918. It was quick and efficient work and the title harks back to the 'Campaign of the Hundred Days', which ended at Waterloo just over a hundred years earlier.

I

Imperial War Graves Commission   The title of the Commission until it was changed on 1st April 1960; it was thought no longer appropriate.

Imperial War Graves Endowment Fund   A fund of £5 million established in 1925 by the then participating governments to provide income for the permanent maintenance of the war graves and memorials. Contributions were made by the countries in proportion to the number of their war graves. The fund was completed in 1940, but has not proved large enough to provide more than a small part of the total funds required by the Commission.

Inscription   See Dedicatory Inscription and Personal Inscription.

Isolated Grave   A war grave which is not in a cemetery or plot and for which the Commission may or may not be responsible. Often the remains were not moved in compliance with the next of kin's request.

J

Jerry   The Commonwealth's most commonly used nickname for a German. Various derivatives have been offered; it possibly comes from 'German'.

Joint Grave   A Commonwealth war grave containing two war dead.

K

Kaiser (Der)   Wilhelm (William) II (1859–1941) was the third German Kaiser (emperor), and ninth King of Prussia. He reigned from 1888–1918 and was head of state of Germany during the 1914–1918 War. He was exiled at the war's end and died in exile at Doorn in the Netherlands.

L

League of Nations   The first attempt to create a worldwide organization of states, an idea inspired by pacifist and liberal ideas and by the experiences of the 1914–1918 War. The League was set up in 1920, created by the victors in the war; but the US stayed out. Neutrals were soon admitted, followed by the vanquished – Germany in 1925 and the Soviet Union in 1934 – and at its peak the League had 56 members; but the absence of the USA rather emasculated it. In 1932 Japan left the League, when her attack on Manchuria was condemned. It was further weakened when Hitler took Germany out, and when it was unable to do anything positive to stop Italy's invasion of Abyssinia. The League was based in Geneva, Switzerland.

Line(s)   In the 1914–1918 War, usually literally a zig-zag line of trenches, facing the enemy's line. In the 1939–1945 War, more often a broad band of defended localities, the defence of which was made possible by the mobility of the tank and self-propelled artillery etc.

Local Defence Volunteers   See Home Guard.

M

Maginot Line   A line of concrete forts, anti-tank obstacles, guns, machine guns etc., which ran along the French border with Germany from the junction with Belgium to Switzerland. It did not run along the border with Belgium. The Maginot line was static and produced static thought; the Germans' invasion of Belgium outflanked it. Named after André Maginot (1877–1932), who, as Minister for War, was its prime mover.

Maps   See Michelin Maps.

Maquis   Secret force of patriots in occupied France in the 1939–1945 War (French for brushwood).

Marker   The headstone (upright) or plaque (recumbent or semi-recumbent). Normally over a grave, but not infrequently indicating that the actual grave is elsewhere.

Master (or Master Mariner)   The officer in command of a ship of the Mercantile Marine or Merchant Navy. The prefix 'Captain' is an honorary title.

Member Country/Countries   The countries which contribute directly to the Commission's funds and therefore provide official Commissioners. They are Britain, Canada, Australia, New Zealand, South Africa and India, and formerly Newfoundland and Pakistan. Member countries are sometimes described as 'participating countries'.

Member of Commission   See Commissioner.

Memorial   A structure which provides wall space on which are inscribed the names of those with no known grave, no grave but the sea, or who have been cremated.

Mention in Despatches   Not a decoration as such, but a recognition of greater than normal duty – when the name is 'mentioned in despatches'. Such a 'mention' could, of course, be made posthumously whereas only the VC and GC among decorations could at one time be so awarded. (All other decorations for gallantry, except the DSO, may now be awarded posthumously.) The badge of the 'Mention' is an oak leaf worn on the war medal, the stalk of the leaf towards the centre of the chest.

Michelin Maps   In Commission parlance, the specially overprinted maps (Nos. 52, 53 and 54; scale 1:200,000) of Flanders and northern France, showing the location of the bigger memorials, cemeteries and plots. They are published by the Commission in conjunction with Michelin. No other similar maps of other areas are in existence, as nowhere else is the concentration of memorials and cemeteries anything like as dense.

Military Cross (MC)   Awarded for bravery in the field to majors, junior officers and warrant officers. It is ranks below the DSO.

Military Medal (MM)   The army non-officer ranks' equivalent of the Military Cross.

Mine
(a)   An explosive device designed to destroy ships. Some float just below the surface, anchored by a cable to the sea bed; these explode on contact. Others lie on the sea bed and are activated by the ship's acoustics, magnetism, etc.
(b)   An explosive device buried at a shallow depth which detonates on being trodden on or driven over.
(c)   A gallery dug underground, usually by army engineers, to a position under the enemy, where explosives are placed and detonated.

Mobile Group   In Commission parlance, a group of gardeners (generally six or less) who are responsible for the horticultural maintenance of a group of war cemeteries and plots. They and their equipment travel in a van.

Mulberry   The codename given to the floating harbours and landing piers which were towed from England to Normandy in June 1944 to form an artificial port at Arromanches (the other was wrecked).

N

Name Panel   A panel (usually of bronze or stone) on which names are embossed or inscribed on Commission memorials of all types. In registers they are referred to either as panels or faces, with, sometimes, a reference to the pier on which the panel is fixed. One panel may consist of more than one section (eg Panel No. 16 may comprise four inscribed stones).

Nazi   A member of the German National Socialist Party. During the 1939–1945 War it was used loosely to mean a German. Nazi derives from National Socialist.

Nederlands Oorlogsgravenstiching (Netherland War Graves Foundation)   The Netherlands (Dutch) equivalent of the Commission; Head Office is at The Hague.

No Man's Land   The term used by the soldiers to describe the land lying between the friendly and enemy lines. It could vary from yards to miles in width, but with a rough average of perhaps 100 to 500 yards.

Non-Commissioned Officer (NCO)   A Commonwealth serviceman holding an army rank from corporal to staff sergeant inclusive (to flight sergeant in the air forces). Lance Corporal is an appointment, not a rank.

Non-World-War Grave   A grave which is in a Commission cemetery or plot, or in a special plot cared for by the Commission, the occupant of which died outside the 'war periods' or did not meet the required criteria, and who was therefore not entitled to war graves treatment.

O

Officer   Short for Commissioned Officer. A Commonwealth serviceman who has received the King's (now Queen's) or Viceroy's Commission.

Old Contemptible   The sobriquet adopted by the original British Expeditionary Force of 1914 (the Regular British Army) because the Kaiser supposedly referred to it as a 'contemptible little army'. Perhaps a better translation would have been a 'contemptibly little army' which by European standards, at five divisions, it arguably was! The name became so firmly established that Old Contemptibles' Associations are only now, in the 1980s, literally dying out.

Other Ranks (OR)   Soldiers other than those of commissioned rank, though sometimes refers only to those below sergeant. 'Soldiers' was a happier term.

P

Panel See Name Panel.

Personal Inscription A text of 60 letters or less chosen by the next of kin for inscription on a grave marker.

Plaque The stone or bronze marker, recumbent or semi-recumbent, used where headstones were deemed inappropriate for climatic or other reasons.

Platoon A body of about 30 men, commanded by a subaltern officer. There are three or four platoons to a company.

Plot
(a) A section of a war cemetery with a number of rows of graves, usually separated from the other sections by paths or grass.
(b) See War Graves Plot.

'Pocket' Battleship The term used to describe the three vessels built by the Germans to circumvent treaties limiting the size of their warships. By clever design, comparatively small (c. 10,000 tons) ships were given near-battleship guns (11 inch) and armour. The *Admiral Graf Spee* is the most famous of the three, because of its scuttling following the Battle of the River Plate in December 1939.

Portland A white limestone of which most of the Commission's headstones, etc. are made. Named after Portland in south England, where it was quarried.

Post
(a) A place, point, fort, etc. for which a soldier is responsible or at which he is stationed.
(b) To move soldiers from one place or unit to another. Units may also be posted from place to place.

President of the Commission There have been four presidents: the Prince of Wales (later Edward VIII) 1917–1936; the Duke of York (later George VI) 1936; the Duke of Gloucester 1937–1970; and the Duke of Kent (1970–   ).

Q

Quartermaster An army officer who has usually served long and well in the ranks and has been granted a quartermaster commission. His job is the issue of, and accounting for, stores, rations, ammunition, and fuels, and the administration of all quarters, barracks, etc. in the regiment or battalion with which he is serving.

Quisling, Vidkun Norwegian diplomat and Fascist leader who became the puppet prime minister of Norway after the German invasion of 1940. After this traitors came to be known as 'Quislings'. He was executed by the Norwegians in 1945.

R

Redoubt   A fortification: a fieldwork usually square or polygonal and without flanking defences.

Register   The books published by the Commission for all cemetery and memorial sites, giving, in alphabetical order of surname (of first names in the case of Indians and certain other nationals) details of those buried or commemorated.

Register Box   The bronze container (usually set in a wall) with a bronze door in which the cemetery or memorial register is kept with the visitors' book.

Register Entry   The details following the surname in a register: first name(s) and/or initials, unit, date of death, age, next of kin, part address (when known) and plot, row and grave (or panel number for memorials). For the 1914–1918 War only the cause of death, if known, was given.

Reich   The German confederation (Reich is German for 'kingdom'). The First Reich was the Holy Roman Empire (962–1806); the Second Reich was from 1871–1918; the Third Reich was the Nazi regime (1933–1945).

Religious Emblem   The Christian Cross, Jewish Star of David, etc. which is inscribed on a marker at the request of the next of kin. Equally the Commission abides by the next of kin's request for no emblem. In the event that there is no contact with the next of kin, a religious emblem is inscribed.

Riding   (eg in 49th (West Riding) Division, 63rd (West Riding) Medium Regiment RA). The county of Yorkshire was divided into three Ridings – East, West and North. They officially ceased to exist in the early 1970s, when county boundaries were greatly altered.

Roadside Direction Signs   The standard green signs with white lettering which indicate the way to, or announce arrival at, war cemeteries and memorials. The Commission has obtained permission to erect these in nearly all countries. The top line of the sign reads 'Commonwealth War Graves' (or 'Memorial') usually in the local language and script.

Roll of Honour   The Commission's volumes kept by the great West Door of Westminster Abbey, London, near the Tomb of the Unknown Warrior, which list the 65,000 Commonwealth civilians who died in the 1939–1945 War. The great majority were Britons killed by bombing and V1 and V2 attacks. The Roll does not give places of burial, as these are not known to the Commission; nor is the maintenance of their graves the Commission's responsibility.

Row   The row, usually lettered (eg Row C), in which a grave is situated.

Royal Naval Division   A 1914–1918 War division of land troops, effectively part of the British Army, but manned by sailors of the Royal Navy. They fought as soldiers on the Western Front and the Gallipoli Peninsula. Those who lost their lives and have no known grave are commemorated on the Army's memorials, not the Navy's.

S

Sailor For Commission purposes, anyone of any rank who was serving in any capacity in the armed naval forces.

Salient For the purposes of this book, a pronounced geographical bulge into the territory of the opposing side. When not prefixed by a name, 'Salient' was often understood to be the Ypres Salient, which existed from late 1914 to 1918 and was probably the best known.

Scars See Honourable Scars.

Screen Wall The Commission term for a monumental wall built to provide space for the inscription of names. Most usually erected in cases of alternative commemoration or multiple burial (eg the burial of 50 dead in a crater cemetery) where individual marking is impossible. As screen walls are not used for no-known-grave commemorations, the layout of names, regimental details, etc. follows no set pattern and is decided ad hoc.

Seaman For Commission purposes, anyone of any rank or grade who was serving in any capacity in the Mercantile Marine or the merchant navies.

Security of Tenure The legal security from disturbance which the Commission has for all its cemeteries and plots, and which it tries to obtain for all its other sites (eg isolated graves, graves in civil cemeteries when the next of kin have died etc.).

Shrapnel Small metal balls exploded from a shell in flight and used against the enemy in the open; not pieces of the shell itself, which are called shell fragments. It is named after Colonel Henry Shrapnel RA, who invented this shell around 1793.

Signs See Roadside Direction Signs.

Site To the Commission, a 'site' is a place where there is one war grave or more (eg a single war grave in a churchyard in Ontario is a site; so is the largest cemetery, Tyne Cot, Passchendaele). To the Commission the terms 'site' and 'burial ground' are interchangeable.

Soldier For Commission purposes, anyone of any rank who was serving in any capacity in the land forces (but not the sailors in the Royal Naval Division).

Special Memorial Headstones Markers erected to commemorate war dead whose remains are elsewhere (eg in an unmaintainable grave).

Special Operations Executive (SOE) British secret organization during the 1939–1945 War, instructed by Churchill to 'set Europe ablaze'. Many Commonwealth men and women served in it, helping to train, arm, and organize nationals of Axis-occupied countries for armed resistance.

SS Abbreviation of the German *Schutzstaffel* – Protection Patrol. A Nazi political policing force of evil reputation gained particularly for their brutal role in extermination camps, such as Belsen and Auschwitz. The *Waffen* (Armed) SS were part of the German armed forces and distinct from the concentration camp guards.

Stone of Remembrance Usually a monolith acceptable to those of any faith (or none) as a focal point for ceremonies and wreath-laying. Normally erected in cemeteries in which there are 400 or more war dead or in, or near to, certain large memorials to the missing. Where transport of a single stone was impossible, the stone is made up of several smaller ones, but this is uncommon.

Subaltern A commissioned army officer below the rank of captain (ie a second lieutenant or lieutenant).

Sword A Crusader-type sword fixed, hilt uppermost, to a Cross of Sacrifice. Originally made of bronze, replacements now are of fibreglass to deter vandals and thieves. The cross made by the hilt and the blade coincides with the arms and shaft of the Cross itself. Where appropriate for aesthetic reasons, there is a sword on both sides of the Cross; elsewhere on one side only.

T

Tail See Teeth Arms.

Tank An armoured and armed fighting vehicle, driven and steered by its tracks. The word was originally a codeword in the 1914–1918 War, used to mislead the enemy over what was being supplied, under covers, to the front.

Teeth Arms An expression of army origin, referring to those arms which are in direct contact with the enemy (ie infantry, artillery, armour, and combat engineers and signals) as opposed to the administrative 'Tail' (eg ordnance, supply, repair, pay, etc.).

Tempietto A rectangular shelter found in some cemeteries; it sometimes forms part of a memorial, as is the case in the Athens Memorial.

Tommy The British public's, and later the Commonwealth's and the Germans' nickname for British soldiers. The original 'Tommy' was the mythical Private Thomas Atkins, the soldier used as an example in various official military publications.

U

U-Boat From U-Boot, the German abbreviation for *Unterseeboot*, a submarine.

Undivided India So far as the Commission is concerned, when dealing with statistics etc. India is undivided (ie as she was before partition on 15th August 1947). There is no sure way of knowing if a man who died would have been from present-day India or Pakistan: the religion (India – Hindu and Sikh, and Pakistan – Moslem) is only a guide. There is now the added complication that Pakistan, at the time of partition, was divided into West Pakistan and East Pakistan with India between. East Pakistan subsequently broke away and is now Bangladesh. The Commission's estimate is that two-thirds of the 160,000 war dead of undivided India came from present-day India, and a third from Pakistan (ie before her partition into Pakistan and Bangladesh).

Unit   The army term for a body of troops up to battalion in size.

Unknown (Sailor, Soldier, Airman)   The remains of one whose name is not known. Everything else (rank, nationality, regiment, date of death) may be known, but positive identification is impossible as two men with the same particulars may have died on the same day and only one of them been found.

Unknown Warrior   The unknown Commonwealth serviceman buried in Westminster Abbey, London, and representing all those who died in wars.

Unmaintainable grave   A grave which is unmaintainable under the present arrangements. The name of the dead person it contains is therefore commemorated elsewhere.

V

VE Day   The official end of the war in Europe (Victory in Europe) on 8th May 1945.

VJ Day   The official end of the war with Japan (Victory over Japan) on 15th August 1945.

Vergeltungswaffen – V1 and V2   Translates as 'weapons of revenge'. V1 was the codename given by the Germans to their jet-propelled, pilotless aircraft with a one-ton warhead. Much used against London from June 1944, it was inaccurate but successful over such a large target area. Also much used against Antwerp, Belgium. Vulnerable to anti-aircraft guns and fighters. V2 was the codename given by the Germans to their large rocket, also with a one-ton warhead. Its speed meant that there was no warning of its arrival and no defence against it.

Versailles   The peace treaty signed at the Palace of Versailles, near Paris in France on 28th June 1919 between the Allies and Germany is often simply known as 'Versailles'. Its harsh conditions are often held to have contributed to the eventual outbreak of the 1939–1945 War.

Vice-Chairman of the Commission   A retired admiral, general or air chief marshal (usually chosen from each service in rotation) who attends part-time to the Commission's business, usually taking the chair at the Commission's formal quarterly meetings.

Viceroy   Ruler exercising royal authority in colony, province, etc. (eg Viceroy of India).

Vichy   The name of the town in France where the French Nazi-approved government was set up following the French defeat of 1940; it was the capital of non-occupied France.

Victoria Cross (VC)   The highest decoration for valour in the Commonwealth forces. It takes precedence over all other orders, decorations, etc., and is equal in merit, but senior, to the George Cross. The act of valour must now be performed in face of the enemy and the VC can be awarded to a person of any rank. The obverse is inscribed simply 'FOR VALOUR'.

Visitors' Book   A book for visitors to sign, if they wish, when visiting a cemetery or memorial. It is normally kept with the register in the register box.

Volksbund Deutsche Kriegsgräberfürsorge   The German 'War Graves Commission', which has its Head Office at Kassel, West Germany.

W

Waffen SS   See SS.

War Cemetery   Any burial site so-named, or more commonly in the 1914–1918 War, any burial site which had its own entrance, was walled or fenced and contained several war graves. An extension to a civil cemetery, or a plot within it, is considered a war cemetery if it meets the latter set of criteria, though it may also be referred to as, for example, a war graves plot.

War Diary   A form (in the British Army, Form C211) which was headed 'War Diary or Intelligence Summary', in which any events of significance were recorded by place, date, hour and references (if any). These, and despatches, are largely the source of official and other histories.

War Grave   The grave of a serviceman or woman, or of a member of certain other organizations, who died in the two world war periods, no matter what the cause.

War Graves Plot   In effect a war cemetery, but usually a separate and recognizable section of a churchyard or civil cemetery.

War Graves Treatment   The Commission's general term for the measures taken to honour and commemorate those dead entitled to such treatment. The measures include the keeping of records of the dead and the maintenance and protection of graves and memorials in perpetuity.

War Office   The British Department of State responsible for all aspects of the Army's operations, supplies, ordnance, pay, manning, etc. (now incorporated in the tri-service Ministry of Defence).

War Periods   For Commission purposes, 4th August 1914 to 31st August 1921 and 3rd September 1939 to 31st December 1947, all dates inclusive.

Warrant Officer Often abbreviated to WO. A Commonwealth serviceman who holds the Royal Warrant and is graded above staff sergeant (flight sergeant in the air forces) and below commissioned officers. Examples are the Regimental Sergeant Major (RSM, whose rank is WOI – Warrant Officer, Class I) and Battery Sergeant Major (BSM, whose rank is WOII – Warrant Officer, Class II). The WOs were, and are, known as the 'backbone of the Army'. No doubt, they are equally respected and valued in the navies and air forces.

World Wars This term means different things to different countries (eg to the USA it signifies the wars of 1917–1918 and 1941–1945; to Belgium 1914–1918 and 1940–1945). For this good reason, the Commission sticks to 1914–1918 War and 1939–1945 War, though the expression 'Great War' was usually used in registers after that conflict and almost always on the headstones of unknown war dead.

XYZ

Ypres Salient See Salient.

Zero Hour See H-Hour.

APPENDICES

A   Distribution of war graves and memorials in the Commission's care

B   Breakdown of numbers of war dead by forces

C   Major cemeteries and memorials by country

D   War graves or commemorations on memorials of VC and GC holders by country

E   Cemeteries described in Chapter 14

F   Memorials described in Chapter 15

G   Addresses of principal offices and agencies of the Commonwealth War Graves Commission

Appendix A*

War Graves and Memorials in the Commission's Care

| Country or Territory | War Burials Commonwealth | | Other Nation- alities | Burial Grounds | Common- wealth War Dead Commem- orated on Memorials | Total Common- wealth War Dead Commem- orated by name (Cols 2 and 6) |
| | Identified | Unidentified | | | | |
1	2	3	4	5	6	7
Algeria	2,041	122	34	13	–	2,041
Antigua	2	–	–	1	–	2
Argentina	15	–	–	2	–	15
Australia	11,416	13	307	900	1,032	12,448
Austria	582	17	1	2	–	582
Azores	51	1	1	3	–	51
Bahamas	51	–	–	1	9	60
Bangladesh	1,415	27	46	3	6,469	7,884
Barbados	23	–	2	9	–	23
Belgium	102,381	47,563	2,546	623	102,429	204,810
Belize	10	–	–	1	40	50
Bermuda	137	–	–	12	–	137
Botswana	–	–	–	–	162	162
Brazil	25	–	–	5	–	25
Bulgaria	240	3	1	2	–	240
Burma	10,938	1,107	622	4	26,919	37,857
Cameroon	47	–	–	3	–	47
Canada	14,108	9	263	2,990	4,074	18,182
Canary Islands	1	–	–	1	–	1
Cape Verde Islands	9	–	–	1	–	9
Chad	4	–	–	1	–	4
Chile	5	–	–	5	–	5
Congo	29	–	–	1	–	29
Costa Rica	1	–	–	1	–	1
Côte d'Ivoire	–	6	–	1	–	–
Cuba	3	–	–	1	–	3
Cyprus	321	2	–	6	58	379
Czechoslovakia	223	34	8	1	–	223
Denmark	991	120	25	127	–	991
Dijoubti	13	–	–	1	–	13
Dominica	3	–	–	2	–	3
Egypt	28,288	2,601	1,863	34	27,589	55,877
Equatorial Guinea	10	–	–	1	–	10
Ethiopia	1,362	61	9	7	–	1,362
Falkland Islands	33	–	–	1	–	33
Faroe Islands	56	3	–	4	–	56
Fiji	75	–	–	2	34	109
France	355,444	110,232	14,634	2,931	219,419	574,863
Gambia	199	1	3	1	70	269
Germany, Federal Republic of	30,562	1,331	211	30	25	30,587
German Democratic Republic	1,173	2	–	4	–	1,173

* Reprinted, with permission, from the Commonwealth War Graves Commission Annual Report 1986–87

War Graves and Memorials in the Commission's Care

Country or Territory	War Burials Commonwealth		Other Nation-alities	Burial Grounds	Common-wealth War Dead Commem-orated on Memorials	Total Common-wealth War Dead Commem-orated by name (Cols 2 and 6)
	Identified	Unidentified				
1	2	3	4	5	6	7
Ghana	612	3	8	6	1,220	1,832
Gibraltar	653	2	39	2	98	751
Greece	12,427	2,373	491	23	5,678	18,105
Grenada	4	1	–	2	–	4
Guatemala	1	–	–	1	–	1
Guinea	2	–	–	2	–	2
Guyana	6	–	–	1	18	24
Honduras	1	–	–	1	–	1
Hong Kong	1,820	621	81	10	4,582	6,402
Hungary	173	3	37	3	–	173
Iceland	228	2	9	6	–	228
India	10,992	521	75	21	51,351	62,343
Indonesia	2,539	584	187	3	518	3,057
Iran	551	13	25	1	3,590	4,141
Iraq	13,350	9,042	514	11	40,951	54,301
Irish Republic	3,042	52	2	571	–	3,042
Israel	8,348	1,425	1,045	20	4,110	12,458
Italy	44,783	1,906	75	121	4,479	49,262
Jamaica	145	–	23	2	87	232
Japan	1,718	53	80	1	20	1,738
Kenya	4,183	77	31	32	53,638	57,821
Lebanon	1,705	12	73	7	–	1,705
Lesotho	–	–	–	–	956	956
Liberia	12	–	–	2	–	12
Libya	7,054	1,462	236	4	–	7,054
Luxembourg	26	–	–	8	–	26
Madagascar	311	3	1	1	–	311
Madeira	6	–	–	1	–	6
Malawi	209	2	10	6	125	334
Malaysia	2,282	2,691	1	14	2,327	4,609
Maldives	–	–	–	–	70	70
Mali	3	–	–	2	–	3
Malta	3,378	9	247	13	2,349	5,727
Martinique	1	–	–	1	–	1
Mauritania	5	2	–	1	–	5
Mauritius	37	–	–	4	66	103
Monaco	2	–	–	1	–	2
Morocco	61	2	2	6	–	61
Mozambique	182	10	1	6	93	275
Namibia (South West Africa)	421	–	217	38	–	421
Nepal	1	–	–	1	–	1
Netherlands	18,205	1,271	283	469	1,061	19,266
Netherlands Antilles	11	–	–	3	–	11
New Caledonia	242	4	–	1	449	691
New Zealand	2,906	–	1	442	570	3,476
Nigeria	983	29	40	35	3,671	4,654
Norfolk Island	4	–	–	1	–	4

War Graves and Memorials in the Commission's Care

Country or Territory	War Burials Commonwealth		Other Nationalities	Burial Grounds	Commonwealth War Dead Commemorated on Memorials	Total Commonwealth War Dead Commemorated by name (Cols 2 and 6)
	Identified	Unidentified				
1	2	3	4	5	6	7
Norway	928	220	1	74	–	928
Oman	2	–	–	2	–	2
Pakistan	999	–	–	2	26,433	27,432
Panama	15	–	–	1	–	15
Papua New Guinea	6,122	1,646	2	8	2,308	8,430
Peru	6	–	–	1	–	6
Philippines	2	–	–	2	–	2
Poland	1,131	53	34	3	44	1,175
Portugal	51	–	–	5	–	51
Puerto Rico	1	–	–	1	–	1
Romania	170	8	–	3	–	170
St Helena and Ascension Island	21	2	–	2	–	21
St Christopher and Nevis	2	–	–	1	–	2
St Lucia	44	–	–	1	–	44
St Vincent	18	–	–	5	–	18
San Marino	2	–	–	1	–	2
Saudi Arabia	1	–	–	1	–	1
Senegal	23	–	–	2	–	23
Seychelles	76	–	–	1	289	365
Sierra Leone	444	9	20	4	1,393	1,837
Singapore	4,453	860	24	3	24,690	29,143
Society Islands	4	–	–	1	–	4
Solomon Islands (Guadaleanal)	5	–	–	1	–	5
Somalia	280	22	3	2	317	597
South Africa	8,202	20	141	568	129	8,331
South Yemen	295	3	10	2	76	371
Soviet Union	153	2	5	5	354	507
Spain	107	7	2	20	–	107
Sri Lanka	1,653	11	60	8	346	1,999
Sudan	395	–	19	1	1,346	1,741
Swaziland	–	–	–	–	77	77
Sweden	149	45	–	11	–	149
Switzerland	136	–	–	1	–	136
Syria	1,273	132	20	2	10	1,283
Tanzania	3,270	87	166	10	2,085	5,355
Thailand	6,324	188	2,209	2	11	6,335
Togo	1	–	–	1	–	1
Tonga	3	–	–	2	–	3
Trinidad and Tobago	105	–	1	1	40	145
Tunisia	7,749	811	5	11	1,955	9,704
Turkey	9,483	13,461	22	36	27,114	36,597
Uganda	373	2	2	13	127	500
United Kingdom	169,516	1,354	10,760	12,227	133,688	303,204
United States	953	3	–	444	–	953

War Graves and Memorials in the Commission's Care

Country or Territory	War Burials Commonwealth		Other Nationalities	Burial Grounds	Commonwealth War Dead Commemorated on Memorials	Total Commonwealth War Dead Commemorated by name (Cols 2 and 6)
	Identified	Unidentified				
1	2	3	4	5	6	7
Uruguay	8	1	–	1	–	8
Vanuatu	2	–	–	1	–	2
Venezuela	1	–	–	1	–	1
Western Samoa	12	–	–	1	–	12
Yugoslavia	609	30	18	8	–	609
Zaire	22	–	–	6	8	30
Zambia	70	–	1	1	1,695	1,765
Zimbabwe	542	8	15	19	132	674
	932,118	204,415	37,950	23,175	762,739	1,694,857

The figures for Bangladesh, India and Pakistan in columns 6 and 7 include the dual commemorations on the Bombay/Chittagong Memorials (6,469) and the Delhi/Karachi Memorials (25,865). The overall totals have been reduced by 32,334 to allow for this.

Appendix B*

Breakdowns of Numbers of War Dead by Forces

Forces	1914–18 War		1939–45 War		Both Wars		Total Commemorated
	Identified Burials and Cremations	Commemorated on Memorials to the Missing	Identified Burials and Cremations	Commemorated on Memorials to the Missing	Identified Burials and Cremations	Commemorated on Memorials to the Missing	
United Kingdom and former Colonies	475,025	413,276	244,391	139,083	719,416	552,359	1,271,775
Canada	45,258	19,514	37,305	8,011	82,563	27,525	110,088
Australia	38,462	23,398	28,268	12,129	66,730	35,527	102,257
New Zealand	11,849	6,299	9,031	2,868	20,880	9,167	30,047
South Africa	6,482	2,815	10,006	1,889	16,488	4,704	21,192
Undivided India	7,891	64,506	18,150	68,951	26,041	133,457	159,498
Total	584,967	529,808	347,151	232,931	932,118*	762,739	1,694,857+

* This together with 204,415 unidentified burials, brings the total burials and cremations to 1,136,533.

+ An overall alphabetical index of all dead of the two wars is held by the Commission and there is an alphabetical register for each cemetery and memorial. There are 23,175 burial places containing Commonwealth War Dead, of which

7,931 contain only 1914–1918 war graves, 8,067 contain only 1939–1945 war graves, and 7,177 contain graves of both world wars.

Of the many civilians of the Commonwealth whose deaths were due to enemy action in the 1939-45 war, the names of 66,375 are commemorated in the Civilian War Dead Roll of Honour, located near St George's Chapel in Westminster Abbey, London.

* Reprinted, with permission, from the Commonwealth War Graves Commission Annual Report 1986–87.

Appendix C

Cemeteries and Memorials

The following are the major sites and memorials by country.
('major' for that country)

Cemeteries	Total war dead	Memorials	Total commem- orated
Algeria			
Bone War Cemetery, Annaba	874		
Dely Ibrahim War Cemetery	505		
El Alia Cemetery, Algiers	376		
La Réunion War Cemetery, Bejaia	212		
Le Petit Lac Cemetery, Oran	220		
Australia			
New South Wales			
Rookwood Necropolis, Sydney	648		
Sydney War Cemetery	932	The Sydney Memorial (in Sydney War Cemetery)	750
Northern Territory			
Adelaide River War Cemetery	434	The Northern Territory Memorial (in Adelaide River War Cemetery)	282
Queensland			
Brisbane General Cemetery	378		
Lutwyche Cemetery, Brisbane	432		
Townsville War Cemetery	222		
South Australia			
Centennial Park Cemetery, Adelaide	224		
Victoria			
Springvale War Cemetery, Melbourne	686		
Western Australia			
Perth (Karrakatta) General Cemetery	229		
Perth War Cemetery	500		
Austria			
Klagenfurt War Cemetery	599		
Bahamas			
Nassau War Cemetery	51		

Cemeteries	Total war dead	Memorials	Total commem- orated
Bangladesh			
Chittagong War Cemetery	751	The Chittagong Memorial (in Chittagong War Cemetery)	6,469
Maynamati War Cemetery, Comilla	736		

Belgium

There are about 200 sites in Belgium and it is impractical to list them all here. The great majority are in the area surrounding Ypres (Ieper) and to its south, to the border with France. Almost all are the result of fighting on the Western Front in the 1914–1918 War. Several sites are so close that they are within sight, and easy walking distance, of each other. Readers who require the names of the sites in Belgium should purchase the Commission's overprinted Michelin Map No 51, which lists and identifies the major sites.

Cemeteries	Total war dead	Memorials	Total commem- orated
Bulgaria			
Sofia War Cemetery	188		
Burma			
Rangoon War Cemetery	1,418		
Taukkyan War Cemetery, Rangoon	7,478	The Rangoon Memorial (in Taukkyan War Cemetery)	26,875
Thanbyuzayat War Cemetery	3,770		
Canada			
British Columbia			
Vancouver (Mountain View) Cemetery	568		
Manitoba			
Winnipeg (Brookside) Cemetery	448		
Ontario			
Kitchener (Woodland) Cemetery	203		
Ottawa (Beechwood) Cemetery	231	The Ottawa Memorial (freestanding in Green Island, Ottawa)	771
Toronto (Mount Pleasant) Cemetery	219		
Toronto (Prospect) Cemetery	629		
Nova Scotia			
		The Halifax Memorial (in Point Pleasant Park, Halifax)	3,262

Cemeteries	Total war dead	Memorials	Total commem- orated
Quebec			
Montreal (Côte des Neiges) Cemetery	469		
Montreal (Mount Royal) Cemetery	450		
Cyprus			
Nicosia War Cemetery	287		
Czechoslovakia			
Prague War Cemetery	265		
Denmark			
Aabenraa Cemetery	156		
Esbjerg (Fourfelt) Cemetery	277		
Egypt			
Alexandria (Chatby) War Memorial Cemetery	2,785	The Chatby Memorial (in Chatby WMC)	981
Alexandria (Hadra) War Memorial Cemetery	3,046		
Cairo War Memorial Cemetery	2,391		
El Alamein War Cemetery	7,943	The Alamein Memorial (in El Alamein WC)	11,868
Fayid War Cemetery	1,199	The Fayid Memorial (in Fayid WC)	265
Halfaya-Sollum War Cemetery	2,060		
		The Giza Memorial, Cairo (plaques in Giza Eye Hospital. The figure is notional; there are no names on this memorial)	10,000
Heliopolis War Cemetery, Cairo	1,830	The Heliopolis (Aden) Memorial (in Heliopolis WC)	618
		The Heliopolis (Port Tewfik) Memorial (in Heliopolis WC)	3,799
Ismailia War Memorial Cemetery	669		
Kantara War Memorial Cemetry	2,000	The Kantara Indian Cemetery Memorial (in Kantara WMC)	283
Moascar War Cemetery	494		

Cemeteries	Total war dead	Memorials	Total commem- orated
Port Said War Memorial Cemetery	1,094		
Suez War Memorial Cemetery	901		
Tel-el-Kebir War Memorial Cemetery	675		

Ethiopia
Addis Ababa War Cemetery	297		
Asmara War Cemetery	279		
Keren War Cemetery	728		

France
There are over 600 sites in France and it is impractical to list them all here. The great majority are on the Western Front of the 1914–1918 War, largely in the departments of Pas-de-Calais, Nord and Somme, with many others in other departments. Some of the sites are so close that they are within sight, and easy walking distance, of each other. The sites which relate to the 1939–1945 War (a comparatively small number) are mainly in the departments of the Pas-de-Calais (Campaign of 1940) and Calvados (Campaign of 1944). Readers who require the names of sites in France should purchase the Commission's overprinted Michelin Maps Nos 52 and 53, which list and identify the major sites. Neither of these maps shows the sites in Normandy (Calvados).

Gambia
Fajara War Cemetery	203		

Germany (German Democratic Republic – East Germany)
Berlin South-Western Cemetery, Stahnsdorf	1,172		

Germany (Federal Republic of Germany – West Germany)
Becklingen War Cemetery, Soltau	2,401		
Berlin 1939–1945 War Cemetery	3,580		
Celle War Cemetery	209		
Cologne Southern Cemetery	2,643		
Durnbach War Cemetery	2,989		
Hamburg Cemetery, Ohlsdorf	2,185		
Hanover War Cemetery	2,412		

Cemeteries	Total war dead	Memorials	Total commem- orated
Kiel War Cemetery	992		
Munster Heath War Cemetery	589		
Niederzwehren Cemetery, Kassel	1,796		
Reichswald Forest War Cemetery, Cleves	7,654		
Rheinberg War Cemetery	3,332		
Sage War Cemetery, Oldenburg	969		
Ghana			
Christiansborg War Cemetery, Accra	419	The Christiansborg Memorial (in Christiansborg WC)	452
Gibraltar			
Gibraltar (North Front) Cemetery	692	The Gibraltar Memorial (freestanding – near the Cemetery entrance)	98
Greece			
Doiran Military Cemetery	1,384	The Doiran Memorial (freestanding)	2,160
East Mudros Military Cemetery, Lemnos	887		
Karasouli Military Cemetery	1,426		
Kirechköi-Hortaköi Military Cemetery	663		
Lembet Road Military Cemetery, Thessaloniki	1,694		
Mikra British Cemetery, Thessaloniki	1,962	The Mikra Memorial (in Mikra British Cemetery, Thessaloniki)	478
Monastir Road Indian Cemetery, Thessaloniki	358		
Phaleron War Cemetery, Athens	2,141	The Athens Memorial (in Phaleron War Cemetery)	2,877
Sarigol Military Cemetery	711		
Struma Military Cemetery	955		
Suda Bay War Cemetery, Crete	1,527		

Cemeteries	Total war dead	Memorials	Total commemorated
Hong Kong			
Sai Wan Bay War Cemetery	1,726	The Sai Wan Bay Memorial (in Sai Wan Bay War Cemetery)	2,071
Stanley Military Cemetery	598	The Hong Kong Memorial (in the Botanical Gardens)	2,439
Hungary			
Budapest War Cemetery	210		
Iceland			
Reykjavik (Fossvogur) Cemetery	204		
India			
Calcutta (Bhowanipore) Cemetery	712		
		The Bombay Memorial (in the Indian Sailors Home)	2,218
		The Bombay 1939–1945 War Memorial (in the Indian Sailors Home)	6,469
Delhi War Cemetery	1,154	The Delhi 1939–1945 War Memorial (in Delhi War Cemetery)	25,865
		The Delhi Memorial (India Gate)	13,502
Gauhati War Cemetery	521		
Imphal Indian Army War Cemetery	1,696		
Imphal War Cemetery	1,603		
Kirkee War Cemetery	1,669	The Kirkee 1914–1918 War Memorial (in Kirkee War Cemetery)	1,810
Kohima War Cemetery	2,337		
Madras War Cemetery	857	The Madras 1914–1918 War Memorial (in Madras War Cemetery)	1,037
Ranchi War Cemetery	705		

Cemeteries	Total war dead	Memorials	Total commemorated
Indonesia			
Ambon War Cemetery, Ambonia Island	2,136	The Ambon Memorial (in Ambon War Cemetery)	460
Djakarta War Cemetery	1,173		
Iran			
Tehran War Cemetery	589	The Tehran Memorial (in Tehran War Cemetery)	3,590
Iraq			
Alwiya Indian War Cemetery, Baghdad	451		
Amara (Left Bank) Indian War Cemetery	5,000		
Amara War Cemetery	4,621		
Baghdad (North Gate) War Cemetery	7,330	The Baghdad (North Gate) Memorial in Baghdad (North Gate) War Cemetery	543
Basra Indian Forces Cemetery	1,401		
Basra War Cemetery	3,180	The Basra Memorial (freestanding)	40,705
Kut War Cemetery	420		
Mosul War Cemetery	336		
Ireland			
County Dublin			
Glasnevin (or Prospect) Cemetery, Dublin City	205		
Grangegorman Military Cemetery, Dublin City	905		
Israel (or Israeli-controlled territory)			
Beersheba War Cemetery	1,239		
Deir-El-Belah War Cemetery, Gaza	734		
Gaza War Cemetery	3,473		
Haifa War Cemetery	342		
Jerusalem Indian War Cemetery	369		

Cemeteries	Total war dead	Memorials	Total commem- orated
Jerusalem War Cemetery, Mount Scopus	2,539	The Jerusalem Memorial (in Jerusalem War Cemetery)	3,366
Khayat Beach War Cemetery	792		
Ramleh War Cemetery	5,363		
Italy			
Agira Canadian War Cemetery, Sicily	490		
Ancona War Cemetery	1,019		
Anzio War Cemetery	1,056		
Arezzo War Cemetery	1,267		
Argenta Gap War Cemetery	625		
Assissi War Cemetery	949		
Bari War Cemetery	2,230		
Beach Head War Cemetery, Anzio	2,313		
Bolsena War Cemetery	600		
Caserta War Cemetery	769		
Cassino War Cemetery	4,266	The Cassino Memorial (in Cassino War Cemetery)	4,054
Castiglione South African Cemetery	502		
Catania War Cemetery, Sicily	2,139		
Cesena War Cemetery	775		
Coriano Ridge War Cemetery	1,940		
Faenza War Cemetery	1,152		
Florence War Cemetery	1,637		
Forli Indian Army War Cemetery	1,264		
Forli War Cemetery	738		
Giavera British Cemetery	417		
Gradara War Cemetery	1,192		
Milan War Cemetery	421		
Minturno War Cemetery	2,049		
Montecchio-Precalcino Communal Cemetery Extension	439		
Montecchio War Cemetery	582		

Cemeteries	Total war dead	Memorials	Total commem- orated
Moro River Canadian War Cemetery, Ortona	1,615		
Naples War Cemetery	1,206		
Padua War Cemetery	517		
Ravenna War Cemetery	988		
Rimini Gurkha War Cemetery	790		
Rome War Cemetery	426		
Salerno War Cemetery	1,848		
Sangro River War Cemetery	3,136		
Santerno Valley War Cemetery	287		
		The Savona Memorial (in Savona Town Cemetery)	274
Staglieno Cemetery, Genoa	352		
Syracuse War Cemetery, Sicily	1,063		
Taranto Town Cemetery Extension	449		
Tezze British Cemetery	415		
Villanova Canadian War Cemetery	212		
Japan			
Yokohama War Cemetery	1,851		
Kenya			
Gilgil War Cemetery	223		
Mombasa (Manyimbo) War Cemetery	227	The Mombasa African Memorial (in Town Centre): Both this and the Nairobi African memorial commemorate 49,617 African soldiers and followers who fell in East African campaigns and have no known grave. The casualties are not commemorated by name and for statistical purposes they have been allocated to Kenya.	49,617
Nairobi War Cemetery	1,953	The East African Memorial (in Nairobi War Cemetery)	2,213
		The Nairobi African Memorial (in Town Centre)	49,617

Cemeteries	Total war dead	Memorials	Total commemorated
Nyeri War Cemetery, Kiganjo	369		
Lebanon			
Beirut British War Cemetery	362		
Beirut 1939–1945 War Cemetery	811		
Beirut (Saida Road) Indian and Egyptian Cemetery	289		
Lesotho			
		The Lesotho 1939–1945 War Memorial, Masuru	956
Libya			
Benghazi War Cemetery	1,240		
Knightsbridge War Cemetery, Acroma	3,670		
Tobruk War Cemetery	2,454		
Tripoli War Cemetery	1,388		
Madagascar			
Diego Suarez War Cemetery	315		
Malaysia			
Labuan War Cemetery	3,941	The Labuan Memorial (in Labuan War Cemetery)	2,327
Taiping War Cemetery	865		
Malta			
Addolorata Cemetery	314	The Malta Memorial (freestanding in Valletta – Floriana).	2,297
Imtarfa Military Cemetery	254		
Malta (Capuccini) Naval Cemetery	1,196		
Pembroke Military Cemetery	323		
Pieta Military Cemetery	1,486		

Cemeteries	Total war dead	Memorials	Total commem- orated
Netherlands			
Amersfoort (Oud Leusden) General Cemetery	232		
Amsterdam New Eastern Cemetery	323		
Arnhem (Oosterbeek) War Cemetery	1,747		
Bergen-op-Zoom Canadian War Cemetery	1,115		
Bergen-op-Zoom War Cemetery	1,303		
Eindhoven (Woensel) General Cemetery	686		
Groesbeek Canadian War Cemetery, Nijmegen	2,613	The Groesbeek Memorial (in Groesbeek Canadian War Cemetery)	1,068
Holten Canadian War Cemetery	1,394		
Jonkerbos War Cemetery, Nijmegen	1,642		
Mierlo War Cemetery	665		
Uden War Cemetery	703		
Venray War Cemetery	692		
New Zealand			
Auckland (Waikumete) Cemetery	282	The Auckland Memorial (freestanding in Devonport).	352
Featherston Cemetery	182		
Karori Great War Memorial Cemetery	200		
Wellington (Karori) Cemetery	189		
Nigeria			
Yaba Cemetery, Lagos	419	The Lagos Memorial (in Tafawa Balewa Square)	947
		The Nigeria Memorial, Lagos (in Tafawa Balewa Square)	1,158
		The Calabar Memorial (in Town Centre, Calabar)	406

Cemeteries	Total war dead	Memorials	Total commem-orated
Norway			
Fredrikstad Military Cemetery	82		
Oslo Western Civil Cemetery	101		
Trondheim (Stavne) Cemetery	155		
Pakistan			
Karachi War Cemetery	642	The Karachi 1914–1918 War Memorial (in Karachi War Cemetery)	568
		The Karachi 1939–1945 War Memorial (in Karachi War Cemetery)	25,865
Rawalpindi War Cemetery	357		
Papua/New Guinea			
New Britain			
Rabaul (Bita Paka) War Cemetery	1,139	The Rabaul Memorial (in Rabaul (Bita Paka) War Cemetery)	1,225
New Guinea			
Lae War Cemetery	2,805		
Papua			
Port Moresby (Bomana) War Cemetery	3,819	The Port Moresby Memorial (in Port Moresby (Bomana) War Cemetery)	741
Poland			
Cracow (Rakowski) Cemetery Commonwealth Plot	498		
Malbork Commonwealth War Cemetery	245		
Poznan Old Garrison Cemetery, Commonwealth Section	475		
Romania			
Bucharest War Cemetery	89		
Slobozia Military Cemetery	83		

Cemeteries	Total war dead	Memorials	Total commem-orated
Sierra Leone			
Freetown (King Tom) Cemetery	397	The Freetown Memorial (outside the Secretariat, Freetown)	1,358
Singapore			
Kranji War Cemetery	5,329	The Singapore Memorial (in Kranji War Cemetery)	24,327
South Africa			
Cape Province			
Cape Town (Maitland Road) Cemetery	991		
Kimberley (West End) Cemetery	410		
Natal			
Durban (Stellawood) Cemetery)	735		
Transvaal			
Johannesburg (Brixton) Cemetery	272		
Johannesburg (West Park) Cemetery	706		
Voortrekkerhoogte New Military Cemetery	293		
Voortrekkerhoogte Old Military Cemetery	258		
South Yemen			
Ma'ala Cemetery, Aden	300		
Sri Lanka			
Colombo Kanatte General Cemetery	366		
Colombo (Liveramentu) Cemetery	778	The Liveramentu Memorial (in Colombo (Liveramentu) Cemetery)	347
Trincomalee War Cemetery	319		
Sudan			
Khartoum War Cemetery	414	The Khartoum Memorial (in Khartoum War Cemetery)	1,346

Cemeteries	Total war dead	Memorials	Total commem- orated
Sweden Kviberg Cemetery, Gothenburg	114		
Switzerland Vevey (St Martin's) Cemetery	136		
Syria Aleppo War Cemetery	252		
Damascus Commonwealth War Cemetery	1,173		
Tanzania Dar-es-Salaam War Cemetery, Bagamoyo Road	1,931	The Dar-es-Salaam British and Indian Memorial (in Dar-es-Salaam War Cemetery)	1,547
		The Tanganyika Memorial (in Dar-es-Salaam (Upanga Road) Cemetery)	352
Morogoro Cemetery	393		
Tanga Memorial War Cemetery	394		
Thailand Chungkai War Cemetery	1,740		
Kanchanaburi War Cemetery	6,981		
Tunisia Béja War Cemetery	396		
Enfidaville War Cemetery	1,551		
Massicault War Cemetery, Borj-el-Amri	1,578		
Medjez-el-Bab War Cemetery	2,910	The Medjez-el-Bab Memorial (in Medjez-el-Bab War Cemetery)	1,955
Sfax War Cemetery	1,255		
Tabarka Ras Rajel War Cemetery	500		

Cemeteries	Total war dead	Memorials	Total commem- orated
Turkey			
Gallipoli Peninsula			
Azmak Cemetery, Suvla	1,074		
Baby 700 Cemetery, Anzac	493		
Beach Cemetery, Anzac	391		
Chunuk Bair Cemetery, Anzac	632	The Chunuk Bair Memorial (in Chunuk Bair Cemetery)	852
Embarkation Pier Cemetery, Anzac	944		
Greenhill Cemetery, Suvla	2,971		
Hill 10 Cemetery, Suvla	699		
Hill 60 Cemetery, Anzac	788		
Lancashire Landing Cemetery, Helles	1,253	The Helles Memorial (freestanding at Cape Helles)	20,765
Lone Pine Cemetery, Anzac	1,167	The Lone Pine Memorial (in Lone Pine Cemetery)	4,932
Pink Farm Cemetery, Helles	602		
Quinn's Post Cemetery, Anzac	473		
Redoubt Cemetery, Helles	2,027		
7th Field Ambulance Cemetery, Anzac	640		
Shell Green Cemetery, Anzac	409		
Shrapnel Valley Cemetery, Anzac	683		
Skew Bridge Cemetery, Helles	606		
The Farm Cemetery, Anzac	652		
Twelve Tree Copse Cemetery, Helles	3,360		
V Beach Cemetery, Helles	696		
Istanbul			
Haidar Pasha Cemetery	566		
United Kingdom			
Brookwood Military Cemetery, Woking, Surrey	5,854	The Brookwood Memorial, Surrey (in Military Cemetery)	3,475
Cambridge City Cemetery, Cambridgeshire	1,020		

Cemeteries	Total war dead	Memorials	Total commemorated
		The Chatham Naval Memorial, Kent	18,626
Gillingham (Woodlands) Cemetery, Kent	1,214		
Harrogate (Stonefall) Cemetery, North Yorkshire	1,007		
Haslar Royal Naval Cemetery, Gosport, Hampshire	1,382		
		The Hollybrook Memorial, Southampton, Hampshire	1,868
		The Lee-on-Solent Fleet Air Arm Memorial, Hampshire	1,928
Liverpool (Anfield) Cemetery, Merseyside	976	The Liverpool Memorial, Merseyside	1,406
		The Lowestoft Naval Memorial, Suffolk	2,398
Manchester Southern Cemetery, Greater Manchester	1,267		
Plymouth Old Cemetery (Pennycomequick) Devon	955	The Plymouth Naval Memorial, Devon	23,196
Plymouth (Weston Mill) Cemetery, Devon	989	The Portsmouth Naval Memorial, Hampshire	24,589
		The Runnymede Memorial, Surrey	20,450
		The Tower Hill Memorial, Greater London	35,700

USA

Arlington National Cemetery, Virginia	28
Long Island National Cemetery, Farmingdale, New York	35
Montgomery (Oakwood) Cemetery Annexe, Alabama	78
St Louis (Jefferson Barracks) National Cemetery, Missouri	38

Cemeteries	Total war dead	Memorials	Total commemorated
Yugoslavia			
Belgrade War Cemetery	481		
Zambia			
		The Abercorn Memorial	1,467
Zimbabwe			
Bulawayo Cemetery	146		
Harare (Pioneer) Cemetery	261		

Appendix D

Cemeteries and Memorials where recipients of the Victoria Cross and
George Cross are buried or commemorated

The following is a list of those recipients of the Victoria Cross and the George Cross who were eligible for 1914–1918 and 1939–1945 War graves treatment. Those shown as having been awarded the Albert Medal (AM) would, had they survived, eventually have had their medals exchanged for the George Cross. In addition there may be other recipients of the VC, the GC and, particularly the AM, whose award has not yet been recorded in this list. Rank and regiment are as at the date of death.

Asterisks indicate Bars. Some sites have very similar titles: care should be taken not to confuse them.

Cemeteries and memorials, in alphabetical order by country, where recipients of the Victoria Cross and George Cross who are entitled to war graves treatment are commemorated.

Country	Cemetery or Memorial	Rank	Name, Initials and Decorations	Service, Regiment Corps etc.
Algeria	Bone War Cemy	FSgt	Aaron A.L. VC DFM	RAF(VR)
		Maj	Kempster A.G. GC	Duke of Wellington's
Australia	Cowra War Cemy, NSW	Pte	Hardy B.G. GC	Aus Inf
		Pte	Jones R. GC	Aus Inf
Belgium	Bedford House Cemy, Zillebeke	2Lt	Hallowes R.P. VC MC	Middx
	Birr Cross Roads Cemy, Zillebeke	Capt	Ackroyd H. VC MC	RAMC
	Blankenberge Communal Cemy	Lt Comdr	Bradford G.N. VC	RN
	Brandhoek New Military Cemy, Vlamertinghe	Capt	Chavasse N.G. VC* MC	RAMC
	Brussels Town Cemy, Evère-les-Bruxelles	FSgt	Thompson G. VC	RAF(VR)
	Canada Farm Cemy, Elverdinghe	Cpl	Davies J.L. VC	RWF
	Essex Farm Cemy, Boesinghe	Pte	Barratt T. VC	S Staffs
	Grootebeek British Cemy, Reninghelst	Pte	Lynn J. VC DCM	Lancs Fus
	Haringhe (Bandaghem) Military Cemy	Spr	Farren J.C. AM	RE
		CSM	Furlonger A.H. AM	RE
		Spr	Johnson G.E. AM	RE

259

Country	Cemetery or Memorial	Rank	Name, Initials and Decorations	Service, Regiment Corps etc.
	Heverlee War Cemy	F O	Garland D.E. VC	RAF
		Sgt	Gray T. VC	RAF
		F O	Manser L.T. VC	RAF(VR)
	Hooge Crater Cemy, Zillebeke	Pte	Bugden P.J. VC	AIF
	La Brique Military Cemy, St Jean-les-Ypres	Cpl	Drake A.G. VC	RB
	Leopoldsburg War Cemy	Cpl	Harper J.W. VC	Yorks and Lancs
		Capt	Swales E. VC DFC	SAAF
	Lijssenthoek Military Cemy, Poperinghe	LCpl	Alderson G. AM	DLI
		Maj	Tubb F.H. VC	AIF
	Mendinghem British Cemy, Proven	Lt Col	Best-Dunkley B. VC	Lancs Fus
	The Menin Gate Meml, Ypres	LCpl	Fisher F. VC	Cdn Inf
		Brig Gen	Fitzclarence C. VC	Cmdg 1st Gds Bde (late RF)
		CSM	Hall F.W. VC	Cdn Inf
		2Lt	Hewitt D.G.W. VC	Hamps
		Lt	McKenzie H. McD. VC DCM	Cdn MGC
		Capt	Vallentin J.F. VC	S Staffs
		Pte	Warner E. VC	Buffs
		2Lt	Woodroffe S.C. VC	RB
	Menin Road South Military Cemy, Ypres	Capt	Colyer-Fergusson T.R. VC	Northants
	Oxford Road Cemy, Ypres	Capt	Robertson C. VC	Tank Corps
	Perth Cemy (China Wall), Zillebeke	2Lt	Birks F. VC MM	AIF
		Maj	Johnston W.H. VC	RE
	The Ploegsteert Meml.	Spr	Hackett W. VC	RE
		Pte	MacKenzie J. (James) VC	S Gds
		Capt	Pryce T.T. VC MC	G Gds
	Railway Dugouts Burial Ground, Zillebeke	2Lt	Youens F. VC	DLI
	St Symphorien Military Cemy	Lt	Dease M.J. VC	RF
	Staceghem Communal Cemy, Harlebeke	Lt	McGregor D.S. VC	MGC
	Tyne Cot Cemy, Passchendaele	Capt	Jeffries C.S. VC	AIF
		Sgt	McGee L. VC	AIF
		Pte	Robertson J.P. VC	Cdn Inf
	The Tyne Cot Meml, Passchendaele	Lt Col	Bent P.E. VC DSO	Leics
		Cpl	Clamp W. VC	Yorks
		LCpl	Seaman E. VC MM	Innisk Fus

Country	Cemetery or Memorial	Rank	Name, Initials and Decorations	Service, Regiment Corps etc.
	Vlamertinghe Military Cemy	Capt	Grenfell F.O. VC	9th Queen's Royal Lancers
	Vlamertinghe New Military Cemy	CSM	Skinner J. VC DCM	KOSB
	Westoutre British Cemy	Maj	Dougall E.S. VC MC	RFA
	White House Cemy, St Jean-les-Ypres	Pte	Morrow R. VC	RI Fus
	Ypres Reservoir Cemy	Brig Gen	Maxwell F.A. VC CSI DSO*	Cmdg 27th Inf Bde (late Middx)
	Zantvoorde British Cemy	Capt	Brooke J.A.O. VC	Gordon Hldrs
		Sgt	McGuffie L. VC	KOSB
	The Zeebrugge Meml	Lt Comdr	Harrison A.L. VC	RN
Burma	The Rangoon Meml	Hav	Abdul Rahman GC MM	9th Jat Regt
		Nk	Fazil Din VC	10 Baluch Regt
		Lt	Horwood A.G. VC DCM	Queen's
		LNk	Islam-Ud-Din GC	9th Jat Regt
		Nk	Kirpa Ram GC	13th FF Rifles
		Sub	Netrabahadur Thapa VC	2/5 R Gurhkha Rifles
		Jem	Parkash Singh VC	13th FF Rifles
		Sub	Ram Swarup Singh VC	1st Punjab Regt
		LNk	Sher Shah VC	16th Punjab Regt
	Rangoon War Cemy	Maj	Seagrim H.P. GC DSO MBE	19th Hyderabad Regt
		FSgt	Woodbridge S.J. GC	RAF(VR)
	The Taukkyan Cremation Meml	Lt	Karamjeet Singh Judge VC	15th Punjab Regt
	Taukkyan War Cemy	Capt	Allmand M. VC	IAC
		Maj	Blaker F.C. VC MC	HLI
		Lt	Cairns G.A. VC	SLI
		Maj	Hoey C.F. VC MC	Lincs
		Lt	Knowland G.A. VC	Norfolk
		Lt	Raymond C. VC	RE
		Pte	Silk J.M. GC	SLI
		Lt	Weston W.B. VC	Green Howards

Country	Cemetery or Memorial	Rank	Name, Initials and Decorations	Service, Regiment Corps etc.
Canada	The Halifax Meml, Nova Scotia	Lt	Gray R.H. VC DSC	RCNVR
	Kildonan Cemy, Winnipeg	Lt	McLeod A.A. VC	RAF
	Smith's Falls (Hillcrest) Cemy, Ontario	LAC	Spooner K.G. GC	RCAF
	Vancouver (Mountain View) Cemy	LAC	Gravell K.M. GC	RCAF
Egypt	Alexandria (Hadra) War Memorial Cemy	BSM	Horlock E.G. VC	RFA
	Cairo War Memorial Cemy	Maj Gen	Campbell J.C. VC DSO* MC	Cmdg 7th Armd Div (late RHA and RA)
	El Alamein War Cemy	Pte	Gratwick P.E. VC	AIF
		Pte	Gurney A.S. VC	AIF
		Sgt	Kibby W.H. VC	AIF
		Pte	Wakenshaw A.H. VC	DLI
	Halfaya Sollum War Cemy	Col	Lyall G.T. VC	RAOC
	The Heliopolis (Port Tewfik) Meml	Resr	Badlu Singh VC	14th Murray's Jat Lancers
	Kantara War Memorial Cemy	Pte	Needham S. VC	Bedfs
England	Alderbury (St Mary) Chyd, Wilts	Lt	Foster W. GC MC DCM	Home Guard
	Basingstoke (South View) Cemy, Hants	Capt	Liddell J.A. VC MC	A & S Hildrs and RFC
	Beck Row (St John) Chyd, Suffolk	P O	Middleton R.H. VC	RAAF
	Birmingham (Yardley) Cemy	Sect Comdr	Inwood G.W. GC	Home Guard
	Birstall (St James) Chyd, Leics	FSgt	Hannah J. VC	RAF
	Boughton-Monchelsea (St Peter) Chyd, Kent	Cdr	Jolly R.F. GC	RN
	Brighton (Bear Road) Cemy, E Sussex	WOII (CSM)	Gristock G. VC	Norfolk
	Brompton Cemy, London	Flt Sub Lt	Warneford R.A.J. VC	RNAS
	The Brookwood Meml, Surrey	Ensign	Szabo V.R.E. GC	WTS (FANY)
		Capt	Thompson J.R.O. GC	RAMC
	Brookwood Military Cemy, Surrey	Cpl	Hendry J. GC	RCE
		Sgt	Rennie J. GC	A & SH of Canada

Country	Cemetery or Memorial	Rank	Name, Initials and Decorations	Service, Regiment Corps etc.
	The Brookwood (Russia) Meml, Surrey	Sgt	Pearse S.G. VC MM	RF
	Camberwell (Forest Hill Road) Cemy, London	AB	McKenzie A.E. VC	RN
	Chalfont St Peter Cemy, Bucks	2nd Hand	Drummond G.H. VC	RNPS
	The Chatham Naval Meml, Kent	Skipper Capt Maj	Crisp T. VC DSC Fegan E.S.F. VC Harvey F.J.W. VC	RNR RN RMLI
	City of London Cemy, Manor Park, Essex	Lt	Drewry G.L. VC	RNR
	Coventry (London Road) Cemy, Warwicks	2Lt Sgt BSM	Campbell A.F. GC Gibson M. GC Parker C.E.H. VC	RE RE RFA
	Cudham SS Peter and Paul Chyd, Orpington, Kent	Sqn Ldr	Moxey E.L. GC	RAF(VR)
	Eston Cemy, Cleveland	Lt	Sandford R.D. VC	RN
	Falmouth Cemy, Cornwall	AB	Savage W.A. VC	RN
	Gillingham (Woodlands) Cemy, Kent	Lt Comdr (A)	Esmonde E.K. VC DSO	RN(FAA)
	Golders Green Crematorium, London	Lt Col	Watson T.C. VC	RE
	Harrow Weald (All Saints) Chyd Extension, Middx	Capt	Robinson W.L. VC	Worcs att RAF
	Haslar Royal Naval Cemy, Gosport, Hants	Lt Comdr	Ryan R.J.H. GC	RN
	Hoylake (Holy Trinity) Chyd, Cheshire	Lt	O'Neill J. VC MM	Pioneer Corps
	Ilkley Cemy, West Yorks	Vol	Maufe T.H.B. VC	Home Guard
	Kettering (London Road) Cemy, Northants	P O	Lewin R.M. GC	RAF(VR)
	Kingston-upon-Thames Cemy, Surrey	F O	Barton C.J. VC	RAF(VR)
	Leicester (Gilroes) Cemy	Ord Smn	Southwell B. GC	RN
	The Liverpool Naval Meml	Lt	Wilkinson T. VC	RNR
	Maidstone Cemy, Kent	Lt Comdr	Humphreys P.N. GC	RN
	Manor Park Cemy, East Ham, Essex	Boy 1st Class	Cornwell J.T. VC	RN
	Parnham Private Cemy, Beaminster, Dorset	Lt	Rhodes-Moorhouse W.B. VC	RFC

Country	Cemetery or Memorial	Rank	Name, Initials and Decorations	Service, Regiment Corps etc.
	Penshurst (St John the Baptist) Church, Kent	Field Marshal	Gort J.S.S.P.V. The Viscount VC GCB CBE DSO·· MVO MC	Commands and Staff (late G Gds)
	The Plymouth Naval Meml, Devon	Sto PO Lt Comdr	Mahoney H.J. GC Sanders W.E. VC DSO	RN RNR
	Portland Royal Naval Cemy, Dorset	Ldg Smn	Mantle J.F. VC	RN
	Portsmouth (Milton) Cemy, Hants	CPO	Ellingworth R.V. GC	RN
	The Portsmouth Naval Meml, Hants	Ord Smn	Carless J.H. VC	RN
		Lt	Fasson F.A.B. GC	RN
		AB	Grazier C. GC	RN
		Comdr	Linton J.W. VC DSO DSC	RN
		Lt	Low J.N.A. GC	RN
		Comdr	Marshall-Adeane W.R. DSO DSC AM	RN
		AB	Miller H.J. GC	RN
		Capt	Peters F.T. VC DSO DSC·	RN
		Lt Comdr	Roope G.B. VC	RN
		PO	Sephton A.E. VC	RN
		Lt Comdr	Wanklyn M.D. VC DSO··	RN
		Lt Comdr	White G.S. VC	RN
		AB	Williams W.C. VC	RN
	Preston (New Hall Lane) Cemy, Lancs	Pte	Young W. VC	E Lancs
	The Runnymede Memorial, Surrey	WO	Campion M.P. GC	RAF
		F O	Gray R.B. GC	RCAF
		Sect Offr	Inayat-Khan N. GC	WAAF
		Grp Capt	McKechnie W.N. GC	RAF
		W Comdr	Nettleton J.D. VC	RAF
		The Rev	Pugh H.C. GC	RAF(VR)
	St Erth (St Ercus) Chyd, Cornwall	Maj	Carter H.A. VC	101st Grenadiers
	St Paul's Cathedral, London	Field Marshal	Roberts F.S. 1st Earl VC KG KP GCB OM GCSI GCIE VD	Commands and Staff (late Bengal Artillery)
	Sunderland (Bishopwearmouth) Cemy, Co Durham	Bdr	Reed H.H. GC	RA
	Swanage (Northbrook) Cemy, Dorset	CPO	Pitcher E.J. VC DSM	RN
	Taunton (St Mary's) Cemy, Somerset	Lt	Andrews W.L. GC	RE

Country	Cemetery or Memorial	Rank	Name, Initials and Decorations	Service, Regiment Corps etc.
	The Tower Hill Memorial, London	Apprentice Master	Clarke D.O. GC Smith A.B. VC	MN RNR
	Ugborough (St Peter) Chyd, Devon	FSgt	Warne A.E. AM	RAF
Eritrea	The Keren Cremation Meml	Sub	Richpal Ram VC	6th Raj Rifles
France	Abbeville Communal Cemy	LCpl	Keyworth L.J. VC	1/24 London
	Adanac Military Cemy, Miraumont and Pys	Sgt Pte	Forsyth S. VC Richardson J.C. VC	NZEF Cdn Inf
	Annoeullin Communal Cemy, German Extension	Capt	Ball A. VC DSO** MC	The Sherwood Foresters att RFC
	The Arras Meml	2Lt	Beal E.F. VC	Yorks
		2Lt Sgt	Cassidy B.M. VC Edwards A. VC	Lancs Fus Seaforth Hldrs
		Sgt 2Lt Maj Capt 2Lt Cpl Lt Maj	Erskine J. VC Harrison J. VC MC Hawker L.G. VC DSO Hirsch D.P. VC Horsfall B.A. VC Jarratt G. VC Jones R.B.B. VC Mannock E. VC DSO** MC*	Scots Rifles E Yorks RE and RFC Yorks E Lancs RF N Lancs RE and RAF
		Lt Col Sgt	Watson O.C.S. VC DSO White A. VC	KOYLI SWB
	Arras Road Cemy, Roclincourt Auberchicourt British Cemy	Capt Sgt	Kilby A.F.G. VC MC Cairns H. VC DCM	S Staffs Cdn Inf
	Aubigny Communal Cemy Extension	Pte	Nunney C.J.P. VC DCM MM	Cdn Inf
	Bailleul Communal Cemy Extension	Sgt	Mottershead T. VC DCM	RFC
	Bancourt British Cemy	Sgt	Jones D. VC	Liverpool
	Barlin Communal Cemy Extension	Cpl	Cunningham J. VC	Leinster
	Bayeux War Cemy	Cpl SBA	Bates S. VC Franconi A. AM	Norfolk RN
	Bellicourt British Cemy	Lt Col	Vann B.W. VC MC*	Sherwood Foresters
	Berles New Military Cemy, Berles-au-Bois	Brig Gen	Lumsden F.W. VC CB DSO***	RMA

Country	Cemetery or Memorial	Rank	Name, Initials and Decorations	Service, Regiment Corps etc.
	Béthune Town Cemy	Lt	de Pass F.A. VC	34th Poona Horse
	Beuvry Communal Cemy Extension	Lt(QM)	Smith E. VC DCM	Lancs Fus
	Bienvillers Military Cemy	Lt Col	Brodie W.L. VC MC	HLI
	Boulogne Eastern Cemy	Capt Sqn Ldr	Campbell F.W. VC Close G.C.N. GC	Cdn Inf RAF
	Bouzincourt Ridge Cemy, Albert	Lt Col	Collings-Wells J.S. VC DSO	Bedfs
	Braine Communal Cemy	Capt	Ranken H.S. VC	RAMC
	Brest (Kerfautras) Cemy, Lambezellec	F O	Campbell K. VC	RAF(VR)
	Brown's Copse Cemy, Roeux	Lt	MacKintosh D. VC	Seaforth Hldrs
	The Cambrai Meml	Pte Pte 2Lt Maj Capt Capt Capt	Clare, G.W.B. VC Dancox F.G. VC Emerson J.S. VC Johnson F.H. VC McReady-Diarmid A.M.C. VC Stone W.N. VC DSO MC Wain R.W.L. VC	5 Lancers Worcs Innisks Fus RE Middx RF Tank Corps
	Carnières Communal Cemy Extension	Pte	Holmes, W.E. VC	G Gds
	Chocques Military Cemy	2Lt	Turner A.B. VC	Berks
	Cojeul British Cemy, St Martin-sur-Cojeul	Capt Pte	Henderson A. VC MC Waller H. VC	A & S Hldrs KOYLI
	Contalmaison Château Cemy	Pte	Short W.H. VC	Yorks
	Corbie Communal Cemy Extension	Maj	Congreve W. LaT. VC DSO MC	RB
	Couin New British Cemy	Sgt	Travis R.C. VC DCM MM	NZEF
	Crouy British Cemy, Crouy-sur-Somme	Cpl	Miner H.G.B. VC	Cdn Inf
	Dartmoor Cemy, Bécordel-Bécourt	Pte	Miller J. VC	Lancaster
	Delville Wood Cemy, Longueval	Sgt	Gill A. VC	KRRC
	Dernancourt Communal Cemy Extension	Sgt	Harris T.J. VC MM	RWK
	Dominion Cemy, Hendecourt-les-Cagnicourt	Sgt	Knight A.G. VC	Cdn Inf

Country	Cemetery or Memorial	Rank	Name, Initials and Decorations	Service, Regiment Corps etc.
	Douchy-les-Ayette British Cemy	LCpl	Woodcock T. VC	I Gds
	Dourlers Communal Cemy Extension	Capt	Lascelles A.M. VC MC	DLI
	Dud Corner Cemy, Loos	Capt	Read A.M. VC	Northants and RFC
		Sgt	Wells H. VC	Sussex
	The Dunkirk Meml	Lt	Furness The Hon C. VC	W Gds
	Escoublac-la-Baule War Cemy	Sgt	Durrant T.F. VC	RE
	Estaires Communal Cemy	Brig Gen	Gough Sir John VC KCB CMG	Chief of Staff, First Army (late RB)
	Etaples Military Cemy	Maj	Reynolds D. VC	RFA
	Etretat Chyd	Sgt	Clarke L. VC	Cdn Inf
	Fillièvres British Cemy	Lt	Baxter E.F. VC	King's Liverpool
	Flatiron Copse Cemy, Mametz	Cpl	Dwyer E. VC	E Surrey
	Foncquevillers Military Cemy	Capt	Green J.L. VC	RAMC
	Fouquescourt British Cemy	Lt	Tait J.E. VC MC	Cdn Inf
	Gordon Dump Cemy, Ovillers-la-Boiselle	2Lt	Bell D.S. VC	Yorks
	Gorre British Cemy, Beuvry	Pte	Mills W. VC	Manchester
	Guards Cemy, Windy Corner, Cuinchy	Maj	MacKenzie J. (John) VC	Bedfs
	Hangard Wood British Cemy, Hangard	Pte	Croak J.B. VC	Cdn Inf
	Heath Cemy, Harbonnières	Pte	Beatham R.M. VC	AIF
		Lt	Gaby A.E. VC	AIF
	Hem Farm Military Cemy, Hem-Monacu	2Lt	Cates G.E. VC	RB
		Pte	Mactier R. VC	AIF
	Hermies British Cemy	Brig Gen	Bradford R.B. VC MC	Commands and Staff (late DLI)
	Hermies Hill British Cemy	2Lt	Young F.E. VC	Herts
	La Chaudière Military Cemy, Vimy	Pte	Pattison J.C. VC	Cdn Inf
	Le Câteau Military Cemy	LCpl	Sayer J.W. VC	Queen's

Country	Cemetery or Memorial	Rank	Name, Initials and Decorations	Service, Regiment Corps etc.
	The Le Touret Meml	Pte	Acton A. VC	Border
		Cpl	Anderson W. VC	Yorks
		Pte	Barber E. VC	G Gds
		Pte	Rivers J. VC	Sherwood Foresters
	Lichfield Crater Cemy, Thélus	SSgt	Sifton E.W. VC	Cdn Inf
	Lillers Communal Cemy	Cpl	Cotter W.R. VC	Buffs
		Maj	Nelson D. VC	RFA
	Longuenesse (St Omer) Souvenir Cemy	Cpl	Noble C.R. VC	RB
	Lonsdale Cemy, Aveluy and Authuile	Sgt	Turnbull J.Y. VC	HLI
	The Loos Memorial	Lt Col	Douglas-Hamilton A.F. VC	Cameron Hldrs
		Rfn	Peachment G.S. VC	KRRC
		2Lt	Wearne F.B. VC	Essex
	Mailly Wood Cemy	Sgt	Colley H.J. VC MM	Lancs Fus
	Marfaux British Cemy	Sgt	Meikle J. VC MM	Seaforth Hldrs
	Masnières British Cemy, Marcoing	LSgt	Neely T. VC MM	Lancaster
	Mazingarbe Communal Cemy	Pte	Dunsire R. VC	RS
	Meharicourt Communal Cemy	P O	Mynarski A.C. VC	RCAF
	Metz-en-Couture Communal Cemy, British Extension	Capt	Paton G.H.T. VC MC	G Gds
	Moeuvres Communal Cemy Extension	Lt	Pope C. VC	AIF
	Mory Abbey Military Cemy	Lt Col	West R.A. VC DSO* MC	Tank Corps
	Namps-au-Val British Cemy	Capt	Flowerdew G.M. VC	Lord Strathcona' Horse
	Naves Communal Cemy Extension	Cpl	McPhie J. VC	RE
	Néry Communal Cemy	Capt	Bradbury E.K. VC	RHA
	The Neuve-Chapelle Meml	Lt	Bruce W.A. McC. VC	59 Scinde Rifles
		Rfn	Gobar Singh Negi	Garhwal Rifles
	Neuvilly Communal Cemy Extension	Pte	Lester F. VC	Lancs Fus
	Niagara Cemy, Iwuy	Lt	Algie W.L. VC	Cdn Inf

Country	Cemetery or Memorial	Rank	Name, Initials and Decorations	Service, Regiment Corps etc.
	Noeux-les-Mines Cemy	Pte Maj	Brown H.W. VC Learmonth O.M. VC MC	Cdn Inf Cdn Inf
	Norfolk Cemy, Bécordel-Bécourt	Maj	Loudon-Shand S.W. VC	Yorks
	Ors Communal Cemy	2Lt Lt Col	Kirk J. VC Marshall J.N. VC MC*	Manchester I Gds
	Péronne Communal Cemy Extension, Ste Radegonde	Cpl	Buckley A.H. VC	AIF
	Péronne Road Cemy, Maricourt	Lt Col	Anderson W.H. VC	HLI
	Pozières British Cemy, Ovillers-la-Boisselle	Sgt	Castleton C.C. VC	AIF
	The Pozières Meml	Pte 2Lt Lt Col	Columbine H.G. VC deWind E. VC Elstob W. VC DSO MC	MGC (Cav) RI Rifles Manchester
	Quéant Communal Cemy	Lt	Honey S.L. VC DCM MM	Cdn Inf
	Quéant Road Cemy, Buissy	Capt	Cherry P.H. VC MC	AIF
	Querrieu British Cemy	Lt Col	Bushell C. VC DSO	Queen's
	Rocquigny-Equancourt Road British Cemy, Manancourt	Sgt	Rhodes J.H. VC DCM*	G Gds
	Roisel Communal Cemy Extension	2Lt	Buchan J.C. VC	A & S Hldrs
	Romeries Communal Cemy Extension	Cpl	McNamara J. VC	E Surrey
	Royal Irish Rifles Chyd, Laventie	CSM	Carter N.V. VC	Sussex
	Sablonniers New Communal Cemy	Capt	Norwood J. VC	5 DG
	Ste Marie Cemy, Le Havre	Sgt	Waring W.H. VC MM	RWF
	St Sever Cemy Extension, Rouen	The Rev	Hardy T.B. VC DSO MC	RAChD
	Sanders Keep Military Cemy, Graincourt-les-Havrincourt	LCpl	Jackson T.N. VC	C Gds
	Senantes Chyd	Sqn Ldr	Bazalgette I.W. VC DFC	RAF(VR)
	The Thiepval Meml, Somme	Capt Pte Lt Rfn Rfn Lt Lt	Bell E.N.F. VC Buckingham W. VC Cather G. StG. VC McFadzean W.F. VC Mariner W. VC Wilkinson T.O.L. VC Young A. VC	Innisks Leics RI Fus RI Rifles KRRC N Lancs SA Inf

Country	Cemetery or Memorial	Rank	Name, Initials and Decorations	Service, Regiment Corps etc.
	Unicorn Cemy, Vendhuile	Cpl	Weathers L.C. VC	AIF
	Vadencourt British Cemy, Maissemy	Lt Col	Dimmer J.H.S. VC MC	KRRC
	Vailly British Cemy	Capt	Wright T. VC	RE
	Vaulx Hill Cemy, Vaulx-Vrancourt	Lt	Sewell C.H. VC	Tank Corps
	Vertigneul Chyd, Romeries	Sgt	Nicholas H.J. VC MM	NZEF
	Vielle-Chapelle New Military Cemy, Lacouture	2Lt 2Lt	Collin J.H. VC Schofield J. VC	Lancaster Lancs Fus
	The Villers-Bretonneux Meml, Somme	Pte	Cooke T. VC	AIF
	Villers-Bretonneux Military Cemy, Fouilloy	Lt	Brillant J. VC MC	Cdn Inf
	Villers-Faucon Communal Cemy	2Lt 2Lt	Dunville J.S. VC Parsons H.F. VC	1R Dragoons Gloucs
	The Vimy Meml	Lt Sgt Pte Sgt	Combe R.G. VC Hobson F. VC Milne W.J. VC Spall R. VC	Cdn Inf Cdn Inf Cdn Inf Cdn Inf
	The Vis-en-Artois Meml	Cpl CPO Sgt	Lewis A.L. VC Prowse G. VC DCM Riggs F.C. VC MM	Northants RNVR Yorks & Lancs
	Vraucourt Copse Cemy, Vaulx Vraucourt	Pte	McIver H. VC MM*	RS
	Wanquetin Communal Cemy Extension	Cpl	Kaeble J. VC MM	Cdn Inf
	Warlencourt British Cemy	Sgt	Brown D.F. VC	NZEF
	Wavans British Cemy	Maj	McCudden J.T.B. VC DSO* MC* MM	RAF
	'Y' Farm Military Cemy, Bois-Grenier	Lt	Moor G.R.D. VC MC	Hamps
Germany (East)	Berlin South-Western Cemy, Stahnsdorf	Maj	Yate C.A.L. VC	KOYLI
Germany (West)	Becklingen War Cemy, Soltau	Gdsm Capt	Charlton E.C. VC Liddell I.O. VC	I Gds C Gds
	Berlin 1939–1945 War Cemy	Sqn Ldr	Parker E.D.J. GC DFC	RAF(VR)
	Hamburg (Ohlsdorf) Cemy	Lt Col Sgt	Elliott-Cooper N.B. VC DSO MC Ward J.A. VC	RF RNZAF

Country	Cemetery or Memorial	Rank	Name, Initials and Decorations	Service, Regiment Corps etc.
	Niederzwehren Cemy, Kassel	Capt	Gribble J.R. VC	Warwicks
	Reichswald Forest War Cemy, Cleves	Pte	Stokes J. VC	KSLI
	Rheinberg War Cemy	Sqn Ldr	Palmer R.A.M. VC DFC*	RAF(VR)
Greece	Phaleron War Cemy, Athens	Brig	Nicholls A.F.C. GC	Commands and Staff (late C Gds)
Hong Kong	Hong Kong (Happy Valley) Colonial Cemy	Dvr	Hughes J. GC	RASC
	The Sai Wan Bay Meml	CSM	Osborn J.R. VC	Winnipeg Gren, RCIC
	Stanley Military Cemy	Capt	Ansari M.A. GC	7th Rajput Rifles
		Capt	Ford D. GC	RS
		Mr	Fraser J.A. GC MC*	British Army Aid Group
		Flt Lt	Gray H.B. GC AFM	RAF
		Col	Newnham L.A. GC MC	Middx
India	The Delhi Meml	Capt	Andrews H.J. VC MBE	IMS
		Capt	Jotham E. VC	51 Sikhs
		Lt	Kenny W.D. VC	Garhwal Rifles
	Imphal Indian Army War Cemy	Jem	Abdul Hafiz VC	9th Jat Inf
	Imphal War Cemetery	Sgt	Turner H.V. VC	W Yorks
	Kohima War Cemy	LCpl	Harman J.P. VC	RWK
		Capt	Randle J.N. VC	Norfolk
Iraq (then Mesopotamia)	Amara War Cemy	Lt Comdr	Cookson E.C. VC DSO	RN
		Lt Col	Henderson E.E.D. VC	N Staffs
		Cpl	Ware S.W. VC	Seaforth Hldrs
	The Basra Meml	Lt Comdr	Cowley C.H. VC	RNVR
		Sgt	Finlay D. VC	BW
		Lt	Firman H.O.B. VC	RN
		Pte	Fynn J.H. VC	SWB
		Capt	Henderson G.S. VC DSO* MC	Manchester
	Basra War Cemy	Maj	Massy Wheeler G.G. VC	7 Hariana Rifles

Country	Cemetery or Memorial	Rank	Name, Initials and Decorations	Service, Regiment Corps etc.
Irish Republic	Cobh Old Church Cemy, Co. Cork	Master	Parslow F.D. VC	RNR
	Modreeny Church of Ireland Chyd, Tipperary	Sgt	Somers J. VC	Innisk Fus
Israel (then Palestine)	Beersheba War Cemy	Maj	Lafone A.M. VC	Middx Hussars
		Capt	Russell J.F. VC MC	RAMC
	Gaza War Cemy	2Lt	Boughey S.H.P. VC	RSF
	Jerusalem War Cemy	Cpl	McCarthy J.F. AM	RIR
	Khayat Beach War Cemy, Haifa	Sgt CQMS	Beckett J.A. GC Harvey, N. VC	RAF RE
Italy	Argenta Gap War Cemy	Sgt Cpl Maj	Banks A. GC Hunter T.P. VC Lassen A.F.E.V.S. VC MC**	RAF(VR) RM Gen List and SBS
	Arrezo War Cemy	Lt	Young St J.G. GC	RAC att Central India Horse
	Bari War Cemy	Cpl	Horsfield K. GC	Manchester
	Beach Head War Cemy, Anzio	Sgt	Rogers M.A.W. VC MM	Wilts
	The Cassino Meml	Swr	Ditto Ram GC	Central India Horse
		Nk	Yashwant Ghatge VC	3/5 Bn, Mahratta LI
	Catania War Cemy, Sicily	Lt	Talbot E.E.A.C. GC MBE	RE
	Faenza War Cemy	Capt	Brunt J.H.C. VC MC	Sherwood Foresters
	Giavera British Cemy	2Lt	Youll J.S. VC	NF
	Minturno War Cemy	Pte	Mitchell G.A. VC	London Scots (Gordon Hldrs)
	Rimini Ghurkha War Cemy	Rfn Rfn	Sher Bahadur Thapa VC Thamman Gurung VC	Gurkha Rifles Gurkha Rifles
	Sangro River Cremation Meml	Sub	Subramanian GC IDSM	QVO Madras Sappers & Miners
	Sangro River War Cemy	Maj	Anderson J.T. McK. VC DSO	A & S Hldrs
	Staglieno Cemy	Capt	McNair E.A. VC	Sussex
	Udine War Cemy	LCpl	Russell D. GC	NZ Inf

Country	Cemetery or Memorial	Rank	Name, Initials and Decorations	Service, Regiment Corps etc.
Kenya	The East Africa Meml, Nairobi	Sgt	Leakey N.G. VC	KAR
	Nairobi War Cemy	Capt	Latutin S. GC	SLI
	Voi Cemy	Lt	Dartnell W.T. VC	RF
Libya	Benghazi War Cemy	Lt Col	Keyes G.C.T. VC MC	Royal Scots Greys
	Knightsbridge War Cemy, Acroma	Rfn 2Lt	Beeley J. VC Gunn G.W. VC MC	KRRC RHA
	Tobruk War Cemy	Cpl	Edmondson J.H. VC	2/17 AIB, AIF
		Capt	Jackman J.J.B. VC	RNF
Malaysia	Labuan War Cemy, Sabah	Lt	Derrick T.C. VC DCM	2/48 AIB, AIF
		Cpl	Mackey J.B. VC	2/3 Pnr Bn, AIF
		Capt	Matthews L.C. GC MC	AIF
	Taiping War Cemy, Malaya	Sqn Ldr	Scarf, A.S.K. VC	RAF
Malta GC	Cappucini Naval Cemy	W Comdr Lt Comdr LAC	Dowland J.N. GC Hiscock W.E. GC DSC Osborne A.M. GC	RAF RN RAF(VR)
	The Malta Meml	F O	Trigg L.A. VC DFC	RNZAF
Netherlands	Arnhem (Oosterbeek) War Cemy	Capt	Grayburn J.M. VC	Para Regt AAC
		Flt Lt Capt	Lord D.S.A. VC DFC Queripel L.E. VC	RAF Sussex
	Groesbeek Canadian War Cemy	Sgt	Cosens A. VC	QOR of Canada
	The Groesbeek Meml	LSgt	Baskeyfield J.D. VC	S Staffs
	Nederweert War Cemy	LCpl	Harden H.E. VC	RAMC
	Sittard War Cemy, Limburg	Fus	Donnini D. VC	RSF
	Steenbergen-en-Kruisland, RC Chyd	W Comdr	Gibson G.P. VC DSO* DFC*	RAF
	The Hague (Westduin) General Cemy	Lt Comdr	Goodman G.H. GC MBE	RNVR
Northern Ireland	Newry Old Chapel RC Cemy, Co Down	Capt	Blaney M.F. GC	RE
Norway	Ballangen New Cemy	Capt	Warburton-Lee B.A. VC	RN

Country	Cemetery or Memorial	Rank	Name, Initials and Decorations	Service, Regiment Corps etc.
Papua New Guinea	Lae War Cemy, New Guinea	Lt	Chowne A. VC MM	2/2 AIB, AIF
		Flt Lt	Newton W.E. VC	RAAF
	Port Moresby (Bomana) War Cemy, Papua	Cpl	French J.A. VC	2/9 AIB, AIF
		Pte	Kingsbury B.S. VC	2/14 AIB, AIF
	Rabaul (Bita Paka) War Cemy, New Britain	Cpl	Sukanaivalu S. VC	Fijian Inf Regt
Scotland	Kirkaldy Cemy, Fife	Lt Col	Marshall W.T. VC	19th Royal Hussars
	Lerwick New Cemy, Shetland Isles	Flt Lt	Hornell D.E. VC	RCAF
Singapore	The Singapore Meml	Gnr	Brown W.E. VC DCM*	RAA
		W Comdr	Nicolson J.B. VC DFC	RAF
South Africa	Capetown (Maitland Road) Cemy	Sub Conductor	Glasock H.H. VC	SASC
	Mafeking Cemy	Capt	Beauchamp-Proctor A.F.W. VC DSO MC* DFC	RAF
South Yemen	Ma'ala Cemy, Aden	Lt Col	English W.J. VC	RUR
Sudan	Khartoum War Cemy	Sgt (Obs)	Parish G.L. GC	RAF(VR)
Sweden	Kviberg Cemy	Comdr	Jones L.W. VC	RN
Tanzania (then Tanganyika)	Morogoro Cemy	Capt	Butler J.F.P. VC DSO	KRR
Tunisia	Béja War Cemy	W Comdr	Malcolm H.G. VC	RAF
	Enfidaville War Cemy	Pte	Duncan C.A. GC	Parachute
	Massicault War Cemy	Capt	Lyell C.A. Baron of Kinnordy, VC	S Gds
		Lt	Sandys-Clarke W.A. VC	Loyals
	Sfax War Cemy	Pte	Anderson E. VC	E Yorks
		Coy Hav Maj	Chhelu Ram VC	4/6 Raj Rifles
		2Lt	Ngarimu Moana-Nui-a-Kiwi VC	28 NZ Bn
		Lt Col	Seagrim D.A. VC	Green Howards

Country	Cemetery or Memorial	Rank	Name, Initials and Decorations	Service, Regiment Corps etc.
Turkey	The Helles Meml, Gallipoli Pena	Maj	Bromley C. VC	Lancs Fus
		Lt Col	Milbanke Sir John Bt VC	Notts Yeomanry
		Capt	O'Sullivan G.R. VC	Innisk Fus
		Sgt	Stubbs F.E. VC	Lancs Fus
		Sub Lt	Tisdall A.W. St C. VC	RNVR
	Lala Baba Cemy, Gallipoli Pena	Brig Gen	Kenna P.A. VC DSO	Cmdg 3rd Notts & Derby Bde (late 21st Lancers)
	Lancashire Landing Cemy, Gallipoli Pena	LSgt	Kenealy W.S. VC	Lancs Fus
	The Lone Pine Meml, Gallipoli Pena	Cpl	Burton A.S. VC	AIF
		Capt	Shout A.J. VC MC	AIF
	Twelve Tree Copse Cemy, Gallipoli Pena	2Lt	Smith A.V. VC	E Lancs
	'V' Beach Cemy, Gallipoli Pena	Lt Col	Doughty-Wylie C.H.M. VC CB CMG	RWF
		Capt	Walford G.N. VC	RFA
Yugoslavia	Belgrade War Cemy	Sigmn	Smith K. GC	RCS

Appendix E

Cemeteries described in Chapter 14

WW I = 1914–1918 War/WW II = 1939–1945 War
B/S = Battlefield site

Algeria	– Le Petit Lac Cemetery, Oran WW II
Australia	– Adelaide River War Cemetery, Northern Territory WW II
Austria	– Klagenfurt War Cemetery WW II
Belgium	– Bedford House Cemetery, Zillebeke WW I & WW II
	– Dickebusch Old Military Cemetery, WW I & WW II
	B/S – Dickebusch New Military Cemetery & Extension WW I
	– Hautrage Military Cemetery WW I
	B/S – Hedge Row Trench Cemetery, Zillebeke WW I
	– Hooge Crater Cemetery, Zillebeke WW I
	– Lijssenthoek Military Cemetery WW I
	B/S – Lone Tree Cemetery, Spanbroekmolen, Wytschaete WW I
	B/S – Passchendaele New British Cemetery WW I
	– Poelcapelle British Cemetery WW I
	B/S – Polygon Wood Cemetery, Zonnebeke WW I
	B/S – St Symphorien Military Cemetery WW I
Burma	– Thanbyuzayat War Cemetery WW II
Egypt	– Halfaya-Sollum War Cemetery WW II
France	B/S – AIF Burial Ground, Grass Lane, Flers WW I
	B/S – Anzac Cemetery, Sailly-sur-la-Lys WW I
	B/S – Sailly-sur-la-Lys Canadian Cemetery WW I
	B/S – Bazentin-le-Petit Communal Cemetery Extension WW I
	– Bény-sur-Mer Canadian War Cemetery, Normandy WW II
	– Béthune Town Cemetery WW I & WW II
	B/S – Bourlon Wood Cemetery WW I
	B/S – Cabaret Rouge British Cemetery, Souchez WW I
	– Dieppe Canadian War Cemetery WW II
	– Etaples Military Cemetery WW I & WW II

	B/S	– London Cemetery & Extension, High Wood, Longueval WW I & WW II
		– Ranville War Cemetery, Normandy WW II
		– St Pierre Cemetery, Amiens WW I & WW II
		– St Sever Cemetery & Extension, Rouen WW I & WW II
		– Terlincthun British Cemetery, Wimille WW I & WW II
	B/S	– Thistle Dump Cemetery, High Wood, Longueval WW I
	B/S	– Toronto Cemetery, Démuin WW I
		– Wimereux Communal Cemetery WW I & WW II
Germany		– Berlin 1939–1945 War Cemetery WW II
		– Reichswald Forest War Cemetery WW II
		– Sage War Cemetery, Oldenburg WW II
Greece		– Salonika (Lembet Road) Military Cemetery WW I
Hong Kong		– Stanley Military Cemetery WW II
India		– Imphal War Cemetery WW II
	B/S	– Kohima War Cemetery, Assam WW II
Italy	B/S	– Beach Head War Cemetery, Anzio WW II
		– Castiglione South African Cemetery WW II
		– Forli Indian Army War Cemetery WW II
		– Moro River Canadian War Cemetery, Ortona WW II
		– Salerno War Cemetery WW II
		– Sangro War Cemetery WW II
Japan		– Yokohama War Cemetery WW II
Libya		– Tobruk War Cemetery WW II
Malaysia		– Labuan War Cemetery, Sabah WW II
Netherlands		– Arnhem (Oosterbeek) War Cemetery, WW II
		– Bergen-op-Zoom War Cemetery WWI & WW II
		– Groesbeek Canadian War Cemetery WW II
New Caledonia		– Bourail New Zealand War Cemetery WW II
Norway		– Oslo Western Civil Cemetery WW II
Papua New Guinea		– Lae War Cemetery, New Guinea WW I & WW II
Thailand		– Kanchanaburi War Cemetery WW II

Turkey	B/S – Azmak Cemetery, Suvla WW I
	B/S – Beach Cemetery, Anzac WW I
	B/S – Lancashire Landing, Helles WW I
	B/S – Shrapnel Valley Cemetery, Anzac WW I
	B/S – V Beach Cemetery, Helles WW I
	B/S – Walker's Ridge Cemetery, Anzac WW I
United Kingdom	– Cliveden War Cemetery, Taplow, Bucks WW I & WW II
	– Dover (St James's) Cemetery, Kent WW I & WW II

Appendix F

Memorials described in Chapter 15

WW I = 1914–1918 War/WW II = 1939–1945 War

NAVAL MEMORIALS

Canada
– The Halifax Memorial WW I and WW II (combined Naval/Land Forces)

United Kingdom – The Chatham, Plymouth and Portsmouth Memorials WW I and WW II

LAND FORCES MEMORIALS

Belgium
– The Messines Ridge New Zealand Memorial WW I

– The Ploegsteert Memorial WW I

– The Tyne Cot Memorial WW I

– The Ypres (Menin Gate) Memorial WW I

Burma
– The Rangoon Memorial WW II

Egypt
– The Alamein Memorial WW II (combined Land/Air Forces)

France
– The Arras Memorial WW I (combined Land/Air Forces)

– The Bayeux Memorial WW II

The Beaumont-Hamel (Newfoundland) Memorial WW I (combined Naval/Land Forces)

– The Delville Wood Memorial WW I

– The Neuve-Chapelle Memorial WW I

– The Thiepval Memorial WW I

– The Villers-Bretonneux Memorial WW I

– The Vimy Memorial WW I

Hong Kong
– The Sai Wan Bay Memorial WW I & WW II

Italy
– The Cassino Memorial WW II

Singapore
– The Singapore Memorial WW II (combined Land/Air Forces)

Turkey
– The Helles Memorial WW I

United Kingdom – The Brookwood Memorial WW II

– The Brookwood (Russia) Memorial WW I & WW II

– The Hollybrook Memorial, Southampton WW I

AIR FORCES MEMORIALS

Malta GC – The Malta Memorial WW II

United Kingdom – The Runnymede Memorial WW II

MERCANTILE MARINE/MERCHANT NAVY MEMORIAL

United Kingdom – The Tower Hill Memorial WW I & WW II

Appendix G

Principal offices and agencies of the
Commonwealth War Graves Commission

Head Office:

2 Marlow Road, Maidenhead
Berkshire SL6 7DX
England .

MAIDENHEAD (0628) 34221

Canadian Agency:

Commonwealth War Graves Commission
284 Wellington Street
Ottawa, Ontario K1A OP4, Canada

OTTAWA (0613) 922-3224

Canada, United States of
America

Office of Australian War Graves

Department of Veterans' Affairs
PO Box 21, Woden
ACT 2606, Australia

CANBERRA (062) 891111

Australia, Norfolk Island, Papua
New Guinea, Solomon Islands
(Guadalcanal)

Department of Internal Affairs New Zealand:

Department of Internal Affairs
Wellington
New Zealand

WELLINGTON (04) 738699

New Zealand, New Caledonia,
Society Islands, Tonga, Vanuatu,
Western Samoa

South African Agency:

PO Box 1554
Pretoria 0001, South Africa

PRETORIA (012) 262100

South Africa, Namibia (South
West Africa)

France Area:

Rue Angèle Richard
62217 Beaurains
France

PAS DE CALAIS (21) 23 03 24

France (including Corsica),
Monaco, Switzerland

Northern Europe Area:

Elverdingsestraat 82
B-8900 Ieper (Ypres)
Belgium

IEPER (057) 20 01 18
(057) 20 57 18

Belgium, Czechoslovakia,
Denmark, Federal Republic of
Germany, German Democratic
Republic, Luxembourg,
Netherlands, Norway, Poland,
Sweden

United Kingdom Area:

Jenton Road
Sydenham, Leamington Spa
Warwicks CV31 1XS, England

LEAMINGTON SPA (0926) 30137

Channel Islands, Faroe Islands,
Iceland, Irish Republic, Isle of
Man, United Kingdom

North Africa Area:

Heliopolis War Cemetery
9 Sharia Nabil el Wakad
PO Box 57, 11341 Heliopolis
Arab Republic of Egypt

CAIRO (02) 669351

Algeria, Egypt, Libya, Sudan,
Tunisia

Western Mediterranean Area:

Viale Pola 27A/29
00198 Rome, Italy

ROME (06) 844 1795
(06) 851 431

Austria, Hungary, Italy, Malta,
San Marino

Outer Area:

2 Marlow Road
Maidenhead
Berkshire SL6 7DX
England

MAIDENHEAD (0628) 34221

All other countries and territories

Additional Address

The Royal British Legion
48 Pall Mall
London SW1 5JY
England

LONDON (01) 930 8131

M

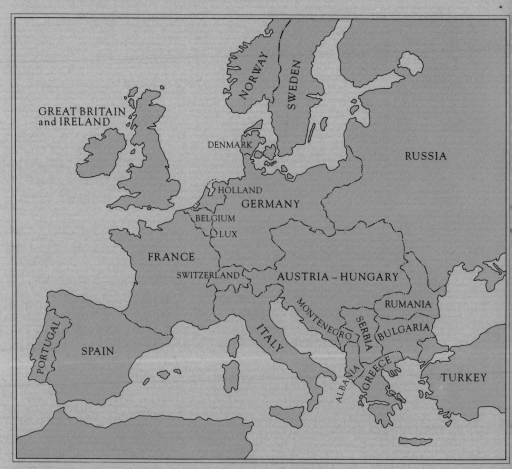

Europe in 1914